AMONG THE RUINS

CHRISTIAN C. SAHNER

Among the Ruins

Syria Past and Present

OXFORD
UNIVERSITY PRESS

Oxford University Press, Inc., publishes works that further
Oxford University's objective of excellence
in research, scholarship, and education.

Oxford New York
Auckland   Cape Town   Dar es Salaam   Hong Kong   Karachi
Kuala Lumpur   Madrid   Melbourne   Mexico City   Nairobi
New Delhi   Shanghai   Taipei   Toronto

With offices in
Argentina   Austria   Brazil   Chile   Czech Republic   France   Greece
Guatemala   Hungary   Italy   Japan   Poland   Portugal   Singapore
South Korea   Switzerland   Thailand   Turkey   Ukraine   Vietnam

Copyright © 2014 Christian C Sahner

Oxford is a registered trade mark of Oxford University Press in the UK
and certain other countries.

Published by Oxford University Press, Inc
198 Madison Avenue, New York, New York 10016

Published in the United Kingdom in 2014 by C. Hurst & Co. (Publishers) Ltd.

www.oup.com

Oxford is a registered trademark of Oxford University Press

All rights reserved. No part of this publication may be reproduced,
stored in a retrieval system, or transmitted, in any form or by any means,
electronic, mechanical, photocopying, recording, or otherwise,
without the prior permission of Oxford University Press.

Library of Congress Cataloging-in-Publication Data is available for this title
Christian C Sahner
Among the Ruins
Syria Past and Present
ISBN 978-0-19-939-670-2 (hardback)

Printed in the USA

CONTENTS

A NOTE FOR THE READER

Certain names, places, and biographical details in this book have been changed in order to protect the identities of the individuals mentioned.

In transliterating Arabic, I have omitted the standard diacritic marks familiar to scholars. I have represented the letter *hamza* with a single backwards quote ('), and the letter *'ayn* with a single forward quote ('). In many instances, I have chosen transliterations of Arabic names and words that conform to popular as opposed to scholarly usage (e.g., Hussein, not Ḥusayn; Hafez not Ḥāfiẓ; muezzin not mu'adhdhin; or Baath not Ba'th).

I have not endeavored to identify every source I consulted. Rather, I have used endnotes sparingly in order to credit the authors and texts that have influenced my thinking, and to point readers to further material should they become interested in particular subjects, both broad and narrow.

ACKNOWLEDGEMENTS

Many friends have supported me over the past six years as I traveled through Syria and the greater Middle East, and later, as I sat down to write this book.

My greatest debt of gratitude goes to those who volunteered to read the manuscript in its entirety. Their confidence in the project buoyed my spirits, and their insights greatly improved the final product. For this I thank Betsy and Peter Brown, Honey Al Sayed, and Luke Yarbrough. The two anonymous referees commissioned by Hurst offered superb advice and saved me from many careless errors. I am grateful for their help.

I would also like to express my thanks to the following individuals, who read portions of the text and gave input concerning the publishing process: Michael Cook, Scott Erwin and Nita Colaco, Simon Fuchs, Jacob Olidort, and Jack Tannous. Likewise, Michael Dwyer, publisher at C. Hurst & Co., early on saw promise in this project and has been a steady champion of it ever since. He and the entire staff of Hurst deserve great thanks for seeing this book through to the end. I would also like to acknowledge the help and support of the staff at Oxford University Press, New York.

For the ability to study and travel extensively in the Middle East, I would like thank the following academic institutions: in Princeton, the Department of History and its chairman, William Jordan; the Seeger Center for Hellenic Studies and its director, Dimitri Gondicas; the Graduate School, the Group for the Study of Late Antiquity, the U.S. Department of Education (whose grants were administered by the Program in Near Eastern Studies), and the Woodrow Wilson School.

In Oxford, I would like to thank the Rhodes Trust, especially the warden during my time, Sir Colin Lucas, Mary Eaton, and the entire staff of Rhodes House; also, St John's College, the Faculty of Oriental Studies, and the Faculty of Classics.

I began and later completed this book while at the Institut français du Proche-Orient in Beirut. I would like to thank Eric Gautier and the teaching staff of the *stage de langue arabe* for creating a stimulating and pleasant environment in which to work.

The initial seeds of this book were planted in 2007 during a memorable summer as a Robert L. Bartley Fellow at *The Wall Street Journal*. I would like to thank Melanie Kirkpatrick, who interviewed me for the job and later shed light on the publishing industry once this book was underway; Eric Gibson, who has continued to publish my dispatches from the Middle East; Robert Pollock and the features group; and L. Gordon Crovitz, the former publisher of the paper. I would also like to thank the *Journal* for the permission to adapt material from several of my previously published essays.

I have profited immensely from contact with many generous teachers over the years, who have shared with me their deep knowledge of the Middle East in various periods. First and foremost, I thank my advisers, Peter Brown and Michael Cook, who supported the project despite its being a significant detour from the real task of finishing my doctoral dissertation. I'm grateful for their confidence in me and thankful for the opportunity to study under two such eminent scholars and fine people.

I would also like to thank the following teachers, scattered among different places and phases of my career: Anne-Marie Bouché, Slobodan Ćurčić, John Fleming, the late Malfono Robert Gabriel, John Haldon, Bernard Haykel, Daniel Kurtzer, Neil McLynn, Emmanuel Papoutsakis, Carol Petrallia, Helmut Reimitz, Roseann Sharo, Onnie Strother, Max Weiss, and Fritz Zimmermann.

I would also like to acknowledge the many people who have contributed to this book in ways both big and small—whether as travel companions, consultants on bibliography, sources of insight, or merely as faithful friends and colleagues. They include: Ryan Anderson, Haley Bobseine, Thomas Carlson, James Casey, Martina Censi, Nick Chatrath, Joseph Clair, John Coleman, Wolfgang Danspeckgruber, Michael Doran, Naseem Ferdowsi and Ern Hlow, Simon and Maria Fuchs, Farès Gillon, Sherif Girgis, Samuel Helfont, Fr Dominique Hélou-Khoury, Julian Hertz, Nate Hodson, Adam Izdebski, Ahmad Al Jallad, Greg Johnsen, Stan Katz, Faysal Lahmami, Nicholas Marinides, Paul Miles, Fr Martin Miller, Caelum Moffatt, Msgr Thomas Mullelly, Douglas Parsons, Alex Petkas, Jenna Phillips, Christine Pisani (who set things in motion by buying me a journal), Michael Reynolds, the Jael Rogers Coalition, Charlie Scribner, Sahar Tabaja, Luis Tellez, Mathieu Tillier, Alex Townson, Lev Weitz, Stefan Winter, and Nadim Zeidan.

Finally, it remains to thank my parents, Ron and Brigid, along with my siblings, Duncan and Elizabeth, for supporting the book as well as my travels in the region (even as they resulted in my absence from important family occasions; *mea maxima culpa*). It has been a special joy to share this great adventure with them.

Lastly, I want to acknowledge the many friends and acquaintances I made during my time in Syria (and the Middle East more broadly), whose stories form the heart of this book. Given the present situation, I have done my best to disguise their identities. I thank them for their warmth and hospitality, and I salute them for their perseverance in trying times. *Tahyaa Suriya*.

Amman   July 2014

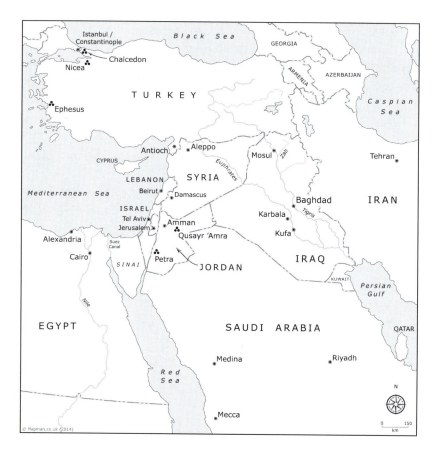

Middle East Region

Syria

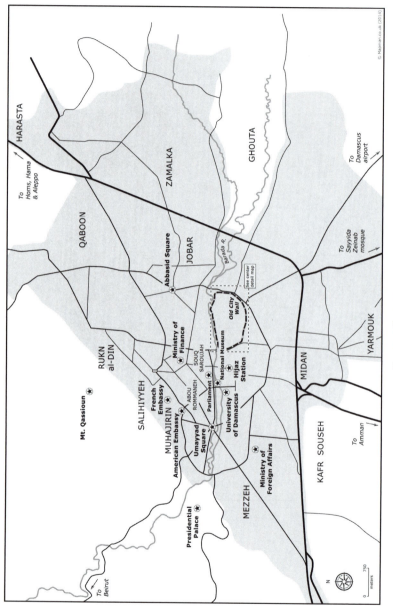

Greater Damascus

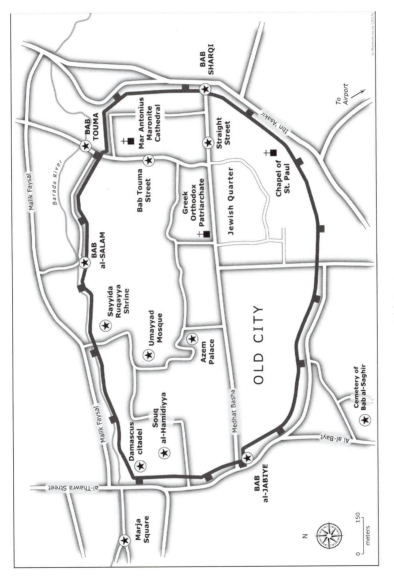

Old Damascus

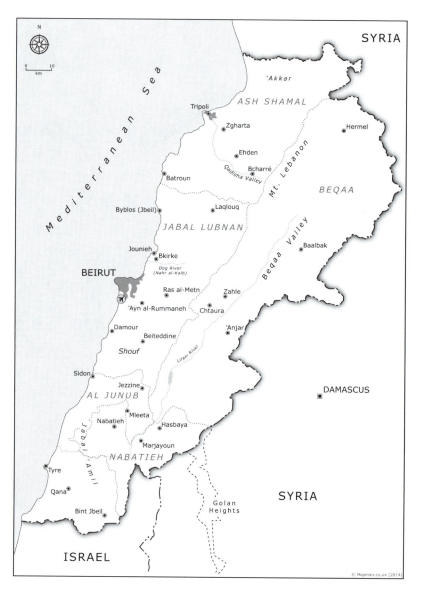

Lebanon

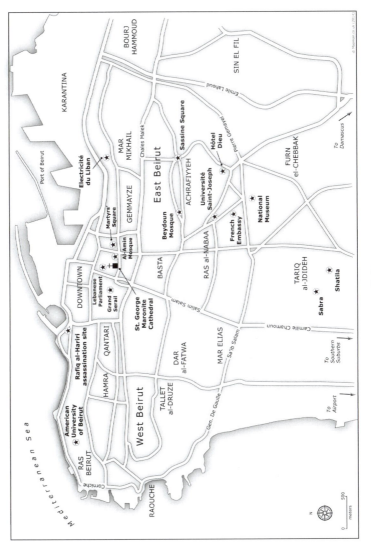

Beirut

AN ODE FOR SYRIA TODAY

Where the quiet-coloured end of evening smiles,
  Miles and miles
On the solitary pastures where our sheep
  Half-asleep
Tinkle homeward thro' the twilight, stray or stop
  As they crop—
Was the site once of a city great and gay,
  (So they say)
Of our country's very capital, its prince
  Ages since
Held his court in, gathered councils, wielding far
  Peace or war.

Now the country does not even boast a tree,
  As you see,
To distinguish slopes of verdure, certain rills
  From the hills
Intersect and give a name to, (else they run
  Into one)
Where the domed and daring palace shot its spires
  Up like fires
O'er the hundred-gated circuit of a wall
  Bounding all
Made of marble, men might march on nor be prest
  Twelve abreast. [....]

In one year they sent a million fighters forth
  South and North,

And they built their gods a brazen pillar high
  As the sky
Yet reserved a thousand chariots in full force—
  Gold, of course.
O heart! oh blood that freezes, blood that burns!
  Earth's returns
For whole centuries of folly, noise and sin!
  Shut them in,
With their triumphs and their glories and the rest!
  Love is best.

Robert Browning, "Love Among the Ruins," 1855

PREFACE

A JOURNEY THROUGH MANY SYRIAS

.

Upon my graduation from Princeton in the spring of 2007, I received from a family friend a handsome leather journal. It had a purple cover, a large metal lock, and a silver monogram—a gift that felt more fitting for a twelve-year-old girl than a man of my age. Throughout my time in college, I was an occasional diarist, filling the pages of cheap notebooks with observations about my overseas travels—the medieval monasteries of Ireland and Scotland, the great basilicas of Rome, the Byzantine ruins of Istanbul. Recording my impressions was a useful way of processing these experiences, as well as of passing the lonely time I spent by myself on the road. The purple diary was not a total waste. But at the same time, I was slightly embarrassed by this gift, and therefore decided to bury it in a bookshelf in my parents' basement, never to be seen again.

Somehow, the diary ended up in my luggage that fall as I embarked on a two-year sojourn at Oxford as a Rhodes Scholar. Warned by relatives not to forget anything that happened, I assiduously recorded my memories of the first few weeks in Oxford, but quickly abandoned the exercise for tutorial essays and the distracting temptations of the city's pubs.

Over the course of that first year in England—as my enthusiasm for the diary waned—I committed myself to the study of Islamic history. In this, I was driven by an intense curiosity about what had become of the ancient Mediterranean after the coming of Islam in the seventh century AD. Anyone who has studied the period knows that the Arab conquests represent a major watershed in human history. In a matter of a few generations, Palestine, Syria, and Egypt went from being the jewels of a Greek-, Syriac-, and Coptic-speaking Byzantine Empire to the center of a new Arabic-speaking Muslim caliphate. To peer from one side of this frontier to the other was to gaze into a brave new world, at once familiar yet deeply alien. And to explore this world I needed one important skill: the Arabic language.

Such was my introduction to the study of Arabic and Middle Eastern history. At a deeper level, though, I'm not entirely sure what prompted me to do it. My only early memory of the Arab world comes from when my father would ask us "who was in trouble." Depending on the headlines of that day's *New York Post*, this might include junk-bond villain Michael Milken; New York real-estate developer Leona Helmsley; or, significant for my development as a future scholar of the Middle East, Hosni Mubarak (the despised former president of Egypt, who ruled from 1981 to 2011).

My interest in the Middle East began to deepen after a visit to Istanbul in the late 1990s. Hagia Sophia—the St Peter's Basilica of the Byzantine world—captured my imagination and refused to let go. In a single afternoon, beneath its mighty dome, I was introduced to the radical idea (at least for a teenager from New Jersey) that there existed a Christianity east of Rome, and what is more, a Christianity which now lay mostly within the domains of Islam.

In the years that followed, my initial curiosity about the Middle East was nurtured by several inspiring teachers who taught me about history and art. In particular, I became fascinated by the great treasures of antiquity and the Middle Ages: the Pantheon of Rome, San Vitale in Ravenna, and again, significant for my future trajectory, the Dome of the Rock in Jerusalem.

There was also a final primordial shock that prompted me to study the Middle East. As for many members of my generation, September 11th, 2001 was a tragic but defining moment. I watched the World Trade Center burn from a hilltop park in my hometown outside Manhattan. This was an event that called out for explanation, and I—along with practically everyone else in America—realized I knew precious little about the region where these attacks had originated, to say nothing of the religion in whose name they had been allegedly committed. I did not set out to chart a clear path from the Prophet Muhammad to Osama Bin Laden, as many irresponsible pundits seemed determined to do. Rather, what 9/11 did was to draw my attention to a world that—had I come of age in 1991 and not 2001—might have seemed otherwise remote, inaccessible, and probably uninteresting.

To supplement my studies at Oxford I spent the summer of 2008 in Damascus working on my Arabic. In hindsight, I'm not sure why I chose Damascus over any other city in the region, though the decision would be propitious. In Syria I found a country different from anywhere else I had visited before, a land of imposing ruins, cultured peoples, complex languages, and still knottier politics. And like a bloodhound refusing to give up the scent, that purple diary followed me too, providing an unforeseen chance to make sense of my new surroundings and experiences.

In certain respects, those many hours I spent writing in my journal took time away from "real life" in Damascus—from the chance to meet people, explore monuments, and sample its many cuisines. At the same time, writing preserved those memories intact, as a fresco is bonded permanently to a plaster wall, its bright colors and sharp lines undiminished by the passage of time. Indeed, my experiences in Syria in 2008–10 and later in Lebanon in 2011–13 seem somehow more real because of having written about them at the time. Now, six years since I first arrived in Damascus, those memories remain fresher, more vivid even, than many things I've experienced since. We live through all seasons of life, but some we remember better than others.

What I did not realize at the time was that the observations I had jotted down in my purple diary formed a picture of Syrian society on the cusp of a huge upheaval. 2008–2010 were years of uneasy calm, a period of superficial normality on the brink of revolution. I certainly didn't sense that a civil war would erupt in Syria in March 2011, a few months after my last visit, and I'd venture to say most Syrians did not either. While change would one day affect Syria's authoritarian system, many people told me, it would never occur today, or tomorrow, or the next day. Such is the difference between living in the thick of history and looking back on it from the comfort of the future. You never see it coming.

At home in the United States, friends and family were interested in my impressions of Syria. For the most part, their views were rather gloomy. At the end of the 9/11 decade, the most that many Americans knew was that Syria counted as an honorary member of the "axis of evil," that exclusive club of rogue states committed to destabilizing the global order, according to the administration of President George W. Bush. In an effort to complicate these views, I wrote occasional essays for *The Wall Street Journal* describing other sides of Syrian society and culture.[1] These essays, which drew on my travels, focused on major historical monuments. Specifically, I was interested in monuments that seemed to reflect the surprising and rich tableau of religions and cultures in Syria that most American readers had never heard about: the mosque built atop the pagan temple and Christian church; the Crusader castle that later became a Muslim fortress; the Roman city that served as the epicenter of an ancient Arab revolt. These short articles were satisfying not only because they offered me respite from the heavily footnoted essays I was writing for my professors at the time, but also because they allowed me to reflect on Syria's ancient and medieval past and how it continued to shape the present.

It was these essays—coupled with my journal-writing—that planted in my head the idea for a longer book. Early concepts included profiles of archaeological sites, a day-by-day account of life in Damascus, and a "then-and-now" travelogue that would follow in the footsteps of a great Muslim writer from the Middle Ages. These ideas were hatched at a time when Syria was at peace, and then it seemed appropriate to undertake a more lighthearted book that would entertain and educate a general audience.

Syria's fortunes shifted dramatically with the onset of the Arab Spring in late 2010 and early 2011. In many ways, Syria was the Johnny-come-lately of that torrid season: it would take more than three months for the protests that ignited in Tunisia and Egypt to spread to the Levant. But spread they would, and in the process, transform Syria into a charnel house. Suddenly, my hopes of writing a book were dashed: I had long planned to spend the academic year 2011–12 in Damascus, but the pace of fighting made this unfeasible, and instead I had to relocate to Beirut. My various ideas for a project now seemed ill-suited to the tragedy of the moment.

All the same, as I settled into Beirut in the fall of 2011—enjoying the illusion of security only fifty miles from Damascus—I realized there remained a rich story to tell. While I could not narrate for readers the events of the Syrian revolution, I could offer them a snapshot of the country on the edge of change. And in certain respects, this was even more needed, for although Syria dominated the world's newspaper headlines, the reporting was often rather thin. While it described the high drama of the battlefield and the diplomatic conference, it skirted round the history of the country— the very long history that had led Syria to these particular circumstances at this particular point in time.

What I found lacking in reporting on Syria, as well as the spate of interesting books that appeared at the onset of the uprising,[2] was a sense of deep historical perspective, especially on the country's social and religious texture. How many superficial articles did I read that paid lip service to this when describing the Syrian revolution as "sectarian," pitting the interests of the Sunni "majority" against those of the embattled 'Alawi "minority"? But how did the 'Alawis come to power? Who were they? And why did the Sunnis despise them so much? What is more, what were the historical roots of this religious tension?

There were other plot-lines that deserved explanation. Periodically, articles would appear that detailed the plight of Christians in Syria. Many pieces would begin with an exclamation of surprise that there *were* Christian communities in this predominantly Muslim country. But how did relations between Christians and Muslims start off and how did they change over the centuries? Furthermore, why were Christians so afraid of the change then sweeping through their country, and in particular, of the possibility that the conflict would turn sectarian?

These and countless other questions buzzed in my head as I combed through the coverage of the Syrian civil war. With so much (appropriate) emphasis on the rising body count and the role of the great powers in the conflict, there seemed neither room nor patience for the kind of deep history I felt was needed. What is more, the war-zone coverage disguised all sense of what Syria had been like on the edge of revolution, indeed, all sense that Syria had been at one point something other than the war-torn, dysfunctional place it has become after early 2011. What were the smells of everyday life in that disappeared Syria? How did Syrians relate to their government? What did they think of the United States and other Western countries? Was there a Syrian national identity? How did the country's various religious communities co-exist?

Amidst this sense of disappointment, I realized that in my own small way I had recorded some preliminary answers to a few of these questions in my journal. To be sure, the answers in that book were incomplete—they came in the form of lighthearted anecdotes about my life as a young American abroad. At the same time, these anecdotes lent a human perspective on Syrian society, not to mention the longer-term historical processes that had shaped it through centuries of change. These personal impressions were chastened and challenged, in turn, by more formal academic study of the region. Upon finishing my master's degree in history and Arabic at Oxford in 2009, I returned to my alma mater, Princeton University, to undertake a doctorate in late antique and early Islamic history, on the side focusing on the modern Middle East.

The great joy of studying Syrian history was for me the chance to understand a society in a near constant process of change. By dint of its strategic location between Europe and Asia and between the traditional domains of Christendom and Islam, it had experienced its fair share of cultural and political shifts through the centuries. Amidst these changes, Syria had become a witness to the manner in which old begets new, and new preserves old. Such layering is characteristic of many cultures around the world, but in Syria especially so. The country stood at the center of numerous tectonic shifts in global history—whether it was the transition from nomadic to urban life in its prehistoric past; from paganism to Christianity, then Christianity to Islam in late antiquity; or from medieval empires to modern nation-states in the present. Syria may be an old place—especially in contrast to these youthful and petulant United

States where I have spent most of my life—but it is also a dynamic and diverse place, shaped and renewed by the very changes that in the near term can seem so destructive.

Now, in the midst of another historical change in Syria, I fear that much of the country's past will be forgotten. I fear this not only because the war has damaged many of Syria's prized antiquities—the very objects that connect Syrians to their deep past. I fear this because many communities are fleeing, perhaps never to return. This is true of the population at large, whether those internally displaced peoples who have fled their ancestral homes for safer havens elsewhere in the country, or the millions of refugees who wait anxiously in tent cities along the borders in Turkey, Lebanon, and Jordan, along with more distant places like Egypt. I fear especially for smaller communities, like the Christians, who have left Syria in droves for neighboring countries and, for anyone with financial resources, to places like Europe and the United States. This is a tragedy not only in absolute terms, but also because it may spell the end of Christianity as a vital and substantial presence in Syrian life, bringing an end to a tradition that stretches back two thousand years.

Perhaps the greatest tragedy yet to take place is the explosion of large-scale violence against Syria's 'Alawi community. President Bashar al-Asad is an 'Alawi, and has relied on their support throughout the war. Not all 'Alawis have profited from his brutal rule—indeed, many have suffered because of it—but they may pay the ultimate price for his brutality. I earnestly hope this does not happen, but like the ethno-religious violence that engulfed the Balkans in the 1990s, this may prove to be the saddest epilogue of an already tragic story.

This book is one person's attempt at making sense of these changes. It is written primarily for non-specialists, who encounter Syria through newspaper headlines and the evening news, but who wish to go deeper. As such, it is not laden with citations like the typical scholarly work, but it does identify key studies in the expectation of offering readers a sense of the rich bibliography on Syria that exists beyond these pages. I hope it will be of interest to specialists, too, particularly my colleagues in the academy. I also write it for myself, as an attempt to make sense of a place I came to love before the onset of war altered it in hitherto unimaginable ways.

Above all, I write this book for the thousands of Syrians who have died in the course of the fighting, as well as the countless others who have suffered and grieved because of it. Among these, I write for the many friends and acquaintances I gained while in Syria and Lebanon. They opened to me their homes, families, and lives. When I met most of them, I had no intention of writing about their countries, much less of showcasing their stories to a general audience. There are some with whom I remain in touch, and they are safe. There are others, however, with whom I have lost contact or whom I cannot reach. I do not know where they are. I suspect some have fled Damascus, perhaps Syria altogether. Others could be dead. I write this book to honor them and their country, to capture a sense of what Syria was and still could be: a land of diversity, elegance, beauty, and tradition.

This is not a happy book. Had I written it against the backdrop of different events, I would have focused on less melancholy themes. The times seemed to call for reflection on the long-term challenges facing Syria—the very challenges that have reared their heads in the context of war, complicating and prolonging the conflict. Every country has its demons and heartaches, not least my own. I present Syria's demons not in an effort to condemn the country, but to complicate stereotypes about its history, culture, and politics by placing them in the messy matrix of day-to-day life.

Furthermore, I focus on certain storylines not in an effort to exacerbate the conflict, nor to tell a tale that is convenient for politicians in my country or any other which is involved in the fighting. This is especially true of my focus on sectarianism. Indeed, I suspect some readers will disagree with my assessments of the importance of religious identity in Syrian history. Before the outbreak of the civil war, it was common to hear that "there is no sectarianism in Syria." According to the preferred interpretation, the barbed sectarianism of the revolution was not the work of normal Syrians, but depending on one's perspective, of either the regime or its foreign enemies, who sought to destabilize the country by stoking hatred between members of different religious groups. Thus, Syria before the war emerges as a supra-sectarian paradise, in which Sunnis, 'Alawis, Christians, and Druze carried on with noble lack of interest in each other's faiths. As in all things, however, the facts lie somewhere in between. True, in recent times, Syria escaped the ferocious tensions that plagued its similarly diverse neighbors, especially Lebanon and Iraq. But the notion that sectarianism suddenly appeared only because of the civil war does no justice to what historical analysis and personal experience show to be deep and unspoken tensions before the onset of the so-called "Arab Spring." These tensions do not deserve celebration, but they do call for explanation, which I hope to provide in my own way here.

Furthermore, it bears underlining that sectarianism is a complex and variegated phenomenon. My interest in its pre-modern roots should not be interpreted to mean that religious conflicts (whether between Christians and Muslims, or between Sunnis and Shi'is) are somehow "unchanging" or "primordial"—far from it. In this book, I return often to ancient and medieval history in the interest of understanding how certain themes resurface and change over time. If we are to be sensitive to sectarianism in the present, we must be sensitive also to how sectarianism was manifested in the past.

I am a historian, and much of this work is concerned with the analysis of events that happened long ago. I weave these passages together with anecdotes from my life in the Middle East. The result is a hybrid style that I hope is both enriching and entertaining for the reader.

The book revolves around five principal themes, each of which features in its own longer chapter. First, the arrival of Islam in Syria in the seventh century and its continuing impact on the country today; second, the history of Christianity in Syria, especially the manner in which Christians relate to the Muslim society around them; third, the emergence of sectarian politics in the nineteenth and twentieth centuries; fourth, the behavior of Syria's autocratic state and its impact on daily life; and fifth, the current war, particularly its human toll and future direction, in which I take cues from Lebanon, a similar post-conflict society on Syria's border. I believe these five themes require clarification for a general audience, especially in the context of the Syrian civil war, in which information and historical perspective are hard to come by.

Finally, as I trust will become clear in pages that follow, I write this book out of a deep affection and respect for Syria and the Syrian people. What criticism I offer comes from a sense of concern and admiration for the country and its inhabitants, from a desire to understand Syria in her many facets: the good and the bad. I only wish I had more time to share in these pages those aspects of Syria which I treasured, especially the friendships, quotidian pleasures, and landscapes that made me feel so welcome in a foreign land. So, as we proceed on a tale that can seem disheartening and at times critical, do not forget that I write this book with a feeling of *'ishq* in my heart: of the faithful love one feels for a friend, for a relative, or your beloved. I hope I do her justice.

1

THE IMPERIAL MOMENT

ISLAM IN SYRIA

Mount Qassioun glowered over Damascus like a silent sentry. It is said that the Prophet Muhammad visited this mountaintop in the early seventh century—years before the armies of Islam fanned across the Middle East—and he took in her beauty. Then, Damascus was a much smaller place, studded with the towers of Byzantine churches, her Roman walls ringed by lush orchards and cool mountain streams. Yet the Prophet refused to descend and enjoy the city up close: man was meant to enter heaven only once.

In 2008, Damascus seemed less like paradise than urban purgatory: from high above, she was a mash of satellite dishes and grey tenements, an expanse of concrete slowly consuming all trace of green on the desert fringe. She wore a thin layer of exhaust fumes upon her head at all times, dancing to a bracing diesel symphony. In the glare of the sun, Damascus struck the onlooker as the quintessential Middle Eastern metropolis—busy, choked with people and traffic, bereft of elegance. Indeed, I suspected that had the Prophet visited in the twenty-first century and not in the seventh, he might have turned on his heel and looked for heaven somewhere else.

Still, Damascus could muster a sense of romance, especially at sunset. For three minutes at dusk, just as the light faded, a cascade of noise washed over the place. Hundreds of mosques erupted in sound, calling the faithful to the *maghrib*, the penultimate prayer of the day. Anyone who has ever visited a Muslim city would recognize it: like the Angelus bell in a European village, the call to prayer provides rhythm to daily life in the Middle East. It is a gentle but tenacious reminder to forget your daily chores, and for a moment, turn your eyes to God instead.

For most of history, the call to prayer was sung by the muezzin, who stood on the balcony of a minaret, the slender tower attached to the side of the mosque. In modern times, many mosques broadcast a recording of the prayer through a loudspeaker. Despite the intrusion of modern technology, however, the effect is undiminished. Each muezzin in Damascus had a slightly different way of singing. Many chanted with a monastic drone that would soar to a solemn crescendo, and then peter out with a perfunctory click at the tape's end. The sound was neither operatic nor angelic—but when amplified across hundreds of mosques in a vast space like the bowl of Damascus, the experience was powerful indeed.

The words of the prayer were hard to pick out from Mt Qassioun. Each mosque followed its own stopwatch, and together, they created a wall of sound. Still harder was trying to pair a ripple of '*Allahu akbar*' with a particular point of light down below. But that's not the reason people came to Mt Qassioun to listen. Sunset over Damascus was not about star performers, but rather about the entire orchestra.

Sunset brought a motley crew to the slopes of Qassioun. I came to the mountaintop on a warm summer night in 2008—one of my first in Damascus—and, looking around, noticed several foreign visitors, willing to swig an overpriced bottle of Barada beer to catch a glimpse of the city at her finest. There were the Syrian soldiers who patrolled the military bases higher up the slopes. There were the taxi drivers eager to ferry visitors back to the city, keeping their eyes open for lonely-looking men who might enjoy a visit to an Iraqi prostitute downtown (rates negotiable). Then there were the holy men, the true locals of Qassioun, who tended the mosques and shrines that peppered the face of the mountain. Since early Christian times, this area was a refuge for ascetics and pilgrims. It was allegedly here that Cain had slain his brother Abel, and where God had lulled forty pious Christians to sleep to save them from

Umayyad Mosque, Damascus, view from the courtyard

the persecution of Roman emperors. Each group rotated in a different galaxy despite the lofty setting they shared.

From the commanding heights of Qassioun, there was one monument down below that could not fail to impress. From high up, it resembled a basilica: long and narrow, crowned by a dome and girded by a large forecourt. On closer inspection, I noticed the small phalanx of towers hemming it in, with sheets of gold mosaic covering the courtyard like screens of chiffon. The entire city seemed to bow in its direction, and with good reason: this was the Umayyad Mosque—the most important building in Damascus and a fascinating window into Syrian history past and present.

After a few minutes, the call to prayer was ending. As the minarets went silent, their last echoes fading into the night, I asked for the bill and headed out of the restaurant.

Packs of hungry taxi drivers swarmed around, offering to spirit me away to places both sacred and profane. "No thanks, no fun for me tonight," I replied with a laugh to one, who cruised beside me in a beat-up Iranian cab, "Just down to the city, thank you." Unlike the Prophet Muhammad, I was ready to visit paradise.

Syria: The Bottleneck of Empires

Damascus claims to be the oldest continually inhabited urban center in the world.[1] It's a boast I heard before in my travels around the Middle East—from Egypt to Turkey and everywhere in between. I also learned to be warily skeptical of this claim. In my experience, ancient history can be a hobby of party bosses, generals, and state propagandists—the kinds of people who profit from tracing the political present to a distant, unknowable past. It's a way of establishing a sense of continuity for the nation, sect, or party. It's also a way of excluding those deemed not to belong.

Despite the hyperbole, Damascus may have a legitimate claim on being the world's oldest city, or certainly one of them. Nomads settled this desert oasis six thousand years ago, and the name *Dimaski* makes its first appearance in written form in tablets from Mari, an ancient city on the banks of the Euphrates, from around the year 2500 BC. Over the centuries, the city expanded and prospered. It was ruled by successive dynasties of Near Eastern kings—Aramaeans, Assyrians, and Babylonians—before falling to Alexander the Great in 332 BC. The Greeks brought order to the ancient metropolis, building grid-like streets, theaters, and other civilized amenities. This process continued under the Romans, who conquered the region in 64 BC, holding sway more or less continuously for another seven hundred years. In 635–36 AD, the armies of Islam took Syria from the East Roman Empire based in Constantinople. It inaugurated an uninterrupted period of Islamic rule through a string of dynasts, including the Umayyads, 'Abbasids, Tulunids, Ikshidids, Fatimids, Hamdanids, Ayyubids, Seljuks, Mamluks, and finally the Ottomans. With the collapse of the Ottoman Empire after World War I, France assumed custody of Syria under a mandate issued by the League of Nations. European colonialism ended in 1946, when the Syrian Arab Republic became an independent state with its capital at Damascus.

As is clear from this potted history, Damascus has seen its share of conquest over the centuries. But what accounts for its constant changing of hands, and what has made the city seem so sweet a prize for so many aspiring rulers?

If Afghanistan is the graveyard of empires, as pundits remind us constantly, Syria is surely their bottleneck. Lying astride the land bridge between the Mediterranean Sea and the Iranian plateau, Syria was where the empires of antiquity traditionally met for battle. While other powers—Hellenistic, Roman, Persian—may have schemed to conquer Syria for themselves (indeed, through most of its history, Syria was ruled from one of three places: Egypt, Persia, and the city of Constantinople-Istanbul) this made it infertile ground for an empire of its own. This is not to say that Syrians did not try. In ancient times, the region saw a steady stream of upstarts and rebels who dared to challenge the great kings from abroad. Most of them ended up defeated and humiliated—like Zenobia, the queen of the desert city of Palmyra in central Syria, who was paraded around Rome in golden chains in 274 AD after an abortive rebellion against the Emperor Aurelian. Aspiring politicos learned to survive as the clients of their more powerful neighbors. These would-be imperialists ended up managing the affairs of absentee landowners, like the

Christian Arab tribes of Ghassan, who policed vast swaths of greater Syria on behalf of the emperors in Constantinople.

Syrians today make much of the geographic and cultural unity of *Bilad al-Sham*—"the lands of Damascus" (*Sham*, the colloquial name for Damascus, is related to the Arabic word *shamal*, meaning "left," or "north," referring to its location in relation to the Arabian Peninsula). These stretch approximately from the Turkish border south to the Negev desert in Israel, and from the Mediterranean coast to the banks of the Euphrates. But talk of Greater Syria—often by Syrian nationalists gunning to exercise control over their weaker neighbors—overlooks the essential diversity of the region. Far from being a geographic and cultural unit, *Bilad al-Sham* is actually a patchwork of fragmented landscapes, from the rugged valleys of Lebanon to the flowing grain fields of Palestine, and from the arid expanses of the Eastern Desert to the lunar crags of southern Jordan. These sub-climates did not always cohere to form a natural ecosystem. Indeed, geographic diversity often sheltered deeper cultural and political divides.

The Lands of Damascus at the Dawn of Islam

Syrians are immensely proud of their ancient past. There is a sense that many of the great tectonic shifts in human history were uniquely "Syrian moments"—whether it was the establishment of city-states along the Euphrates River in the far east of the country or the invention of the alphabet by seafaring Phoenicians on the coast. That said, despite an appreciation of the breath of history that has unfolded across these lands, there is an equally pronounced sense among some that history really began with the coming of Islam.

I could occasionally see this feeling on display when I visited monuments around Syria: on the forlorn-looking ticket booths owned by the Ministry of Tourism were posted different prices for Syrians and for foreigners. Foreigners often paid ten or twenty times more than locals. Despite weighing entrance prices in their favour, it was rare to see large numbers of Syrians visiting these treasures aside from the occasional busload of students or the chance family excursion. This was especially true of monuments from the pre-Islamic period—the sprawling classical cities, Byzantine churches, and Neolithic settlements—which were usually abandoned save for a handful of European visitors milling around, as well as a few locals who tended the grounds or sold souvenirs. Meanwhile, the Islamic monuments—especially the early mosques, madrasas, and tombs of fallen heroes—were often besieged by crowds. True, this was partly a result of accessibility: the pre-Islamic sites were usually located in remote areas and were—well—dusty ruins; meanwhile, the great Islamic monuments remained in use for prayer and study, and more often than not, stood in the hearts of living, breathing cities. This was a history that was alive to people, and I often wondered whether the manifestly lower level of interest in the relics of the distant past reflected a sense among some Syrians that history had really begun with the coming of Islam. What had happened before it was a *jahiliyya*, or an age of ignorance. What came after was a golden age.

Whatever the case may be, it is undeniable that the advent of Islam in the early seventh century *did* change Syria in a profound way.[2] Whether for commercial or religious reasons, the Prophet Muhammad always showed a special interest in these lands. He died in 632 AD, four years before the fall of Damascus, but we know he harbored early ambitions to bring *Bilad al-Sham* into the Muslim fold, as evidenced by a string of campaigns he dispatched to southern Jordan at the end of his life. Under his immediate successors, the caliphs Abu Bakr and 'Umar, the conquest of Syria proceeded in earnest. It concluded in 640, with the surrender of Caesarea Maritima, a coastal city in modern-day Israel which was the last outpost to resist the conquering armies.[3]

The attention of Muslim leaders was understandable. As Arabia's closest northern neighbor, *Bilad al-Sham* was a natural point of expansion for the young movement. It was home to a large Arabophone population, most of it tribal in structure and Christian in faith, not unlike communities in the Arabian Peninsula. Moreover, many leading Muslims were familiar with the area thanks to years of land-owning and commerce. As a boy, the Prophet Muhammad is said to have visited Syria with a caravan owned by his uncle, Abu Talib.

In the wake of the conquests, Syria emerged as the most stable, powerful, and influential of the new Islamic provinces. This owed to several factors, none more important than its talented governor, Mu'awiya Ibn Abi Sufyan.[4] Mu'awiya was a pious and sober man, a scion of the aristocracy of the city of Mecca and a longtime secretary of the Prophet. His family, the Banu Umayya (meaning "the Tribe of Umayya"), were formerly leaders of the pagan resistance against Muhammad (indeed, Mu'awiya's mother, Hind, is said to have eaten the liver of the Prophet's uncle after he was killed in battle in 625). But after Muhammad captured Mecca in 628, the family fell into line and converted to the new religion. Appointed governor in Damascus in 638, Mu'awiya ruled Syria with relative independence for the next twenty years, building his power base as war and dissent simmered elsewhere in the empire.

These troubles came to a head in 658 when a rebel killed the third caliph, 'Uthman Ibn 'Affan. The Prophet's nephew 'Ali—today venerated as the first Imam by Shi'a Muslims—took control of the caliphate, but 'Uthman's supporters demanded revenge. Mu'awiya was the perfect choice to lead them. Not only was he independently powerful as the governor of Syria, but as a member of the Banu Umayya and a kinsman of the slain caliph, he had a strong moral claim against 'Uthman's killers. Civil war erupted between the governor Mu'awiya and the caliph 'Ali, and after a complex and tragic string of events, in 661 Mu'awiya emerged the victor, moving the capital of the caliphate to Syria. Henceforth, the fate of Damascus would be tied to the fortunes of its ruling family, the Umayyads.[5]

The Umayyads: Masters of the Syrian Century

At first glance, Mu'awiya's victory over 'Ali is all we need to explain Damascus' rise to power in the mid-seventh century. It had more to do with the great man who happened to govern Syria in those crucial decades than anything special about Damascus itself. As we have seen, Syria had a poor track record as an incubator of empires, and furthermore, it was neither the richest nor the most populous province of the expanding Islamic empire. At the same time, there is another view, popular among Syrian nationalists, which discounts this way of thinking. For them there was nothing surprising about the turn of events. Rather, what happened in the seventh century, when Syria became the center of an expanding Arab and Muslim world, was a matter of destiny, and not merely the exceptional man who initiated the process. In my judgment, the truth lies somewhere in between. There were deeper reasons why it was the governor of Syria who managed to wrest control of power in the 660s and put Damascus on the map, inaugurating what I call the "Syrian century."

As I noted above, Syria enjoyed relative stability between the 640s and 660s. During these trying years, Muslims elsewhere in the empire grappled with deep internal divisions and struggled to establish control over their ever-expanding domains. Meanwhile, Mu'awiya kept his post as governor in Damascus. He did so by drawing support from an especially loyal and relatively homogenous base of Arab tribesmen, who had settled there after the conquests of the 630s. The Syrian army was the single most important weapon at Mu'awiya's disposal. As governor, his greatest accomplishments were essentially those of this army: the creation of the first Arab naval fleet, the construction of coastal defenses against the Byzantines, and the successful securing of the northern frontier. When Mu'awiya challenged 'Ali for control of the caliphate in 661, it was his Syrian troops who provided him with the crucial boost needed for victory.

The dominance of the Syrian army in the early period owed partly to its size. We know from the reign of a later Umayyad caliph, al-Walid I (r. 705–715), that the troops of the Damascus *jund*, or military district, numbered some 45,000 men, with the total number throughout greater Syria approaching 175,000. By contrast, the total number of troops in the army of Khurasan, an important province in northeastern Persia, was a paltry 50,000. Across the decades, this army functioned as the main guarantor of Syrian hegemony, pushing the pace of conquest and quelling troubled hotspots throughout the empire.

Scholars sometimes refer to the Umayyad caliphate as a "jihad state," since it spent most of its time and resources conquering new territory.[6] Given that its armies were engaged in conquest across the ancient world—from Spain to China—Syria became a strategic base for monitoring and managing the action. The caliph Hisham Ibn 'Abd al-Malik, for example, ruled at a time with fronts as far flung as Poitiers in southern France (732) and Navsari in western India (738–39), which he could monitor effectively from his capital in Syria. Furthermore, Syria was close to the most important military front of all, that with the Byzantine Empire. In pre-modern societies, in which the government's footprint is usually light and control of territory often tenuous, wherever the army is based tends to be where the state resides, as well. Syria's strategic location proved crucially important. Indeed, this location would keep Syria in the center of regional and global affairs for centuries to come, including today, when its importance stems partly from its proximity to geopolitical hotspots including Israel, Lebanon, and Iraq.

Why did Syria succeed?

Aside from these strategic considerations, there were other factors that propelled Damascus and the lands around it into the epicenter of Islamic history. Many of these owed much to the legacy of Roman rule. The province was easily governed in the decades after the conquest due to its long and proud history of central government and urban life. Some of the wealthiest and most prosperous cities of the ancient world were located there, including Antioch in modern-day Turkey; Tyre and Heliopolis (Baalbek) in Lebanon; Apamea, Emesa (Homs), and Damascus in Syria; as well as the cities of the Decapolis, which are spread today between Jordan and Israel-Palestine. Of these a number were in a sorry state of disrepair when Muslim armies arrived in the 630s, and many more withered over the coming century. But their shining colonnades, stately agoras, and richly appointed churches were living proof of Syria's stability, wealth, and sophistication. Archaeological evidence suggests that certain Syrian cities continued to flourish well into the seventh century, in comparison to other parts of the eastern Mediterranean, which were hit hard by economic contraction, demographic decline, and even plague. In short, Syria was fertile ground for a new empire when the Muslims entered Damascus for the first time in 634.[7]

Once the conquests were over, the inhabitants of Syria proved relatively submissive to their new Muslim overlords. Local rebellions did not figure prominently in the history of the region in the early Islamic period, leaving Mu'awiya and his Umayyad successors time to consolidate control elsewhere. Furthermore, many Syrian elites—the kinds of military and political leaders who had the resources to spark a rebellion against Muslim rule—fled to the safety of Byzantium instead. The power-brokers of early Islamic Syria included descendants of the Byzantine remnant that chose to stay behind—especially the Christian Arab tribes of Ghassan, whom we have already met, many of whom converted to Islam and formed an important part of the Umayyads' power base.[8]

The absence of serious resistance is also attested by the history of Muslim settlement in Syria. Unlike Iraq or Egypt, where the Muslims sequestered themselves in *amsar*—military camps that evolved into cities, with the goal of separating the Muslim soldiers from the surrounding populations—in Syria Muslims settled mostly in existing cities like Damascus, Homs, and Aleppo.[9] Apparently, security in Syria was such that there was not much need for special "safe houses" to protect the new settlers; plus, there were abandoned riches aplenty to enjoy in the cities.

Finally, Syrian society then—as today—was divided by linguistic, regional, and sectarian differences. There were tensions between city and countryside; between Greek metropolitan society and the Syriac culture of the villages; between the Chalcedonian Christianity of the imperial capital and the Jacobite Christianity of the local "nonconformist" churches. These tensions created a stunning array of "micro-climates" in Syria, but they also made it a difficult place to rule. Syria's Roman masters—by dint of their long stay in the region—had a stake in practically every one of these fights. Therefore whenever their will clashed with those of the locals, control invariably suffered. In some respects the Muslims were blissfully unaware of this "inside game." They were savvy rulers, and learned the Syrian terrain well. But on the crucial questions that had long divided the region and foiled Roman hegemony—the politics of Christian theology, in particular—the Muslims had no stake in the fight. It helped them rule with an efficient impartiality toward the concerns of their Christian subjects, who continued to form a demo-graphic majority in the region deep into the Middle Ages.

All in all, the legacy of late antiquity made Syria generally, as well as Damascus specifically, an attractive base for running an empire. Thanks to the Umayyads, Damascus could finally claim its place among the great capitals of the world, instilling in its inhabitants a sense of grandeur and purpose. As we will see, the feeling lingers to this day. Let's return to the city and discover how and why.

The Psalm and the Mosque

There are relatively few traces of Umayyad rule left in the Middle East. The passage of time—not to mention the efforts of treasure hunters, plunderers, and armies—has erased most of their patri-mony. Today, this consists of a few desert castles, caravanserais, and bathhouses peppering the eastern desert of Syria and Jordan. It makes the survival of the Umayyad Mosque in the center of Damascus all the more remarkable.

When I first visited Syria in 2008, what drew me to the Umayyad Mosque was its soulful voice. Indeed, the only thing finer than sunset atop Mt Qassioun was to recline on the rooftop of my home in Damascus' Old City and listen for the mosque's muezzins, espe-cially on Friday, the Muslim holy day. It is exceptionally rare to hear the call to prayer sung in a chorus. Yet at the Umayyad mosque, a group of men would gather around a bank of micro-phones in a side room and solemnly intone the prayer all at once—producing a melody as stirring as a great cathedral choir.

Most visitors approach the Umayyad Mosque via the command-ing promenade of the Souq al-Hamidiyya, the great covered market where hawkers try to unload carpets, training bras, and digital Qurans with equal zeal. I preferred a different path to the mosque, one that began at the eastern end of the city and wound lazily through less congested territory. Letting the call to prayer lead me west, I would pass Hammam al-Bakri on the right, the bath house run by an old Damascene family claiming descent from the first caliph, Abu Bakr. Further along, someone had nailed an Israeli flag to the middle of the pedestrian way—naturally, passers-by swerved

Umayyad Mosque, Damascus, blocked door with Psalm inscription

to trample it. High above, flowers with dense blooms concealed bundles of power cables that hung lazily across the street. I would then pass the high-end antique shop beside the low-end cobbler; t-shirts for candidate Obama scribbled in Arabic; and a young Syrian romancing a still younger Swedish tourist. This was the city at its exuberant best.

The mosque offered no pretentious greetings when I finally reached her eastern wall. The stone masonry raced skyward high above the cluttered neighborhood. As I turned the corner, about half-way down the much longer southern wall, something would always catch my eye: a blocked door, about ten feet across and fifteen feet high, crammed awkwardly beside a box framing the back wall of the *mihrab*, or prayer niche, inside the building. The faithful, who were streaming out of the mosque after Friday prayers, never seemed to notice the blocked entrance, and I figured it was probably better that way. The lintel bore a Greek inscription with a surprising message: "Thy kingdom, O Christ, is an everlasting Kingdom, and Thy dominion endures throughout all generations." How did a version of Psalm 145 end up on the outside of the holiest Muslim sanctuary in Syria? To puzzle it over, I headed to the main entrance of the mosque, finding the courtyard quiet and all to myself.[10]

Temple, Church, and Mosque in the Heart of Damascus

The Umayyad Mosque, standing in the heart of the Old City, occupies a plot that has been home to religious worship since the second century BC.[11] The Romans built a temple there dedicated to the god Jupiter. It was a vast complex, typically Syrian in design, with a small inner sanctuary surrounded by a vast sacred enclosure. The outer ring of that enclosure, which once spanned nearly a quarter of a mile on its northern and southern sides, no longer survives, but traces of the inner enclosure, or *temenos*, can still be spotted at the beginning of the Souq al-Hamidiyya, where a stately arch sheltered merchants selling all varieties of religious kitsch. More modest traces of the enclosure can be found at the eastern end of the mosque, the path I took on that hot summer day.

Christianity spread to Damascus soon after Jesus' death. Indeed, its moment in the sun happened early on, when a heavenly voice knocked St Paul from his horse, as recounted in the Acts of the Apostles. It then instructed him to go to Damascus and find "a street called straight." It was there, at the home of Ananias, the local Christian leader, that St Paul was baptized and launched in his career as a missionary and apologist for the faith he had once persecuted. Although Christianity gathered steam in Damascus over the next three hundred years, it was not until the late fourth century—after Christianity had become the official religion of the state—that the Temple of Jupiter was converted into a church. Shortly before the Arab conquest, this church came to possess the head of John the Baptist, a prized relic that drew pilgrims from far and wide.

Muslim armies entered Damascus in September 634, and around three decades later, the city became the capital of a fledging state under the Umayyad dynasty. Despite the changing of the guard, the church carried on as a center of Christian worship. Christians remained in the majority here—as throughout Syria—and it was only reasonable that the sizeable Christian population should preserve its glittering church.

For the first seventy years, Muslims worshipped alongside Christians in the existing Byzantine basilica. According to historical reconstructions, Muslims prayed in the southeastern end of the complex, in a special space known as a *masalla*, outfitted with a *mihrab* that pointed the faithful toward Mecca. Meanwhile, Christians continued to conduct their liturgy at the western end of the church, around the existing altar and apse. Scholars believe that the blocked doorway mentioned above served as an entrance for both groups, with Christians turning left and Muslims right into their respective sections of the complex. This arrangement was not so unusual: we know about similar arrangements at other sites from the early Islamic period, where the first generation of Muslims prayed in spaces borrowed from their Christian subjects.

Whether this arrangement reflected the ecumenism, magnanimity, or pragmatism of the conquerors is tough to say. What is easy to imagine is how the arrangement eventually unravelled, having became a source of embarrassment for the Umayyads. The Muslims of Damascus—which, by the turn of the eighth century, had become the capital of the greatest empire in the world at the time—were squatting in "rented space," and what is more, "rented space" belonging to their religious rivals. This had to change.

Thus it was that the caliph al-Walid I (r. 705–15) razed the church.[12] In its place, he built the most magnificent mosque ever seen, abruptly purging Christianity from the city center and establishing Islam as the main show in town. It remains so today.

Damascus' Long Late Antiquity

As I removed my shoes and walked into the courtyard of the Umayyad Mosque, it was easy to imagine how once this had been a church complex. The main part of the mosque, on my right, was essentially a basilica in plan, long and narrow like the great churches of Rome or Florence. But instead of finding a sacred enclosure on the eastern end, as one would in a church, the faithful directed their attention to the southern wall, where a string of five *mihrab*s (each one representing a different school of Islamic law, with one large *mihrab* uniting them in the middle) indicated the direction of prayer. In the middle of this hall—high above the main *mihrab*—was a dome inscribed with dense lines of Arabic text.

Al-Walid and his architects incorporated many elements of the old Byzantine church in their new mosque: the lower masonry of the prayer hall, for example, was left over from the church complex, as were the columns of the inner courtyard, recycled for a second time from the Roman temple. Meanwhile, around the perimeter of the complex were three minarets, which stood atop the bases of the old corner towers. According to tradition, the minaret on the southeast corner, the Tower of Jesus (in its present state dating back to the thirteenth century), marks the spot where Christ will one day descend from the heavens to oversee the Final Judgment—a (happy) thought to contemplate as I would dine occasionally on the rooftop terraces of nearby restaurants, which were level with the base of the tower.

In late antiquity, these towers were the homes of Christian ascetics, some of whom stayed put after the demolition until they were

Umayyad Mosque, Damascus, tomb of John the Baptist

forcibly evicted by Muslim builders. According to a colorful anecdote from the great historian of Damascus, Ibn 'Asakir (d. 1175), one monk refused to come down from his cell, prompting the caliph al-Walid to ascend the tower, seize him by the scruff of his neck, and throw him out of the church. In a twist of fate, after the complex was transformed into a mosque, Muslim holy men ascended the new minarets, much like the monks in the towers before them, in a vivid symbol of religious continuity.[13]

The most important example of religious continuity was to be found back inside the prayer hall. Walking to the eastern end, I discovered a lavish domed shrine, sheathed in green glass and studded with metal grills. Pious men and women crowded around it. I took special note of a man visiting from the east of Syria, who struggled to stuff a wad of cash through the grate; rich tourists from the Gulf who peered warily at the shrine; and an old mystic rocking back and forth as he recited the Quran. This shrine contained the head of John the Baptist—known as Yahya to Muslims—the very same relic that had made the cathedral so famous in Byzantine times. A report from the medieval historian al-Raba'i describes how al-Walid's workmen discovered the relic while excavating a subterranean shrine beneath the nave of the old church. Far from destroying the Christian relic, they promptly restored it to a place of honor in the prayer hall, where it remains today.[14]

For many visitors, the greatest attraction at the Umayyad Mosque are its mosaics, and so they were for me.[15] Originally, they lined the perimeter of the entire courtyard, though a devastating fire in 1893 destroyed many of the originals. Heading outside, I gazed at the "Barada Panel" on the western arcade, a lush scene of riverbeds, palaces, and gardens, reminiscent of descriptions of paradise in the Quran. They reminded me immediately of late antique mosaics I had seen in Istanbul, Ravenna, and Rome, and with good reason: reports suggest that al-Walid hired Christian craftsmen to execute these panels. Robert Byron surmised as much when he visited in the early twentieth century, speculating, "They must have been done by Greeks," since for him they seemed to foreshadow the abstract style of a latter-day Greek master, El Greco.[16]

The direct line between al-Walid and El Greco might have been tenuous, but Byron's general observation was accurate. The mosa-

Umayyad Mosque, Damascus, 'Barada Panel' mosaic

ics were Byzantine in all respects, save for one major difference: the curious absence of human and animal imagery, thus complying with the emergent consensus among early Muslim scholars, who, like the ancient Jews, regarded such depictions as idolatrous. The Barada, for which the mosaics were named, is a river that runs from the mountains northwest of Damascus into the city center. Today, once it reaches the capital, it can look more like a polluted creek, reduced by irrigation and heaps of rubbish. Still, by gazing at these mosaics, I had an immediate sense of what Damascus must have looked like for the Prophet and his Umayyad heirs as they gazed upon it from the heights of Mt Qassioun—a veritable slice of heaven on earth.

The Killing Fields of Karbala

Every time I visited the Umayyad Mosque, it seemed ever more like a palimpsest of Syrian history. The word "palimpsest"—referring to a page from a manuscript that has been scraped clean of older layers of writing for reuse, but which preserves traces of this writing—offers a convenient metaphor for understanding the layers of cultural interaction in the city, if not Syria at large.[17] In the transition from temple to church, and from church to mosque, we realize that all efforts to erase the past invariably depended upon it. Indeed, the process of innovation at the Umayyad Mosque was both destructive and productive, giving rise to dynamic new forms by transforming the residue of the old. This was true of the transition from paganism to Christianity in antiquity, and even more so, of the transition from Christianity to Islam in the Middle Ages. As we will see, it is also a metaphor for Syrian history beyond Umayyad times.

By this point, I had spent more than an hour poking around the mosque, trying to avoid the stares of old men by looking dutifully pious. It seemed to have worked: the old men who had lingered after the prayers took an interest in me, perhaps tipped off by the unkempt beard I had grown that summer. I started getting greetings of "Salaam alaykum! Where are you from? Sit with us, will you?" I declined politely, asking instead for directions to "Imam Hussein".

After a few quizzical looks, they gestured to the great courtyard. I made my way to the northeast corner of this courtyard, to a rather decrepit-looking room lined with ragged carpets but packed with people. This was the final stop of my tour—the shrine (*mashhad*) of Hussein, grandson of the Prophet Muhammad, the son of the fourth caliph 'Ali, and the greatest martyr of Shi'i Islam.

As we saw earlier, the Umayyads rose to power by wresting control of the caliphate from 'Ali, the Prophet's cousin and son-in-law. Although Mu'awiya, then governor of Damascus and founder of the dynasty, did not actually kill 'Ali, his death followed their famous settlement at Siffin in Iraq in 661, where negotiations were more or less rigged in Mu'awiya's favor. As Mu'awiya marched victoriously back to Damascus, 'Ali remained in Iraq, and soon after, while completing the dawn prayer one day, was assassinated by a Kharijite rebel.

In Islamic culture, the conflict between Mu'awiya and 'Ali is referred to as the *fitna*, or temptation, coming from the Arabic root meaning to "seduce," "charm," or "enthrall." Often this word is rendered as "civil war," but this translation doesn't capture the texture—or the tragedy—of what transpired. It was a conflict of geopolitics—pitting 'Ali's Iraqi powerbase against Mu'awiya's in Syria. More than that, in the minds of many Muslims (and especially the followers of 'Ali, from which we get the term *Shi'a*, meaning "the partisans"), the *fitna* had disastrous implications for the Muslim community, opening a ragged breach in the heart of a people who had stood under a single banner more or less continuously since the Prophet's death.

In many ways, the *fitna* represented a conflict over competing ideas of leadership within this community, and thus, over the kind of ruler who could conduct the faithful to their place in heaven. In this vein, there developed a conviction among 'Ali's supporters that this power belonged to the Prophet's family and to no one else. The family—known in Arabic as *Ahl al-Bayt* ("The People of the House")—was thought to have a special spiritual charisma that passed from father to son. Because the Prophet left no sons of his own (he had three, but all died in childhood) the mantle fell to his cousin 'Ali, and in turn, to 'Ali's sons Hassan and Hussein. When

'Ali was assassinated in 661, these brothers were expected to take up the fight and challenge the Umayyad usurpers.[18]

Hassan, the older of the two sons, did not wish to lead the Shi'a. All the same, recognizing the potential threat he posed to them, the Umayyads retired him to a large estate near the city of Medina, where he carried on in solitude until his mysterious death in 669. His younger brother Hussein, on the other hand, eagerly assumed the cause of their slain father. For several years, he led the partisans of the *Ahl al-Bayt*—who were mostly concentrated in Iraq—against the Umayyads in Syria. This happened against the backdrop of a still wider struggle for power inside the caliphate, which came to be known as the second *fitna*. It was during this time that another challenger, 'Abdallah Ibn al-Zubayr, established his own Islamic state based in the Arabian Peninsula. It was a singularly tumultuous moment for the young community of believers.

The conflict between the Umayyads and the *Ahl al-Bayt* came to a head in 680, when the Umayyad general 'Ubayd Allah Ibn Ziyad marched to the Iraqi city of Karbala, about sixty miles southwest of modern Baghdad. It was there that the Umayyads cut off Hussein and his small band of supporters, who were then heading from Mecca to the Iraqi city of Kufa. They were vastly outnumbered by the Umayyads, who crushed them swiftly and harshly. Karbala was a turning point in Islamic history. Though the Umayyads succeeded in quashing the Shi'i threat in the near term, they did so in the most brutal and least decorous way possible: by savagely executing Hussein, a member of the Prophet's house, fondly remembered by many Muslims for having bounced on the Prophet's knee as a child. Muslims of all stripes realized that the victory had come at great cost to the Umayyads, whom many henceforth regarded as blood-thirsty and impious. Moreover, it is worth bearing in mind that prior to their conversion to Islam, the pagans of the Banu Umayya had been the Prophet's staunchest enemies. Thus, to see them usurp the sacred office of the caliph was equivalent to watching Hitler or Mussolini take over the United Nations after World War II.

In the coming decades, a sense of tragic loss spread among the supporters of 'Ali and Hussein. History had stolen their moment in the sun, and they were left to dream—and to curse—what might

Umayyad Mosque, Damascus, *Mashhad* of Imam Hussein

have been. These feelings would fester over the coming decades, giving rise to the recognizable religious movement we now call Shi'ism.

Shi'a Pilgrims in a Sunni Mosque

After Karbala, the head of Hussein was sent to the caliph Yazid in Damascus. There, it was displayed as a trophy of a failed revolt, a reminder to his subjects to respect the authority of the real "deputies of God," the Umayyads.[19] The caliph installed the head in a niche in the Umayyad Mosque, where I found myself staring on that particularly warm summer afternoon.

Although most Muslims in Syria are Sunnis, the *mashhad* of Hussein always attracted large crowds of Shi'i pilgrims—some from Lebanon and Iraq, along with many from Iran. Perhaps this explains why the place seemed rather forlorn, as if the mosque's Sunni caretakers had forgotten about it. Given the historic tensions between Sunnis and Shi'is, it was a fair bet.[20] But what the shrine lacked in plush carpets and good lighting like the rest of the mosque, it more than made up for in feeling.

Around the silver-plated niche where Hussein's head was once displayed—a square box roughly a foot long on each side—stood women dressed in flowing black robes, struggling to hold back their tears. They were contemplating the death of Hussein and the tragedy of Karbala. It would have been a ritual familiar to anyone who had witnessed the Shi'i festival of 'Ashura, which falls on the tenth day of the holy month of Muharram. In Lebanon, where I lived several years later, many members of the Shi'i community celebrate 'Ashura by restaging the high drama of Karbala. In town squares across the south, though especially in the city of Nabatieh, individuals take on the roles of various heroes and villains in the story—the valiant Hussein, the wicked general Shimr who led the Umayyad troops, and the droves of mourning women who witnessed the carnage. Famously, the Shi'a of Nabatieh—taking a cue from the Iranians, who introduced the practice to the area in the early twentieth century—march in boisterous processions in which groups of men cut themselves with razors, creating a steady trickle of blood that falls across their faces and shirts (the Shi'a of

Damascus performed a similar ritual at the shrine of Sayyida Zeinab on the south side of town).[21] To mimic the tortures of Karbala in this way was to enter the slipstream of sacred history, to taste the blood of the martyrs and to weep the tears of their inconsolable families.

Indeed, Karbala has played a crucial role in the Shi'i conception of history—a moment of tragic loss when the Muslim community lost its way. The tears of the women at the Umayyad Mosque were also personal: they cried for lost children, for husbands who had abandoned them, for the poor in the street, for the soldiers slaughtered in battle. This was the melancholy genius of Shi'i spirituality: to encourage the faithful to return to the killing fields of Karbala, and in so doing, to comprehend the suffering of their slaughtered imam. It was not unlike the way Christians sometimes imagine themselves nailed to the cross beside Jesus on Calvary, co-redeeming the world by entering those dark moments of the crucifixion.

Upon arriving, I realized that Hussein's head was actually not in the mosque. There are rich and varied traditions about where it was brought after Damascus: some say to Cairo, others to Medina. Whatever the case may be, I saw Iranian pilgrims pressing wads of money (bearing the likeness of Ayatollah Khomeini) into the shrine as if the head were still there. The existence of this place—and the streams of Shi'a pilgrims who visited it—was a testament to the complex religious ecology of the Umayyad Mosque, and of Syria generally. It was also a testament to the political alliance that made their visit possible, namely, the close relationship between the Baathist regime in Damascus and the Islamic Republic in Tehran.

At the door of Hussein's shrine, an efficient-looking tour operator from Iran looked at his watch. It was time to go. This shrine was one of several pilgrimage sites in Damascus that drew thousands of visitors from Iran each year. Their circuit also included a mosque just to the north in the Old City containing the tomb of Hussein's daughter, Ruqayya, as well as a much larger golden-domed mosque on the south side of the city, home to the tomb of Hussein's sister Zeinab (where Shi'i militias from Iraq and Lebanon presently stand guard). Both of these mosques were relatively new—constructed with funds from Tehran in the past thirty

Cemetery of Bab al-Saghir, Damascus, tombs of the Prophet's descendants

years—and they had a certain gauche aesthetic to them: the mosque of Sayyida Zeinab, for example, was lined in not unattractive blue tiles from the Iranian city of Isfahan, but its interior was covered in garish mirror panels, creating an otherworldly ambiance designed to conjure the dome of heaven (but which came much closer to a forgotten set from the television show *Lost in Space*). I decided to follow these crowds to a more modest, but no less important spot on their pilgrimage route: the ancient cemetery of Bab al-Saghir.

Rival Histories in an Ancient Graveyard

I left the pilgrims to their air-conditioned buses and decided to walk to the cemetery myself. The graveyard was a short fifteen-minute stroll from the Umayyad Mosque, southwest on the edge of Damascus' old city. It was in a gritty neighborhood that included a few handsome mosques and madrassas of the sixteenth century, as well several purveyors of funerary goods (among the most popular wares were headstones emblazoned with the bright yellow logo of the Lebanese Shi'i militant group, Hezbollah).

The cemetery of Bab al-Saghir was among the most important, but little-known monuments from the early Islamic period in Damascus.[22] It was here that a number of kinsmen of the Prophet were buried, including 'Ali's daughter, Umm Kulthum, as well as Hussein's daughter, Sukayna. Before the onset of the war, Syria received over a million religious tourists annually. Around 200,000 of these were Iranian pilgrims, who would flood into these and other green-topped shrines in the cemetery as a standard part of their visit. They were modest versions of the much larger shrines mentioned above, with large above-ground tombs draped in green, around which the faithful circumambulated at a rather sluggish pace.

As an undergraduate, I had taken a course on Chaucer's *Canterbury Tales*, a bawdy poem about a group of medieval pilgrims en route to the shrine of St Thomas à Becket at Canterbury. Throughout the class, I found it difficult to imagine what these pilgrims would have done once they eventually reached Canterbury at the end of the poem—weep, pray, sleep. Chaucer is mute on the subject, though knowing the chronic misdemeanors of his motley crew, I imagined they'd probably head to the nearest alehouse. A few months before visiting the old cemetery in Damascus, I had gone to Rome on my own Easter pilgrimage, where I was struck by the secularity of the experience—by the blurry line between tourism and prayer, between the avowed obligation to light candles and a more intense interest in investigating the gelaterias where I could break my Lenten fast.

Thus, I was curious—and a bit intimidated—to see these Iranians moving around with such pious purpose: the tears, the wailing, the wads of cash dispensed liberally wherever they went. I was relieved to discover, therefore, that at least a few of the penitents in the cemetery of Bab al-Saghir might have enjoyed the company of Chaucer's rowdy misfits. In one of the shrines, I noticed two young men in tight jeans and much hair gel arranging their camera. The first one walked towards the sarcophagus with the studied nonchalance of a young James Dean. As he approached, he suddenly summoned up a primal feeling of grief, grabbing the tomb and weeping dramatically. Meanwhile, his friend stood behind him snapping pictures, like Annie Liebovitz conducting a photo shoot for *Vanity Fair*. After a minute, the flash went dark and the first one returned to the confined sidelines to inspect the photos taken by his friend. I couldn't understand their exchange in Farsi, but the disappointment in the eyes of the first spoke for itself. "Let's do this again," he seemed to say. So as his companion held up his cell phone for a second time, the young man stepped back to the tomb and erupted in a show of grief more intense than the first. On this occasion, he practically mounted the tomb (the Syrian caretaker by the door looked on with a mix of suspicion and indifference—one suspects he'd seen this before). Once this finished, the cameraman showed his friend the photos, and this time, smiles abounded. Real grief! I could only imagine the conversations that would ensue back in Iran among these pilgrims and their friends: "Successful pilgrimage! Great wailing!"

As I followed the visitors, I noticed another domed sanctuary about two hundred feet away. No one was milling around this one, so I decided to inspect it. The tomb was a large stone mausoleum, about ten feet deep by fifteen feet long, girded by a rusting metal grill. The building was unadorned, save for an Arabic inscription stretching across a lintel on the south side, which read: "In this place are buried several companions of the Messenger of God, and they are Fadl Ibn 'Ubayd Allah and Suhayl Ibn al-Akhtal Ibn Wa'is al-Thuqafi and Wa'il Ibn al-Usqu', and they are among those who pledged their loyalty to the Messenger under the tree; and also Mu'awiya Ibn Abi Sufyan, the founder of the Umayyad state." Mu'awiya's tomb—now this was a surprise!

I glanced back at the Shi'a pilgrims and hoped nobody had noticed me. After all, in their version of history, Mu'awiya was the bloodthirsty tyrant who had wrested power from the hands of the Prophet's rightful heir, 'Ali. Furthermore, it was his accursed son, Yazid, who had ordered the murder of Hussein in 680 at Karbala. The Shi'a have no love for these Umayyads, and that's why the location of Mu'awiya's grave—in the same complex frequented by the Shi'a pilgrims—struck me as so ironic, and so eminently Damascene. Here in the crowded concrete expanse of the cemetery of Bab al-Saghir, two conflicting visions of Islamic history lay uncomfortably adjacent to one another. It was as if Jefferson Davis and Abraham Lincoln—the great rivals of the American Civil War—happened to be buried a hundred feet apart in the same graveyard. Judging from the forlorn state of Mu'awiya's tomb, these visions of the Islamic past had come into conflict in a real way even in our modern present. Yet there was something wondrous and impressive about this city that managed to contain so many contradictions in such a small place. Fearing retaliation for the crimes of the seventh century, I decided not to inform the pilgrims from Iran of what I had found.

The Impious Caliph

Despite the general anonymity of Mu'awiya's grave, someone *had* been there. Peering inside the metal grate, I found a modest tomb close to the ground, with a faded wreath draped across it. It had the look of officialdom, as if some delegation had visited and dutifully left it behind. When I returned the following year, I noticed a still fresher wreath atop the cenotaph, as well as a new coat of paint on the dome. Mu'awiya was on someone's radar, but it was not the Shi'a's.

Though the Shi'a harbor universally negative feelings towards the Umayyads, Sunni Muslims—especially in Syria—tend to see more gray in the picture. I was reminded of this when I reported my discovery to my friend Muhammad, a young father and Arabic teacher, who disapproved of my tomb-hunting, regarding it as a kind of vestigial paganism (though he was too polite to say it out loud). "You found Mu'awiya, I see," he told me the next day. "I went there once myself, just to see it, but I didn't want to linger. You know for us Syrians, we have mixed views of Mu'awiya. The Umayyads were not good Muslims: they drank, they womanized, they disobeyed the law of Islam. But they did some great things: without the Umayyads, Syria would be nothing."

Muhammad's balanced assessment rang true. The next summer, while traveling through the deserts of Jordan, I came across what is perhaps the strangest relic of the Umayyad age: the bathhouse of Qusayr 'Amra, erected between 723 and 743 by the prince al-Walid II while he was still caliph-in-waiting.[23] The bathhouse stood about fifty miles east of 'Amman. Built of sand-colored limestone, it struck a low profile against the desert expanse. The main hall was not large, comprising three barrel-vaulted aisles around 45 feet long and 35 feet wide. A door on the western wall led into an attached bath complex, once fed by rain water that was stored in an underground cistern.

More noteworthy than Qusayr 'Amra's architecture was its interior decoration. Brightly colored frescoes covered practically every inch of wall and ceiling—depicting great desert hunts, symbols of the zodiac, and various mythological creatures. For a bathhouse that once belonged to a Muslim prince, the imagery was shockingly profane—especially in contrast to the restrained mosaics of the Umayyad Mosque back in Damascus, built by al-Walid's uncle, al-Walid I. They showed little regard for modesty, much less for religious prohibitions on the depiction of human and animal forms.

This was in keeping with what we know about the man who built it. Medieval Arabic texts portray al-Walid II as a feckless and profligate character. He allegedly used the Quran for target practice; planned to build an open-air "cocktail deck" atop the Kaaba in Mecca, where he could sip wine and gossip about the passers-by;

Qusayr ʿAmra, Jordan, fresco of bathhouse attendant

and once, upon hearing the call to prayer ring out from a nearby mosque, he withdrew from the singing girl lying beneath him and ordered her to lead the prayers in his stead.

Qusayr 'Amra perfectly expressed al-Walid's alleged love of debauchery and power. All around the bathhouse, he placed frescoes of naked women—some dancing, others lifting basins of water, all of them flirting from above. They had little in common with lithe models like Kate Moss, instead resembling the zaftig beauties of Michelangelo's Sistine Chapel ceiling. When I visited, I pointed them out to my Jordanian driver, who seemed embarrassed at the sight of such erotic paintings. Then, overcoming his sheepishness, he removed a cell phone from his pocket and started snapping pictures. He blushed again when I asked whether he would show them to his wife.

Aside from the delights of the flesh, al-Walid was also concerned with his *muruwwa*, or manliness. Across the walls of Qusayr 'Amra leapt packs of antelopes, dogs and hunters in hot pursuit. They stood as a probable record of what took place when al-Walid was in residence—great desert chases, like the hunting parties of ancient Persian literature and pre-Islamic Arabic poetry. For al-Walid, the hunt was both high sport and political theater, an opportunity to demonstrate his skill and dominance over the natural environment.

Many scholars dismiss caricatures of the Umayyads as fun-loving, sensual, and impious as polemical fiction. They argue that these reflect the propagandistic views of writers living under the 'Abbasids, the dynasty which deposed the Umayyads during a bloody revolution around 750, and who had a vested interest in sullying their memory.[24] The Umayyads were worldly and ruthless men, to be sure, but perhaps we read too much into the contradiction between their profligacy and their piety. What mattered was that the Umayyads governed a state that was constantly expanding: on their watch, the caliphate reached its greatest geographical extent. No matter how much boozing, sex, or killing they engaged in, the success of the Umayyad-led jihad was proof that God approved—or at least, didn't really mind—the rule of this family over the domains of Islam.

This is precisely the message of a second group of frescoes at Qusayr 'Amra, which seemed to me to convey concisely the religious and political ideology of the Umayyad court. The most important was a portrait of an enthroned ruler, possibly al-Walid himself, who faced me as I entered the main hall. The image drew on a long tradition of imperial portraiture in Byzantium and Persia, though according to scholar Garth Fowden, the closest icono-graphic parallels may be images of Adam found on church floors throughout the Levant. Early Islamic legends regarded Adam as the prototype of earthly royalty, one of two people in the Quran given the title "caliph" (meaning literally "successor" or "deputy"). For a member of al-Walid's entourage who entered Qusayr 'Amra for the first time, the portrait would have emphatically underlined the role of the Umayyads as heirs of Adam, or as poets of the period proclaimed, "God's rope" to earth.[25]

Al-Walid included another political statement on the hall's east-ern wall. Here, I saw six kings paying obeisance to al-Walid and his sons, who were shown on the adjacent wall reclining on a cush-ioned litter. Thanks to inscriptions in Arabic and Greek, scholars have identified them as rulers of Persia, Byzantium, Spain, and Ethiopia, along with the Khazar khaqan and an Indian raja. They were among the most powerful kings of the ancient world, and by the time of al-Walid, nearly all of them had fallen to the forces of Islam. In this, we see how the Umayyads imagined themselves as both conquerors and caretakers of the ancient past. The coming of Islam eclipsed this so-called "age of ignorance" (*jahiliyya* in Arabic), but the new civilization continued to mix old colors to pro-duce striking new ones. Therein lay the cultural vitality of Umayyad civilization, apparent to anyone who has visited Damascus or this sun-scorched corner of Jordan's eastern desert.

Asad and the Baath: Heirs of the Umayyads?

The Umayyads were not saints. But whatever their personal pec-cadilloes—concubines, wine, murdering the Prophet's grandson—they are rightly remembered as state-builders. As we saw at the beginning of this chapter, Syria often aspired—but never suc-ceeded—to establish an empire of its own. Thus, the creation of a Syria-based state under the Umayyads in the seventh century marked a turning point in the history of the region. For the first time, Damascus lay at the heart of a vast global empire, one which stretched impressively from the Atlas Mountains of present-day Morocco to the Hindu Kush of modern Pakistan.

This fact was not lost on the Baathist regime that has governed Syria under military rule since 1963. For them, the Umayyad period represented the undisputed zenith of pre-modern history, a proud moment when Syria stood front and center on the world stage. Government-sanctioned school books, for example, presented the period as among the crucial steps in the forward march of the Syrian nation. In a sense, the Baathists came to imagine themselves as heirs to Mu'awiya, Yazid and the rest—not for their tyranny (though this comparison was not lost on many Syrians as the decades went by), but as state-builders and nationalists. We can sense this historical affinity on the western façade of the Umayyad mosque, on the edge of a square where teenagers once mingled on BMX bikes and merchants squeezed great mounds of fruit into juice for the passers-by. Here hangs an inscription commemorating the renovations of the 1990s conducted under then-President Hafez al-Asad. By all reports, Asad (who died in 2000) was not a religious man, and even if he were, as an 'Alawi Muslim—a member of a small branch of Shi'ism, regarded as heretical by many—he probably would not have been inclined to pray here, at the heart of Syrian Sunnism except on official occasions. Still, Asad's renovation efforts and the plaque commemorating them (which refers to him *al-ra'is al-mu'min*, "the believing president") serve to place him in a direct line with the mosque's builder, al-Walid I. So did the thousand-pound notes issued by the Syrian central bank, which show a smiling Asad beside the Umayyad mosque, along with a coin of roughly the same vintage bearing the legend: "There is no God but God, and Muhammad is the messenger of God."

The connection between Umayyad past and Baathist present wasn't only a matter of Syrian chauvinism. It was about something deeper: the importance of Arab unity. As we saw earlier, the opening decades of Islamic history were rife with internal divisions. In many ways, these conflicts were part of a longer-term effort to create stable forms of leadership that would help transfer power from one generation of Muslims to the next.[26] For the second caliph, 'Umar—who reigned 634–44—the most important criterion for leadership was the principle of *sabiqa*, or preeminence. Authority and riches went to those members of the Muslim community who had converted first, men who were not necessarily powerful in their own right, but who were respected for their early fidelity to the Prophet.

'Umar's successor, the caliph 'Uthman (644–56) nursed his own set of favorites among the Muslim elite. While 'Umar had suppressed the power of the Arab tribes, 'Uthman concentrated power in the hands of one particular tribe, his kinsmen in the Banu Umayya. He appointed family members to key governor posts throughout the empire, riding roughshod over many of 'Umar's supporters.

With the murder of 'Uthman in 656, a disputed election brought 'Ali to power, and with him the family of the Prophet and their allies, who felt they had been sidelined under the previous caliphs. Thus, by 'Ali's reign, the Muslim community had lived under three different caliphs with three different visions of leadership. At each turn, these shifts splintered the elite, stroked resentment, and fomented war.

Into this void stepped Mu'awiya and his Umayyad successors. They realized that the only way to bring stability to a Muslim community rife with internal dissension was to place power in the hands of a hereditary elite. The Muslims were famously skeptical of monarchies: they regarded them as the flawed legacy of the Byzantines and Persians and a sure path to tyranny. But under the Umayyads, monarchy proved the most effective way of bringing order to the caliphate. Faced with the choice of free-wheeling chaos or autocratic stability, the choice for many was clear.

There was another dimension of Umayyad rule that made it unique in the course of Islamic history: the Umayyad power base in Syria consisted mainly of Arab tribes. Like all things Umayyad, this would eventually become a weakness, as inter-tribal fighting consumed the energies of the court. But in a seventh century world in which most Muslims were still Arabs and old tribal networks still exerted great influence, the "Arab" character of the Umayyad state was a powerful asset.[27]

AMONG THE RUINS

Revolution and the End of the Syrian Century

Autocratic and monarchical, staunchly Arab and Syrian: there is much in the forgoing description that could connect the Umayyads to the Baathist rulers of today. Of course, these similarities are more impressionistic than historical. In my experience, history tends *not* to repeat itself, despite the famous maxim which suggests otherwise. Rather, what tends to happen is more subtle: modern peoples attempt to ground the innovations of the present in a seemingly familiar but actually unreachable past. It has a powerful legitimizing effect on the present.

This is certainly the case in modern Syria, where the Umayyad past still excites a powerful allure. I focus on it in this chapter not because I believe Syria has *not* moved on from what happened many years ago—far from it. Over twelve and a half centuries have elapsed since the dynasty fell in 750: twelve and a half centuries of innovation, creativity, and change in Syria. Rather, I focus on the Umayyads because, for all intents and purposes, they were the makers of Syria's imperial moment, a touchstone in the long history of a region shaped by long periods of foreign occupation. For that brief ninety-year stretch, Syria was the political center of the world. Perhaps more importantly, it was the cultural cauldron in which Islamic civilization was first brewed. If we wish to understand Syria's present, we must begin with this moment of triumph at the end of late antiquity.

History may not be doomed to repeat itself, but that doesn't mean there aren't other maxims that still carry weight. One which rings true in the context of modern Syrian history is that no state, regime, or power is destined to carry on forever. It was true of the Umayyads in the eighth century, as it is true of the Syrian Baath today. As for the Umayyads, what brought about their tragic end?

The policies of *Realpolitik* that proved so effective at consolidating power during the late seventh century came back to haunt the Umayyads in the 740s. Indeed, the Umayyads had once been content to rely on the support of Arab tribes: they formed a small and fairly homogenous elite ruling over a vast sea of non-Muslim subjects. Over time, however, the ranks of the Muslim community came to be filled with non-Arabs. They included Greeks from the

Levant, Berbers from North Africa, Copts from Egypt, and Persians and Turks in the eastern provinces. Each of these communities had its own culture and traditions of government. If anything, these new Muslims regarded the tribal elites as a deeply exclusionary presence in Arab Muslim society, one that ran counter to the radical egalitarianism of Muhammad's preaching, which stressed equality among believers.

The 'Abbasid revolution, which would succeed in toppling the Umayyads, was a response to the perceived political failures of the eighth century.[28] Its leaders were not members of the tribal aristocracy of Syria, but Muslims of mixed ancestry, many of them from the province of Khurasan in northeastern Iran, on the frontiers of the empire. These revolutionaries found inspiration in the struggles of the *Ahl al-Bayt*—the descendants of the Prophet, including 'Ali and Hussein—who like them, had been sidelined in the ruthless game of Umayyad politics. Theirs would be a movement of the oppressed, a revolution notionally free of factionalism, injustice, and impiety. Their message proved powerful, and their military prowess even more so.

The end of the Umayyad dynasty in Syria (a branch of the family would carry on for another three hundred years in Spain) took place on the banks of the river Zab in northern Iraq, where the last caliph, Marwan II, was soundly defeated in the year 750. Marwan managed to escape the carnage, fleeing to Egypt with 'Abbasid forces in hot pursuit. On their way south, these armies stopped in Damascus and beheld all that the Umayyads had wrought. They left the Great Mosque intact, along with the caliphal palace, and they even allowed members of the old Umayyad bureaucracy to remain in their posts. But they did not spare the graves of the caliphs.[29] According to medieval accounts, the 'Abbasids went around Damascus desecrating graves, exhuming, scattering, and even crucifying the remains of the old tyrants. This is what the ancient Romans called *damnatio memoriae*—literally, the condemnation of memory—whereby one obliterates the memory of a dead person by desecrating his remains and defacing his likenesses. In the case of the 'Abbasids, it was a cruel but brilliant strategy that helped bring a symbolic end to Umayyad power.

'Abbasid troops would continue on to Egypt and eventually kill Marwan. Within a decade, they established a glistening new capital in Baghdad, inaugurating what many scholars regard as the "Golden Age" of Islamic civilization, when Greek and Syriac philosophical texts were translated into Arabic, and when artistic production reached an all-time high. Meanwhile, in Damascus, as we have seen, memory of the Umayyads lingered long after their fall.[30]

In the coming chapters, we will continue to reflect on the role of history in the shaping of Syrian identity, especially as it stretches into the modern period. For now, let us turn to another community that was transformed by the arrival of Islam in Syria and has played an important role in the life of the country ever since: Syria's Christians.

2

ONCE "OUR LAND"

CHRISTIANITY IN SYRIA

On the northeast corner of the Old City of Damascus, about a fifteen minute walk from the Umayyad Mosque, there is a neighborhood called Bab Touma, so-named for the Roman gate just outside the walls (the Gate of St Thomas). At first blush, the area was indistinguishable from other neighborhoods in the city. Winding alleyways girded old Damascene homes, with makeshift balconies peering precariously over the foot traffic. Swarms of children spilled out of these buildings in the late afternoon cool, mingling with the hawkers, who in a high-pitched, nasal cry summoned the locals to watermelon and cucumbers from their horse-drawn carts.

There was something surprising in Bab Touma that made it different from the rest of Damascus—indeed, most other parts of the Arab world. On practically every street corner, there were shrines dedicated to the Virgin Mary. These were Technicolor Virgins—of electric blues and rosy pinks—decked out in lights and surrounded by make-shift grottoes. I sipped lemonade beside one on a particularly hot afternoon. Out of the corner of my eye, I noticed an ancient woman making her approach. Sheathed in black, she was hobbled by old age, with leathery skin, blotted tattoos on her hands and wrists, and a nose like Ayers Rock, worn vast and smooth by the ages. She lit a candle, said a prayer, and shuffled away: only in Bab Touma, the heart of Christian life in Damascus.

Bab Touma was my home in Syria from when I first visited the country in 2008. In summertime, it was flooded with foreign students—American, British, German, and Korean—who enjoyed the ambience and cheap rents. More than that, they enjoyed the chance to live with Syrian families and to practice their Arabic. It was not so easy to find intimate accommodation in Muslim parts of town. There, curfews could be tighter and prohibitions against fun-loving Italians even more so. There were greater freedoms in Bab Touma, but Syrian Christians and Western students still made strange bedfellows. The students—wearing sumptuous linen pants, scarves, and heavy silver jewelry, the preposterous uniform of many who headed "east" for a few weeks of study—kept to themselves mostly, their progress in Arabic hampered by the widespread use of English, as well as the distracting presence of the Old City's bars and nightclubs. All the same, they formed an essential part of the strange ecology in Bab Touma.

I came to the neighborhood for different reasons: its churches. Nearly fifteen of them from different Christian denominations lay scattered throughout the area. During my years in Damascus, I got to know one of them—the Maronite Catholic Cathedral of Mar Antonius (St Anthony)—especially well. On an oppressive August afternoon, when the air of the city hung thick with pollution, the air-conditioned sanctuary of the cathedral felt like paradise.

Mar Antonius was inhabited by a distinctive cast of characters. My favorite was a stocky middle-aged man with a constant five-o'clock shadow and a clutch of religious medals around his neck. He was mentally handicapped, and each evening before the six-o'clock mass, would waddle with purpose around the perimeter of the nave, kissing and stroking the statues and icons. His faith was exceptional—his style of piety less so. Many Christians in Bab Touma, as well as the greater Middle East, have a remarkably tactile sense of the holy, of the otherworldly lurking just beyond this side of ordinary objects. It was not uncommon to see Christians of all stripes, though especially women, massaging the hands of the alabaster statues. These statues of Mary and Jesus had fielded many requests over the years: their hands had been worn down to slender stubs like white lilies, but there seemed no urgency to replace them. They were clearly efficacious.

There were other Christian neighborhoods in Damascus—many of them wealthier and more orderly than smelly old Bab Touma. Yet there was something special about this one. Perhaps it was the antiquity of the place. Perhaps it was the medieval walls that physically—and notionally—cordoned her off from the rest of the city. For at the heart of Bab Touma lay a very old-fashioned idea of what Damascus was and in the eyes of many residents—still should be: a Christian city. Here, memories of the past shape the way Christians perceive the present. This, in turn, can help us understand the role of minorities in modern Syria.

The Leap from Byzantium to Islam

According to popular legend, the armies of Islam entered Damascus through the Gate of St Thomas. In fact, it was a man named Sergius Ibn Mansur—a Christian official of the Byzantine fisc—who unlocked the gates and allowed the Muslims inside. Over the coming decades, Damascus remained a predominantly Christian city, its skyline dominated by the monuments of the Byzantine past, a past that many Christian continued to perceive as a Byzantine present—and with good reason. After all, as we saw in the last chapter, not much changed in the fabric of the city during the first decades of Muslim rule.

In the immediate aftermath of the conquests, many Syrian Christians saw Muslim dominion as a temporary hiccup. The Middle East had faced its fair share of barbarian hordes over the centuries, most recently a Persian occupation that had dragged on in Syria between 611 and 628. At first, the Arabs were greeted as simply another manifestation of the same plague; it too would pass. If anything, Christians looked upon the conquests with an anxiety that was more religious than it was political. In a culture deeply concerned with the economies of sin and forgiveness, the conquests were proof that God was chastening His People for years of unbelief.[1] But a forgiving God also lifts His curses. Soon enough, Christians believed, once the church had done its penance, God would lift the Arab occupation and restore Christianity to its rightful place as the faith of the realm. Nearly fourteen centuries later, some Christians in Syria are still waiting for this to happen.

Even as Christians awaited their deliverance, many learned to accommodate Arab rule in surprising ways. A remarkable document discovered in the treasury of the Umayyad Mosque of Damascus at the beginning of last century contains a bilingual text of Psalm 78 in Greek and Arabic.[2] The Arabic portion is written phonetically in Greek letters, leading some scholars to surmise that it served as a kind of didactic tool for Christians learning to speak the language of the conquerors. There is a dispute regarding the document's exact date—according to the latest research, the original text seems to have been written in the fourth or fifth century, but the surviving copy dates to a century or so after the conquests. Whatever the case may be, it is a striking testament to the changing identity of a community caught squarely between Byzantium and Islam.

Today, the Christians of Syria are all Arabic-speakers, and proudly so. All the same, that doesn't stop them from nursing a sense of distinctiveness from the predominantly Muslim population.

During my years in Damascus, I lived with the Khoury family, whose modest home was buried in the heart of Bab Touma. As my Arabic improved, our friendship deepened, and with it, the chance to engage in long, winding conversations once the sun went down. At this time, I took to visiting the Umayyad Mosque on Fridays: mostly to observe the great gathering of souls at prayer, but also to sharpen my Arabic by listening to the sermons of the mosque's famous director, Sa'id Ramadan al-Bouti (whom we will encounter again below). Some of my friends in Bab Touma had a hard time understanding why I went. As a priest once asked me quizzically: "Why go there to watch the prayers? Why study Islam at all? They don't show the same interest in us."

At home, Maryam Khoury—who worked part-time at a nearby store—greeted my visits with resigned bewilderment. Since I headed to Catholic mass most afternoons, she didn't view me as a "flight risk" to Islam. All the same, mine was a peculiar choice which she neither understood nor entirely approved, I suspected. As a Christian, and a woman to boot, the Umayyad Mosque was in her mind off-limits.

"You know the Christians built it?" she asked me once during an evening chat, as the tobacco of our water pipe perfumed the summer air.

Bab Touma from above, with minaret and belfry, Damascus

"What do you mean?" I asked, suspecting the thrust of her question, but wanting to tease the story out of her.

"The cathedral once belonged to the Christians, then the Muslims conquered the city and turned it into a mosque. Even the head of Mar Yuhanna (St John the Baptist) is inside. When the Pope came to visit in 2001, he went there, too, with President Asad at his side."

"Interesting," I said, "Have *you* ever prayed inside? After all, Mar Yuhanna was your saint before he belonged to the Muslims."

"No. I've not been inside," she replied, raising her head slightly and tisking, a common gesture in the Levant used to convey disagreement (and in my case to rebuke a stupid question).

So, despite a life spent in the shadow of Syria's most famous monument, one with a rich pre-Islamic history of its own, Maryam had never spent time inside it. The Islamic conquests had evidently altered the geography of Damascus in ways I had not appreciated when I stared at the maps in my scholarly sources. The conquests had created notional quarantines where some people felt others could venture and they could not. I heard much the same from Muslim friends regarding the Christian neighborhoods of Damascus, especially their churches. For these Syrians—who mixed freely with friends, co-workers, and neighbors of different religions under practically every other circumstance—there were some frontiers you could not cross comfortably without a proper invitation or purpose (that said, a Muslim acquaintance once told me how he and his high-school friends used to congregate at the back of the churches in Bab Touma to pick up Christian girls—apparently they saw them as easier targets than the girls in their Sunni neighborhoods; all the same, they rarely succeeded, especially after introducing themselves as Ahmad, Muhammad, etc.).

This sense of partition among neighborhoods and religions was not always healthy. To be sure, Maryam had avoided visiting the Umayyad Mosque out of a sense of respect for the Muslims who prayed inside, and probably a still deeper confusion about what she would do once she actually entered. Yet I sensed in her voice something else. To don the hijab and visit disputed property—as some Christians regarded the Umayyad Mosque—was a small indignity of major importance.

"Go to a Street Called Straight"

Although the Christians of Syria look upon the Arab conquests as a great watershed in their history, it was by no means the earliest or most important moment in the development of their religion in the country. It was in greater Syria—in Antioch (now in modern Turkey), to be precise—that the followers of Jesus "were first called Christians" (Acts 11:26).

According to scholars, in the early years after Jesus' death, the faith spread largely among Hellenized Jews in different parts of the Middle East, with a large community based in Damascus. It was on his way to Damascus to confront this growing Christian presence that Saul of Tarsus was struck down by a great light that was accompanied by the voice of Jesus, who asked him: "Saul, Saul, why do you persecute me?" (as recounted in Acts 26 and depicted in countless Renaissance paintings). The vision temporarily blinded him, but it changed his convictions and the course of Christian history forever. Saul was instructed "to go to a street called straight," and there, he would find the home of a man named Ananias. The "street called straight" was the Roman *decumanus maximus*, known in Arabic today as *al-shari' al-mustaqim*, which serves as the principal east-west thoroughfare in the Old City. Ananias was the leader of the Christians of Damascus, and upon meeting Saul, baptized him and provided him with his initial instruction in the faith. Rechristened "Paul," he renounced his efforts to persecute Christians, and instead, set off as an apologist for the new faith. Over the coming years, he would visit and advise countless churches throughout the empire, communicating with them through rich and textured pastoral letters that now form the core of the New Testament canon. He was beheaded on charges of treason in the city of Rome around the year 67 AD.

Memory of St Paul remains alive in Bab Touma today. Indeed, the house of Ananias still stands behind a white stone wall at the end of a quiet road off Straight Street (still remarkably straight after all these years). Centuries of detritus have built up around the site, but visitors can still descend ten feet underground to see the Roman home that now serves as a chapel and pilgrimage center run by Franciscan Friars. Archaeological research indicates that the chapel—today, more of a rough-hewn cave—may contain elements of Roman domestic architecture from the first century AD, making it a possible location for Paul's visit.[3] There is a second Pauline monument south of here, planted in the medieval city walls, where the Apostle is said to have been lowered in a basket to escape angry Jewish crowds (Acts 9). This identification, however, is probably apocryphal. All the same, these sanctuaries are reminders of a Christian tradition in Damascus that dates back two thousand years.

Symeon Stylites: The Angel and his Column

The most important Christian visitor to Damascus may have come early on, but the golden age of Syrian Christianity would flower much later. Over the course of the fifth and sixth centuries, Syria found itself at the center of an increasingly global Christian faith whose adherents stretched from the British Isles all the way to India, speaking tongues as varied as Irish, Latin, Greek, Syriac, Arabic, and Persian. As the geographic hub of this world, Roman Syria became a center of Christian thought, art, and missionary activity. What made it truly unique, however, were two distinctive features: its eccentric saints and the boisterous theological debates that thundered throughout its churches and monasteries.

The greatest relic of this golden age is the church of St Symeon Stylites, located about two-hundred miles northwest of Damascus, not far from the bustling city of Aleppo. St Symeon was born around 390 AD, the son of a pious shepherd. Driven by a burning love of God, he embarked on the monastic life at a relatively young age. According to his Greek biography, written in the mid-fifth century by his disciple, bishop Theodoret of Cyrus, he would fast for long stretches of time, refusing to sit down as a kind of self-imposed penance. As Symeon's fame increased, so did the crowds massing near his cell. The sudden celebrity prompted him to seek more isolated quarters and he took refuge atop a column amidst a cluster of ruins. Of course, news of his move to the top of the column only increased his allure. As the crowds grew and grew, Symeon went up and up, ascending to a height of almost thirty feet by the time of his death thirty-seven years later. His regimen atop the column was strict: he ate very little, subsisting on scraps of bread and milk provided by his attendants. For exercise, he is said to have touched his toes 1,244 times every day—a feat of concentration for the monk, to say nothing of the miserable disciple who had to do the counting!

From high above, Symeon could dispense his justice, blessings, and counsel. According to a famous anecdote recorded by Theodoret, a large delegation of Bedouin tribesman once came to speak with Symeon. The saint is said to have tamed the desert dwellers like a circus trainer soothing an angry beast, urging them to abandon their feral ways for a life of piety. They responded in kind, "breaking up their idols in [Symeon's] presence... foreswearing the ecstatic rites of Aphrodite.... and renounce[ing] also the diet of the wild ass or the camel."[4] The Bedouin had discovered the law of God, and it trickled like honey from the lips of the holy man. Such was Symeon's effect on the crowds who swelled at his feet.

Upon Symeon's death in 459, his body was whisked away to the nearby city of Antioch. His memory lingered on as new generations of holy men, inspired by his example, began climbing columns, abandoned towers, and even trees. Like armies of angels, these monks collapsed the vast expanse between heaven and earth, acting as bridges between God and man.[5]

Between 476 and 491, a massive pilgrimage complex was built around Symeon's abandoned column. Once completed, the church attracted visitors from around the Mediterranean and beyond. Qal'at Sim'an, as the church is known today in Arabic (literally, "the Fortress of Symeon"), lies in the heart of the Limestone Massif, a vast highland region stretching south and west of Aleppo.[6] In antiquity, this area was home to networks of prosperous villages, which grew wealthy on trade and agriculture, and to this day the region remains a center of Syria's productive olive industry.

I visited Symeon's church twice and on each occasion was awed by the otherworldly beauty of the place. The slope before the church plunged precariously along the western front, down to a rolling plain that loped dozens miles towards the horizon. From his commanding perch—lush and verdant in spring, dusty and over-cooked in summer—Symeon could survey God's creation. The centerpiece of Qal'at Sim'an was an octagonal court containing the base of the column. Centuries of wind and pilgrims had eroded the mighty pillar, now about ten feet high, but the effect was undiminished, even in 2010 when I last visited. Attached to the courtyard were four basilica naves, each about one hundred feet long, corresponding more or less to the points of the compass. Further along, traces of a triumphal arch and processional road rose along the south side of the complex, marking the area where pilgrims would enter the site. Along with these, there were the administrative buildings and hostels where pilgrims stayed. So famous did Symeon become that ancient sources tell of pilgrims coming from as far away as Britain and Persia. Centuries after his death, another admirer, the Umayyad caliph 'Umar II (r. 717–20), is said to have been buried near here, a testament to the saint's enduring popularity, even among Muslims.

There are few pilgrims today at Qal'at Sim'an—they were mostly tourists—but in antiquity accommodating the crowds proved to be a logistical challenge. Indeed, as I stood beside Symeon's column, it was tempting to imagine simultaneous liturgies taking place in each of the four basilicas, much like the dueling masses that occur in the side chapels of St Peter's in Rome. And as at St Peter's, security was also a major concern at Qal'at Sim'an: around the perimeter of the column, I could still make out traces of what was once a protective screen separating the saint's marble perch from the foot traffic down below. It was important to keep grubbing hands at bay: after all, as any late antique churchman would tell you, pilgrims were among the most determined thieves of all. According to an exemplary tale, a visitor to Jerusalem in the fourth century was allegedly venerating the relic of the True Cross at the Church of the Holy Sepulcher when he decided to take a bite of it for himself. He absconded with the wooden chunk in his mouth—much to the initial confusion of the attendant priests.[7] Whether in Jerusalem or at Qal'at Sim'an, pilgrims always deserved extra scrutiny.

While architecture may have been the main attraction at Qal'at Sim'an, its sculpture was also impressive. Indeed, as I gazed up from the floor of the ruins, you could make out detailed stone carving along the arches and entablature, still crisp after these many

Church of St Symeon Stylites, Aleppo Province, view of column

years. Especially impressive was a series of Corinthian capitals, whose acanthus leaves seem to have been rustled by a sudden zephyr, leaving them swaying in mid-air. Around the portals of the four basilicas, there was also delicate stone tracery resembling strings of flowers liberated from the surrounding limestone. Qal'at Sim'an was an austere place, to be sure: even the masonry seemed to have lost its luster in the midday heat. For me, however, it was a reminder of the tremendous wealth, creativity, and dynamism of Syria's ancient Christian past.

Dissent and Division in the Christian Roman Empire

As I mentioned above, Syria was renowned in late antiquity for its saints as well as for its tumultuous religious politics. Perhaps it was inevitable that in a place like this—a veritable crossroads of Greek, Jewish, Aramaic, Arabic, and Persian civilizations—that no one interpretation of the faith managed to prevail over the others. How was this Christian culture first born?

Late antiquity (ca. 300–800 AD) is often said to be the era of the triumph of monotheism: it was over the course of late antiquity that belief in the One God—once the eccentric doctrine of the relatively tiny Jewish people—found favor among vast new flocks of believers, thanks largely to the efforts of Christian and Muslim missionaries. Structurally, the triumph of monotheism had several obvious advantages.[8] For kings, emperors, and caliphs, monotheism offered a universalizing ideology that could help consolidate control over far-flung domains, imposing a sense of unity among peoples who had previously followed different religious customs. But monotheism had one major structural flaw. As a belief system, it was terrifically capacious *and* dangerously narrow—universal in its ambition to save mankind, but deeply resentful of competing understandings of salvation.

Over the centuries this paradox had the positive effect of creating "orthodoxies," that is, proscribed ways of "doing things right"—or as a sociologist of religion might put it, doctrines that enjoy hegemonic status at a particular place and time. On the flipside, it had the negative consequence of creating "heresies," that is, recognized ways of "going rogue" (of course, most heretics refused the label, continuing to call themselves "orthodox" well after they were jettisoned from the mainstream of the Christian church).

When it comes to Christianity, there were two specific areas that tended to inspire dissent and division in late antiquity. The first was the relationship between God and the man known as Jesus of Nazareth, and later, the relationship of the human and the divine in the person of Jesus. Indeed, these questions inspired disagreements more fundamental and more rancorous than any Catholic-Protestant dispute with which most Americans and Europeans are more familiar. At first glance, the New Testament seems to state the basics of Christian dogma quite clearly: Jesus, son of God, died for the redemption of mankind. This is Sunday school Christianity plain and simple. But underlying the clarity of these words is in fact a vast ocean of theological uncertainty that required the intensive charting of bishops, emperors, and theologians, who attempted to sort things out in great meetings called "ecumenical councils." We can see these councils—the most important of which took place between 325 and 787 AD—as efforts at articulating the implicit Christology of the Gospels in the philosophical language of the pagan Greeks. By and large, this articulation proved elusive.

At stake in these councils was the "orthodox" definition of the person of Jesus: was Jesus, as the Son, created by the Father and therefore subordinate to Him, as a very important group known as the Arians taught? (Arians no longer exist as an institutional church, though their particular Christology has remained appealing to many groups over the centuries.) Or was Jesus of the same substance as the Father, as the victors of the Council of Nicaea decreed in 325, whose view would become the belief of most Christian denominations to this day?[9] Later, Christians tried to figure out how exactly Jesus could be both human and divine at the same time.[10] Some groups started from the idea of Christ being Two—human and divine—and argued that there was a full union between these elements in the person of Jesus. Others started from the notion of Christ being One—and said that the One Jesus existed in two natures, human and divine. The first group, which followed the theological views of the important Christian center of Antioch in

Syria, worried that the second group venerated a Jesus who was more divine than human; the second group, which followed the theological traditions of the city of Alexandria in Egypt, worried that the first group did not venerate a single person, but actually believed in two separate Christs.

Disagreements over the nature of the union of the human and divine in Christ came to a head at the Council of Ephesus in 431, which attempted to resolve the controversial matter of whether Mary deserved the title "Mother of God" or merely "Mother of Christ," a question whose answer had profound implications for how to understand the union of the human and the divine in Jesus.

The Council of Ephesus inadvertently set off a third great dispute, this time surrounding the number of "natures" in the person of Christ. A group known as the Monophysites argued that the divine nature of the Son had existed separately before the Incarnation, and had come into union with the human only after the visit of the angel Gabriel to the Virgin Mary. Hence, the divine nature was thought to have engulfed the human, leaving behind a single nature (hence, the Greek term *Mia-Physites*, the believers in the "single nature"). Their opponents—the party that prevailed at Chalcedon—believed that Christ's human and divine natures were tied up inextricably and yet distinctly in a single being—fully man and fully God. The ancestors of this conflict live on in the so-called Oriental Orthodox Churches (Syrian, Coptic, Ethiopic, and Armenian Orthodox), who rejected the council, on the one hand, and the Eastern Orthodox Churches (Greek, Russian, Bulgarian, Romanian, *inter aliae*) and the Roman Catholic Church (along with its historical progeny, the various Protestant denominations), who accepted them, on the other.

Despite the seemingly narrow terms of debate, these councils were responsible for clarifying the major theological controversies of the early Church. But in sanctioning some positions and anathematizing others, the councils forced the dissenters into separate ecclesial institutions with their own hierarchies, beliefs, and customs. These "rogue institutions," as the victorious fathers of the councils saw them, included the Arian, Nestorian, and Monophysite churches (also known as Jacobite, referring to the sixth-century bishop Jacob

Baradeus, who was instrumental in the establishment of a separate Monophysite hierarchy in the Roman east).[11] Theology lay at the root of their disagreements, but politics also played a role in perpetuating them. The emperor was often responsible for convening these councils, and it fell to him to enforce what he and his allies perceived as the "orthodox" consensus (which could change from one emperor to another, though by the time of the Arab conquests, imperial Christianity was resolutely anti-Arian, anti-Nestorian, and anti-Monophysite). As a result, there were fierce, sometimes bloody struggles between the imperial church in Constantinople and the "heretical" sects scattered throughout the empire, though especially in the eastern provinces of Syria and Egypt.

What does all this mean for Syria? Well, throughout the empire, theological disagreements often became a proxy for still deeper cultural and political disputes. In Syria, where practically all the ancient forms of Christianity flourished at one time or another, religious disagreements tended to fall along still deeper cultural divides. For example, the Orthodox Christianity of the imperial church gained traction among Greek-speaking city-dwellers, while Monophysite Christianity found favor among Aramaic-speaking monks and villagers in the Syrian countryside. As scholars have shown, the distinction between the two communities was not watertight. (Indeed, we have evidence that Syrian Christians tended to look past their disagreements when it came to matters of everyday life, such as intermarriage, burial of the dead and even the Eucharist; we also have evidence that the use of Syriac was widespread among Chalcedonian churches, not just among the Monophysites.)[12] What is certain is that the long struggle between "orthodoxy and heresy" left behind a deeply divided society in ancient Syria. It was one singed by dissension, a place where religious belief sheltered still more profound regional, cultural, and political differences. Far from being a confessional monolith, Syria was a mosaic of clashing colors in the mid-seventh century when the Arab armies first arrived. This intractable relationship between political and religious identity—the unintended byproduct of the monotheist revolution—would become one of the defining legacies of late antiquity down the centuries.

Muslim Masters of a Christian World

The fruits of this divided culture still exist along the streets of Bab Touma. One day, to understand it, I headed south from the House of Ananias where Paul had been baptized. Turning right onto Straight Street, I could see churches of the Armenian Orthodox, the Syrian Catholics, and the Greek Catholics in rapid succession (the Eastern Rite, or Uniate Catholic churches, which observe the traditions and liturgies of the Orthodox but recognize the authority of the Pope, were founded in the eighteenth century and later). Around the corner, along the road leading back to Bab Touma Square, I saw the churches of the Syrian Orthodox and Latin Catholics, along with those belonging to the Maronites and Armenian Catholics buried in the alleyways behind. These were elegant buildings, mostly dating from the nineteenth and early twentieth centuries, but many of them stood on ancient plots. According to medieval sources, including the *History of the City of Damascus* by Ibn 'Asakir, when the caliph al-Walid I resolved to raze the church of St John the Baptist to make room for his mosque, he negotiated with the city's Christians to compensate them for their lost property.[13] Apparently, these negotiations were bruising, and the Christians, not pleased with the initial outcome, continued them with al-Walid's successor, 'Umar II, several years later. In the end, the Umayyad authorities agreed to compensate the Christians by granting them land for churches in perpetuity elsewhere in the Old City. This led to the establishment of four churches in and around the neighborhood of Bab Touma, where Christians would be free to worship. According to tradition, churches still occupy these ancient parcels of land, most notably the Greek Orthodox Patriarchate, known as the Maryamiyya, which stands at a historic crossroads on Straight Street (now beside one of the poshest restaurants in Damascus).

Whatever justice al-Walid and 'Umar rendered unto the Christians in the short term, the long-term effect of razing the basilica was unambiguous. Henceforth, Christianity was exiled from the center of Damascus, pushed to the outskirts of the Old City where it was meant to carry on in quiet anonymity. It was one of the most important steps in the transformation of Damascus from a Byzantine Christian metropolis into an Arab Muslim capital.

Damascus, Bab Sharqi (the Eastern Gate), with Straight Street in foreground

If Christianity can be said to have profited from the experience of conquest and exile, it is that the arrival of Islam led to a general calming of sectarian differences among the local churches. Indeed, while tumultuous debates among Monophysites and Orthodox Christians continued throughout the medieval period, in many ways disagreements over Christology and the authority of a given patriarch were overshadowed somewhat by the more robust (and shared) threat of Islam. Especially today, many Christians in Bab Touma dismiss denominational differences as insignificant. It's easy to find Catholics and Orthodox marrying one another, indeed, to find Catholics receiving the Eucharist at Orthodox churches, and Orthodox receiving it at Catholic churches. At mass at the Maronite Cathedral of Mar Antonius, for example, I was surprised to discover that the woman who sang the prayers over the microphone was herself Greek Orthodox, while others came from Armenian and Syrian Orthodox congregations.

As a Catholic priest in nearby Lebanon once explained to me, "For all intents and purposes, we have achieved full communion among the Christian churches of Lebanon and Syria. Of course, this doesn't apply to the clergy: we have to represent our churches in official capacities, and therefore, cannot celebrate the mass with one another. But among our flocks, they do not always recognize the disagreements that once troubled Christians in these lands—the difference between Orthodox and Catholics, between Greeks and Syrians. In this respect, we are a message to the world, of overcoming Christian difference."

Overcoming centuries of sectarian acrimony is a mighty achievement for the Christians of Syria—but it has come at a considerable cost. In many ways, Christians of different denominations have been forced to reconcile as their overall numbers have dwindled. From the beginning of the Islamic period to as late as the thirteenth or fourteenth century, after the Crusades were over, Christians constituted a demographic majority in Syria.[14] But conversion to Islam brought with it obvious advantages, not least of them financial and social.[15] It offered relief from the despised poll-tax, or *jizya*, which was levied on non-Muslims in commutation for military service.[16] In practice, the *jizya* created a vast and profitable tax base for the Muslim authorities, and at a symbolic level, it enforced a sense of hierarchy between Muslims and their Jewish and Christian subjects (see Quran 9:29).[17] But the simple act of reciting the *shahada*—the Muslim profession of faith—could grant relief to a Christian facing hard times. Especially in the medieval period, a Christian who converted to Islam not only liberated himself from the *jizya* but also had the opportunity to obtain higher social and political status, whether in the service of the state, the army, or certain sectors of the economy dominated largely by Muslims.

It is important to stress that religious conversion in the medieval Middle East was not a one-way street. Early works of Islamic law speak with urgency and anxiety about the prospect of Muslims converting to Christianity and Judaism.[18] Though rare today, this kind of conversion at the dawn of Islam should not surprise us, especially when we consider the demographic realities of this world. In the post-conquest Middle East, a tiny Arabic-speaking Muslim elite came to rule over a vast sea of Christian, Jewish, and Zoroastrian subjects, essentially unchanged in culture, language, and belief from Byzantine and Sasanian times. We often imagine Christians as a minority in this world, and indeed, they were a political minority, largely excluded from the highest echelons of state and society. But we must remember that a political minority is not the same thing as a demographic minority. Given the imbalance between the numbers of Christians and Muslims, Muslims were at least theoretically at risk of conversion to Christianity much as Christians were at risk of conversion to Islam.

There are a few other factors to consider when trying to understand this convert culture. The religion of the early Muslim elite was still in the process of stabilizing through much of the first century of Arab rule. To be sure, early Muslims had a pronounced belief in the unity of God, in the Arab identity of their movement, and in the threat of a looming apocalypse, among other things. But the Muslim community was open to a far wider array of beliefs and practices than we typically imagine when we look back from the present.[19] Islam was, after all, a faith born in the cauldron of conquest, and later civil war, and in certain respects the early Muslim elite seems to have expended more energy discharging its political responsibilities than clarifying doctrine, which would take place in later centuries. What is more, given that the early Muslims were themselves almost always converts from something else—whether Arab paganism, Christianity, Judaism, or Zoroastrianism—they brought with them the residue of their old faiths as they joined the new. Thus we find stories of Muslims seeking baptism for their children; of Muslims praying in churches; and of Muslims receiving spiritual direction at the feet of Christian holy men. At first puzzling and even shocking, these anecdotes provide glimpses into a dynamic convert culture in which Muslims and Christians kept a foot in both worlds.

This age of ambiguity came to an end eventually. We can sense this in the rising incidence of Christian "martyrdom" in the mid-eighth century onwards, when confessional flip-floppers—who converted from Christianity to Islam and back, many of them the children of mixed marriages between Muslims and Christians—were executed by the Muslim state on charges of apostasy.[20] It also came about as Christian and Muslim theologians began plotting the theoretical frontiers between their two faiths, debating and disputing key doctrines such as the Trinity, the Incarnation, and Muhammad's status as a Prophet. By the end, this confluence of factors—not to mention the financial pressures underlying conversion, like the burden of the *jizya*—would help initiate the long process of Christian demographic decline that continues to this day (though now because of politics, war, and migration less than conversion).

The Mosque outside the Christian Quarter

As we have seen, there were not many Muslims in Bab Touma when I lived there between 2008 and 2010. But that does not mean there was no Muslim presence in the neighborhood. Down the street from the Maronite Cathedral stood a small but handsome mosque with a butcher's shop on the ground floor. From what I could tell, the mosque was mostly empty, staying open for a few locals, workers, and others who might be passing through. The next closest mosque lay just outside the medieval walls, on an island in the middle of the traffic that led into Bab Touma Square.

Bab Touma mosque, Damascus

I confess that the voice of the muezzin at the mosque wasn't particularly mellifluous. Quite the opposite, actually, it was downright irritating, soaring over the neighborhood like the cry of a tired bird. This particular muezzin near my home in Bab Touma had not learned his trade particularly well. I vividly recall one day, having been jolted from my siesta nap one too many times by his grating voice, I descended to the quarters of the Khoury family, from whom I rented my room, to ask my friend Fares (the eldest son and an engineer) why the worst muezzin in all of all Damascus sang outside the gates of a Christian area like Bab Touma. At first, he looked at me quizzically, so accustomed had he become to life with this Syrian "Frank Sinatra" that my complaint failed to register at first. Then a smile spread across his face.

"Oh him! Yes, what a voice!" laughed Fares, "But we've gotten used to him."

"Does it strike you as funny that this muezzin—with his particular voice—sings beside a neighborhood where there aren't almost any Muslims to actually pray with?" I said.

"Well," Fares replied in a hushed and joking tone, as he did whenever we turned to sensitive subjects, real or merely imagined, "Perhaps this is the price we pay for remaining Christians in Damascus!"

The entire experience reminded me of what I had read in medieval Christian sources about the call to prayer. For some polemicists, there was no sense of the dignity or beauty of the prayer, as I felt atop Mt. Qassioun or inside the Umayyad Mosque. Instead, it reminded these Christians of the braying of a donkey, as one especially caustic source from ninth-century Spain put it.[21] Polemics aside, my exchange with Fares was deeply instructive. On the one hand, it revealed the extent to which the rhythms of Muslim life washed naturally, almost imperceptibly over the Christians of the city. But on the other, it underscored how these very same rhythms could, in a Christian neighborhood, give the impression of a very gentle siege.

Nearly all the Christians I met in Syria were eager to dispel this impression of religious tension between them and their Muslim neighbors. They spoke lovingly of Syria as a country in which

Muslims and Christians lived together in peace, and for the most part, they were right. In comparison to places like Egypt, where discrimination against the Coptic Church remains endemic, or in Iraq, where targeted violence has led to the exodus of nearly half of the country's Christians since 2003, Syria's Christians have enjoyed security and prosperity. Indeed, they have fared better than the majority of their countrymen, especially when it comes to levels of education, wealth, and political influence. What is more, I knew many Christians who socialized and worked with, dated, and even married members of different communities, challenging the outsider's assumptions about a deeply divided culture on the ground. I could summon countless other examples of co-existence among members of different religions: of the Muslim clergy who attended Christian high holy days; of the Ramadan *iftar* dinners filled with Muslims and Christians; even a young Christian I heard about who was arrested by the security services for distributing Easter eggs bearing Biblical and Quranic verses to children of different sects.

Such were the positive fruits of the Baathist regime that ruled Syria since 1963. It was a regime dominated by a particular religious minority—the 'Alawis—who in turn cultivated the support of other minorities to offset the strength of the Sunni majority. Thus, Christians—along with Ismailis, Druze, and Shi'is—enjoyed a measure of privilege in Syria they would not in practically any other part of the Middle East. As we will see in the coming chapter, the game of minority politics could have disastrous consequences for those who played it, but in the near term, it allowed Syria's minorities to thrive as their counterparts in neighboring countries languished.

Despite the rosy picture, when I dug beneath my friends' plaudits for diversity, I discovered that much was left unsaid. I learned this one day when I returned home to Bab Touma to find Maryam Khoury visibly rattled. She had been on a bus somewhere in Damascus when two men spotted the gold cross around her neck. As she recounted the incident, these men had pointed at the cross and insulted her before she quickly dismounted and fled. Maryam was an intensely private person, hesitant to share her opinions about practically anything sensitive, above all, the question of sectarianism in her country. Her normal script—like that of the government she quietly supported—was that there was no sectarianism in Syria. But under duress, her real opinions became clear.

"I worry that this represents the future of my country," she confessed. "How can we expect to carry on here when we are made to feel unwelcome in our own homes?" She then looked into the courtyard of the family's home, where her young nephews were splashing around in an inflatable pool. "What future is open for them in Syria in twenty or thirty years? To find themselves under the thumb of the Muslim Brothers? To emigrate? To leave our lands? But we were here first: Syria was once a Christian country."

Aramaic in Syria: The Afterlife of a "Dead" Language

This was a recurrent theme in my conversations with many Christians in Syria, especially on my visits to Maaloula, thirty-five miles northwest of Damascus in the foothills of the anti-Lebanon Mountains. Maaloula is famous as one of three Aramaic-speaking villages in Syria. Prior to the coming of Islam, many Christians in the Levant spoke dialects of Aramaic, a Semitic language related to the one Jesus himself used. In late antiquity, Syriac—a dialect of Aramaic that originated in the city of Edessa, now in south-eastern Turkey—blossomed into an important literary and theological language. [22] Today, it lives on in the liturgy of the Syrian Orthodox, Chaldean, and Maronite churches. Most modern descendants of these ancient Syriac speakers know only Arabic, but many residents of Maaloula remain adamantly bilingual.

I discovered this one day while talking with an acquaintance named Boutros—the retired patriarch of a large family in Damascus, who returned to the village where he was born during the hot summer months. Like most houses in Maaloula, his was modest and concrete. Coated in lavender paint, it was perched high above the village square, providing Boutros with a clear view of the Greek Catholic monastery of Mar Sarkis on the other side of town. On the opposite hill, just down the road from his home, was the Greek Orthodox monastery of Mar Takla, a companion of St Paul who, according to local lore, had escaped a group of soldiers by fleeing through a narrow canyon on the north side of the village (hence the

Maaloula, view from the east, with Mar Sarkis monastery, top right

Aramaic root of the word Maaloula, related to the word "entrance"). On September 14th each year, the Christians of Maaloula light fires atop these hills to commemorate the recovery of the True Cross in Jerusalem in 326, soon after the Peace of the Church. According to tradition, Maaloula was part of a relay of mountaintop beacons that conveyed the good news from Palestine to crowds in the imperial capital of Constantinople.

I recall one of my several visits to Maaloula, when Boutros and I were discussing the role of Aramaic in the village—"It's disappearing among the younger generations," he lamented—and the phone suddenly rang. It was Elie, the golden son of the family who worked in the Gulf, a not-uncommon destination for well-educated Syrians seeking their fortunes abroad. After an exchange of pleasantries in Arabic, their conversation shifted suddenly, and I could no longer follow what they were saying. It was because they were speaking Aramaic. I leaned back and enjoyed the scene, struck that Boutros' ancestors could have never imagined their descendants speaking this ancient language via satellite from the Persian Gulf (though in pre-Islamic times, Syriac-speaking monasteries did pepper the coasts of the Arabian Peninsula)![23] In many cultures around the world, language enshrines identity, and for the residents of Maaloula, it was no different. Indeed, the stubborn survival of Aramaic was a tangible connection to a past when Syria was neither entirely Arabic-speaking, nor Muslim. This was a point of pride in the village, especially for its Christian residents: a connection to a long-lost world in which Syria remained a major center of global Christianity.

While many Christians looked upon the disappearance of this culture with obvious regret, their melancholy was infused with a strange sense of pride. As I heard from many of them, the Muslim culture of modern Syria was built on the foundations of a Byzantine past: Boutros, for one, pointed out that even the Muslim minority of Maaloula—the descendants of Christian converts to Islam—still spoke some Aramaic. A Lebanese friend who was a great enthusiast for the Syriac language went so far as to tell me that Levantine colloquial Arabic was nothing more than Aramaic suffused with Arabic vocabulary: "Everyone in this part of the Middle East still speaks Syriac!" he told me, "and they don't even realize it!"

Linguistically, this may have been stretching the truth, but it is undeniable that the language of everyday life in Syria—for both Christians and Muslims—was the product of creative mixing of Arabic, the language of the conquerors who arrived here in the seventh century, and Aramaic, the tongue of a large portion of the subject population since antiquity. Most of these would eventually convert to Islam, embracing Arabic in mosques, schools, and marketplaces. But they blended it—as well as their new identities—with the language and culture of the old.

The Prophet Muhammad and his Christian Teacher

Debates over language may seem academic, but they are part and parcel of the way some Christians in Syria looked upon the surrounding culture: not as an Arab Muslim culture, but as a Christian culture tossed from its historic moorings by the conquests. Indeed, some friends went so far as to insist that many Muslims still harbored a kind of "crypto-Christianity" behind closed doors—residual pieties that survived the transition from church to mosque centuries ago.

For example, a Syrian Orthodox friend in Beirut once told me about Kurdish-speaking Muslim communities in his ancestral village in southeastern Turkey. These people—mostly peasant farmers—had been forced to convert to Islam under duress about a century ago. But on a recent trip to the region, my friend was shocked to discover many Muslims wearing crosses under their shirts. What is more, thanks to the efforts of a small but energetic community of Syrian Orthodox clergy in the area, many of these Muslims were returning to church—baptizing their children and teaching them Aramaic.

I had seen versions of this religious "syncretism" during my own travels in the Middle East. Again and again I was interested to come across Christian holy sites filled with Muslim pilgrims, especially women seeking the intercession of saints for quotidian ailments such as aching backs and fruitless wombs. At the famous monastery of Sednaya outside of Damascus, for example, the writer William Dalrymple noted that Muslim women would spend the night in the monastery's church praying to conceive a child.[24] In the course of their stay, they would nibble the candles in front of the icons and sip the holy oil inside the sanctuary lamps—as a kind of spiritual fertility treatment. In my own experiences in the churches of Bab Touma, on more than one occasion I saw young Muslim women in the pews. I remember one in particular—ragged-looking, perhaps a visitor from outside Syria—who came to mass over the course of several days before disappearing. I could see her whispering prayers in front of the statues and icons.

Some Christians I encountered in Syria persisted not only in thinking of their country as a Christian place, but indeed, in imagining Islam as a "Christian religion." It was a story I had heard from countless Western academics—the so-called "revisionists," who argue that early Islam was an eccentric blend of Jewish and Christian beliefs that emerged as a distinct religion long after the Prophet's death in 632. Despite familiarity with their arguments, I was not prepared to hear essentially the same thing from less educated folk in the Middle East.

Several years after leaving Damascus, I was riding in a taxi in Beirut when I struck up a conversation with the Christian driver. He had an image of Jesus hanging from his rearview mirror, and I asked where he had been born. "Damascus," he said, "but actually, a village just north of it; perhaps you know it? Maaloula?" I explained my connection to the village, and I suppose this put him at ease, because the conversation turned quickly to his not-so-rosy views of Islam. "Let me tell you something," he began, "Islam is nothing more than Christianity gone bad. Read the Quran, and there you'll find David, John the Baptist, Mary, and Jesus—all of them, our saints—and the Muslims worship them as we do!"

"Do you know who Buhayra is?" he asked me, with a look of mischief in his eyes, as if about to unload some damning scrap of evidence. As a matter of fact, I did know about Buhayra: according to medieval Islamic sources, Buhayra (pronounced Bahira in classical Arabic) was a monk in the southern Syrian city of Bosra, who encountered the Prophet Muhammad as a child.[25] At the time, the Prophet was passing through Bosra on a caravan headed from his native Hijaz to the markets of Syria. Though Buhayra was a com-

Roman ruins, Bosra, Dera'a Province

mitted Christian, he observed on Muhammad something strange: between his shoulder blades was a birth mark, which he recognized as the so-called *khatim al-nabawi*, or "Prophetic Seal." According to lore, whoever bore this mark was destined to become the last and greatest of the prophets of God. After seeing this on Muhammad, Buhayra proclaimed the good news to the caravan, announcing the start of a prophetic career. Whether the meeting actually happened is irrelevant. In medieval times, the legend had an important didactic and polemical purpose for Muslim audiences: in recognizing Muhammad as a Prophet, Buhayra placed a Christian imprimatur on the new Muslim faith. What is more, his recognition of Muhammad was thought to foreshadow the eventual eclipse of Christianity by Islam centuries later.

This was the story I had in the back of my head as my driver launched into his own surprising retelling of events. "Buhayra was a monk from Syria," he began, "but had problems with his community, so he went into exile. He wandered down to Mecca and there he met Muhammad. At the time, Muhammad was a powerful trader and political leader, but Buhayra helped him to write the Quran and to assume his most powerful role yet, that of prophet. In other words, the holy book of the Muslims is really just the work of this one monk, and like I said, Islam is just a version of Christianity. Of course, the Muslims don't realize this, and those that do wouldn't admit it, but that's the truth."

My driver's revisionist history was remarkable: remarkable for the strange manner in which he narrated Islamic origins, and from my perspective, remarkable for the contents of the story he told. For as ancient as the Bahira legend was among Muslims, Christians had been telling their own less flattering version for nearly as long. Indeed, sources in Syriac, Greek, and Arabic reveal that the Bahira legend has been circulating among Christians since at least the eighth century. And although the details of the Christian story vary from account to account—including the name of the monk who taught Muhammad (Bahira, Buhayra, Sergios) and his denomination (Nestorian, Arian, Jacobite)—the basic bones of the legend have remained constant. What is more, its polemical impact was essentially unchanged: by attributing the rise of Islam to the influence of a heretical monk—and not to divine revelation—the Christian authors of the Middle Ages (as well as my driver in Beirut) dismissed Islam as an offshoot of their own, "the flavor of the month" in a long procession of heretical Christianities that had flourished in the Middle East from ancient times to the present.

Christians, Muslims, and Neighborly Disputes

The legend of Buhayra can tell us a great deal about the stability of anti-Muslim polemic over the centuries. During my time in Syria, I discovered that anti-Christian polemic among Muslims could work in much the same way. I learned this one summer while reading medieval accounts of Syrian history with my Arabic teacher Muhammad, whom we met in chapter one, a hard-working father of two and a devout Muslim. We were making our way through a book called *Futuh al-Sham*, or "The Conquest of Syria," by the eighth-century historian al-Azdi. In one section of the book, al-Azdi states that the caliph 'Umar, who oversaw the conquest of the Levant, dispatched an envoy to speak with the Byzantine army before a major battle. The envoy was a man named Mu'adh Ibn Jabal, a companion of the Prophet renowned for his piety and distaste for worldly pleasure. Thus, it was with a measure of disgust that he stepped into the tent of the Byzantine commanders and discovered it adorned with cushions, carpets, and other sumptuous amenities.[26] The Christian commanders invited Mu'adh to recline with them as equals, but he refused, stating that God had forbidden the Muslims such careless and trivial luxuries.

The scene was typical of al-Azdi's work: throughout *The Conquest of Syria* he carefully juxtaposes Arab Muslim culture—brave, pious and ascetic ("They fight like lions by day and pray like monks by night," al-Azdi once remarked of the Muslim soldiers in those early years)—with that of the Byzantine Christians—pleasure-seeking and unbelieving. The not-so-subtle suggestion was that the Christians had lost Syria as punishment for their moral and spiritual laxity. It was a point my friend Muhammad was only too eager to drive home as we wound our way through Arabic vocabulary and grammar in the text.

"Do you see?" he asked me, "Syria was a place without faith. Then the armies of Islam came to purify it."

My friend's rather lopsided view of Syria's Christian past—decadent, begging for reformation—was part and parcel of how he perceived the country's Christian culture in modern times, too. For him, Bab Touma was an island of excess amidst a sea of Muslim restraint. He would describe to me walking by the churches of Bab Touma on a Sunday afternoon and noticing the young women parading through the streets. He would refer disapprovingly to the availability of liquor in corner shops, the temptation of the bars and nightclubs in the area known as Bab Sharqi, and the general libertine ambiance. "The older Christians are like us Muslims," he once explained, "Their clothes are not flashy, and if they drink, it is in the privacy of their homes. They worship God and mind their business. But the *shabab* (the young people) behave as if they lived in Europe."

For Muhammad, this was the crux of the matter. Modern Christianity promoted values that were un-Syrian. As practitioners of a Western religion—or so he thought—the Christians were complicit in the excesses of the West. The younger generation had traded their Syrian culture for a foreign lifestyle unmoored from serious faith. "Do you think the young people are praying when they go to church?" he asked me. "I suspect not. Islam is a religion of freedom—a Muslim is free to do as he pleases in the sight of God. But freedom without limits amounts to a kind of slavery. It is no freedom at all. That is the problem I sense among the Christians of Syria today."

Muhammad's caricature of life in Bab Touma was mostly untrue. In my experience, at least, the neighborhood had much more in common with the culture and temperament of a conservative city like Cairo than with a liberal place like San Francisco or Amsterdam. Indeed, many of the fun-loving Italian students who flocked to Bab Touma discovered their Christian hosts to be sometimes surprisingly strict, and in certain ways, invasive: no members of the opposite sex inside the house, no parties, no visitors without advance approval.

Like many stereotypes in Syria, Muhammad's carried a kernel of truth. It was undeniable that Christians, especially in urban places like Damascus, held to "more liberal" values by the standards of Syrian society than many of their Muslim neighbors. The sexes mingled more freely; women walked around with their heads uncovered; and the general cultural orientation—by dint of religion and higher levels of education—was more Western. That did not mean, however, that Bab Touma was a liberal place.

Muhammad's critique fell short on other counts too. The Muslim neighborhoods of Damascus, while sometimes more conservative in appearance, were well acquainted with drink and sex. As Ahmad, another Muslim friend, put it to me, apparently speaking from experience: "Don't be tricked by the *hijab*. They're less overt about it than the Christian girls, but appearances can be deceiving." This applied to men, too: gelled hair and tight jeans could disguise a pious Muslim who prayed five times per day, and by the same token, a long beard and traditional dress could mask a taste for the good life. Appearances could be deceiving, even if it was often women who were the only ones held up as examples of moral rectitude.

Better off without Diversity?

My teacher Muhammad viewed the Christians of Bab Touma the way someone back home complained about his neighbor: his cars were too flashy; his children had no discipline; his parties raged at all hours of the night. In other words, his was a neighborly dispute born of close proximity and clashing worldviews. I also heard Muslims making remarks about Christian culture that were less innocent than his.

One afternoon, I found myself chatting with 'Abdallah, a young Syrian friend, about the challenges facing Christians in the broader Middle East: the bouts of violence, social discrimination, pressures to emigrate from increasingly conservative societies. I also noted to my friend that as Christians left, there left with them an important element of religious and cultural diversity—the kind of diversity that reminds the people of the Middle East and the outside world that their societies are not monolithic.

My friend nodded politely, but I could tell he didn't agree. We had chatted about other sensitive issues before—the Baath party, the crackdowns on the Muslim Brotherhood, even homosexuality in Syria—the sorts of taboos most locals would avoid discussing with an outsider. Sensitivity wasn't his problem. Rather, what seemed to bother 'Abdallah was the unacceptable proposition that diversity might exert a constructive influence on society, and furthermore, that it was the Christians who acted as guarantors of this diversity. "As an American, you like diversity," he began. "You have all these races and ethnicities in your country, even a black president. But what if diversity in my society isn't the same as diversity in yours? What if diversity here is a source of weakness?"

"Wasn't it diversity that created the violence in Iraq," he pressed on, "the existence of all those different groups: Sunni, Shi'i, Kurdish, Christian? I would rather live in a place that did not have diversity and was stable, than live in a diverse place that was at constant risk of falling into a civil war. A country that is culturally and religiously united is resistant to dissent. The opposite is the problem inherent in a place with many different kinds of people."

Herein lay 'Abdallah's problem with the Christians of Syria: "You look upon these people and say 'How nice, they're like me' but maybe you should look upon them and think, 'What problems do they create for the majority?'" In my friend's judgment, Syria's Christians were faint-hearted participants in their own culture: "They denigrate the Arabic language, because they prefer English or French; they abandon their country at the first opportunity to work abroad; and they have 'un-Syrian' lifestyles like the Americans or Europeans. Out in the streets, we all say 'Everything is okay,' but in private, there are disagreements."

My friend was a Sunni Muslim, both well-educated and reasonably religious—not the kind of person who would publicly admit to disliking Christians. But in his remarks I saw the banal logic of sectarianism in Syria, indeed, in many countries throughout the Middle East. It was a sectarianism born of resentment: resentment toward the minority as the achiever, as the outlier of dubious foreign loyalties, as the dissenter who rejected the culture of the mainstream. It was also a sectarianism born of a certain view of society: a view that said Syria would be better off without its weak parts, left as a monolith impervious to internal division. Iraq was 'Abdallah's "worst case scenario" when it came to the consequences of diversity. In Iraq, like Syria, he saw a country rich with difference. But in Iraq, he also saw a place that had been raped and torched by these very same differences. Syria had to avoid this fate at all costs.

The Christians' Dilemma: Assimilation or Separation?

'Abdallah's views were not representative of all Syrians. I appreciated his candor, but other friends and acquaintances of mine held views that ran counter to his. Many examples come to mind: the Syrian Orthodox archbishop of Aleppo, whose church school educated countless Muslim children; the Muslim journalist who dated Sunnis, Christians and 'Alawis without regard to their families' faith; and the Christian family in Damascus who shared Christmas and Ramadan with their Muslim neighbors. In many ways, when I lived in Damascus, the Syria of religious cooperation was more real than the Syria of sectarian strife we have come to know since the onset of the war. Indeed, it is important to remember that Syrian society was for the most part not rife with the kind of deep disagreements over identity that bubbled so close to the surface in nearby countries, including Lebanon, Iraq, and Egypt. All the same, it is also important to remember that as a matter of political expediency, the government and the religious institutions it had co-opted made confessional *convivencia* practically the national slogan. It would be wrong to assume that Syrians of different sects never got along before the revolution. But it would be equally misguided to assume that the sectarianism of wartime Syria materialized out of thin air.

For their part, some Christians I encountered seemed torn between worlds. This was born of the tension between assimilation and secession, between the rightful sense of belonging to a wider Syrian nation, and at the same time, a sense of historical distinctiveness. This tension was nourished by particular views of Syria's past, each of them enshrining opposite attitudes toward Islam and the possibility of belonging inside a predominantly Muslim society.

Some Christians, especially the Greek Orthodox—who form the single largest Christian denomination in the Levant, and who figure prominently in the history of nationalist movements in the region—imagined themselves as full participants in the surrounding Muslim society. They did so by de-emphasizing religious elements in their own culture and focusing on shared ethnic and cultural character-istics with their neighbors. As a result, many developed a deep loyalty to the notion of *'uruba*, or "Arabness," an inclusive identity grounded in ethnicity, language, and culture, instead of the particu-lars of sect and creed.

With this in mind, some Christians in Syria could look upon the Islamic conquests not as a tragedy, but as the high-water mark in the spread of Arab civilization. This was the view of Nadra Mutran, a Christian writer and a member of a prominent Greek Catholic family from the Beqaa Valley just across the border in modern-day Lebanon, who in 1913 described "racial pride [as] a fundamental virtue."[27] Looking back to the time of the conquests, Mutran argued that it was a sense of racial solidarity that had compelled the Arab Christian tribes to reject the suzerainty of their Byzantine Greek overlords and to embrace the dominion of the Arab Muslim conquerors instead. According to the favored reading of history, these Christian tribes—like the Ghassanids we met in Chapter One, as well as the family of Sergius Ibn Mansur, who opened the gates of Bab Touma to the armies of Islam—were Arab nationalists *avant la lettre*. They had jettisoned the weak bond of faith they shared with the Byzantines in favor of the far deeper bonds of ethnicity they shared with the Muslims. Thus, he wrote, "Instead of fighting the Muslims and standing in their faces, [the Christian tribes], stirred by the sentiment of brotherhood, abandoned the religious bond and the political tie which made them the clients of the Romans and contracted friendship with and fidelity to the speakers of their language, and the sons of their fathers."

In today's day and age, when the bonds of religion seem to over-power all sense of racial or ethnic solidarity, Mutran's words have a bracing quality. But what he wrote rings true for many Christians in Bab Touma today, who find in Arab nationalism a powerful logic for belonging.

That said, as attractive as assimilation could be for some Christians in Syria, I met many others who preferred to tell a story of isolation.

I learned this first-hand at the Maronite Cathedral of Mar Antonius, where I began this chapter. For several weeks each summer, the faithful would recite prayers to the "Blessed Masabki Brothers"—not exactly popular saints at back in New Jersey, but, as I discovered, virtual celebrities among the Catholics of Syria and Lebanon.

The Masabkis were three brothers born in Damascus in the nineteenth century. They worked in the silk trade, then a booming industry in the region, and used their considerable wealth to patronize the church. Though they were married, each had a deep, almost ascetical piety, faithfully attending mass, praying the rosary, and venerating the Eucharist. In 1860, fierce fighting broke out between the Maronites and the Druze of Mount Lebanon, fueled by disputes over land, profits, and rapid changes in the demography of the mountain (we shall return to this point below).[28] Thousands of Christians were massacred, and the conflict swept quickly to Damascus. There, in conjunction with the Ottoman authorities, mobs of Sunni Muslims flooded Christian neighborhoods, including Bab Touma, where they terrorized and killed.[29] Homes were looted and destroyed, women were raped, and by the end of fighting in July 1860, Bab Touma lay in ruins. Between 500 and 10,000 people lay dead (records from the time vary widely). During the fighting, the three Masabki brothers fled to a Franciscan convent. When the mob finally discovered them, they offered the brothers the choice of conversion or death. The brothers refused and were promptly chopped down, their blood spilling across the floor of the church. The bones of the Masabki brothers can still be seen today, browning inside a crystal reliquary at Mar Antonius.

The feast of the Masabki brothers was extremely popular in Bab Touma—popular not only because the Masabkis were neighborhood saints, but because memories of 1860 remained fresh in many people's minds. The events of that year are considered by many scholars as the sectarian watershed of modern Middle Eastern history—a moment when tensions between Christians and Muslims erupted suddenly into open violence, spurred by disruptive reforms in Istanbul, the empire's integration into the wider global economy, and the resultant shifts among local power brokers in Syria. Furthermore, they are remembered as the first time European powers really began to meddle in the affairs of minority groups, using their protection of local Christians in the wake of these events as a pretext for wider interference. But what seemed to energize the Catholics of Bab Touma even more was a sense of identification with the martyrs.

One could sense this in the priest's homily on the feast of the Masabki brothers, July 10. Without ever identifying their killers as Muslims, the priest spoke movingly of the need to persevere in the face of temptation, prejudice, and indignity. Indeed, as I listened to the homily, I felt like I was hearing a pep talk to a congregation confronting the events of 1860 all over again (never mind that many of the Christians sitting in the cathedral were probably wealthier, better educated, and more secure than their counterparts in the nineteenth century). What was important was not the date of the saints' martyrdom; rather, it was the notion that Christians had faced persecution of this kind in Syria for centuries. It was a call to continue surviving.

As the clergy and the faithful spilled into the streets of Bab Touma, I realized that their attitude was utterly opposite to what I had noticed when reading about Nadra Mutran. If Mutran had attempted to paper over distinctions between Muslims and Christians by appealing to a shared sense of "Arabness," the Catholics of Bab Touma preferred—at least on that day—to dwell on the bitter moments of conflict. They were two utterly opposite solutions to a common problem: how should Christians in the Middle East create a sense of belonging to a world and a history which are not fully their own?

In the coming chapter, we will extend this story to the modern period, examining how different minority groups in Syria—including Christians—have balanced the particulars of sect with the universal impulses of nationalism, Arabism, and Baathism.

3

OUTSIDERS BECOME INSIDERS

SECTARIANISM IN SYRIA

The road from Latakia to Qardaha wound gently along the Mediterranean coast. From here, the blue waters seemed to race to an endless horizon, to a world still wider than crowded Damascus, over one hundred and fifty miles inland. But the beachside view obscured the intimacy of the moment. Plato referred to this sea and the cities perched on its shores as a pond crowded with frogs.[1] In antiquity, as today, these frogs came in a dizzying menagerie of shapes and colors—Arabs, Phoenicians, Jews, Egyptians, Greeks, Romans, and Spaniards—yet their diversity disguised their essential unity. There was more uniting these far-flung peoples than dividing them. It was a sense of a common heritage held together by the relentless flow of merchants, philosophers, and missionaries across this small pond.

Latakia—ancient Laodicea—is Syria's principal port. It is located along a narrow coastal strip in the northwest of the country, between the Lebanese and Turkish borders. With its beachside resorts, open-air cafes, and relaxed ambiance, the city was a salutary reminder that Syria—at least in these parts—was very much one of Plato's frogs, a Mediterranean country with its eyes trained on the sea.

Nevertheless, not everyone who basks in the Mediterranean sun enjoys its riches. For just as Syria's geography and culture are divided between coast and desert, there is an equally pronounced rift between the coasts and mountains, which rise mightily from the waters' edge. Here, the rugged peaks shelter villages that form the once-destitute heartland of Syria's 'Alawi community, a region known as Jabal Ansariyya. One hot day in July 2009, I headed to one of the most important of these mountain villages—Qardaha—to try to understand how a once-marginal group came to control this country during the course of the twentieth century.

About ten miles south of Latakia, the road began to climb steeply. I was riding in a rickety van that had crawled the streets of Beijing or Seoul in another life, but was now covered with kitschy images of Syria's president, Bashar al-Asad. The van shook to the songs of a Lebanese chanteuse, but the volume waned as we hit a steep incline. I was the only foreigner in a cabin filled with locals, many of them chain-smoking and forlorn-looking. Between them sat crates of peaches, parsley, and what looked like bottles of arak, that alcoholic nectar of the Levant.

The road leveled off eventually and the electronic rhythms resumed their punishing pace. Amidst the rugged landscape, the Mediterranean became harder and harder to see. She appeared occasionally with a coquettish wink, her sparkling blue eyes disguised between olive groves and mountain wadis. Up here, the sea was only seven miles away, but it felt like hundreds. Qardaha and its people were born of a sense of isolation from Plato's world, not of belonging to it.

Qardaha enjoyed little notoriety throughout history: it was one of many faceless farming communities that dotted the mountains of Syria's northwest, whose 'Alawi inhabitants made meager returns selling tobacco, lemons and other crops to coastal merchants. For centuries, poverty here was endemic. Families were sometimes forced to make ends meet by selling their daughters into servitude in the homes of Sunnis grandees down below. By all reports, Qardaha was not a happy place, or much of a place at all; as Gertrude Stein once remarked of a very different city, Oakland, California: "There is no there there."[2]

All this would change in the early twentieth century, when contacts between the mountain and the coast began to increase. Among the beneficiaries was a young man named Hafez al-Asad, born in 1930, destined to become Qardaha's most famous son. He descended the mountain for schooling and never looked back. As an adult, he rose up through the ranks of the Syrian Air Force, Baath Party leadership, and the government, serving as defense minister. In 1970, he seized control of the state in a successful coup, ruling Syria with cruel determination until his death thirty years later. You can tell a lot about a man by where he chooses to be buried, and despite a career forged in the cut-throat government halls of Damascus, Asad wished his body to return here, to the mountain village where he was born.

After a forty-five minute ride, I stepped out of the bus: Asad's mausoleum sat on the edge of Qardaha's still-humble, even derelict-looking downtown. The ragged streets improved as I approached his grave, with newly planted trees and flowers lining a wide boulevard. Despite the inviting entrance and luxurious appointments, the mausoleum was strange: an eight-pointed star surmounted by a flat, onion-shaped dome—reminiscent of a spaceship in an old science fiction movie. An intricate Arabic inscription ran along the façade of the building, and on a large wall facing the entrance hung a sepia-toned portrait of the deceased leader. In it, an elderly Asad wore a page-boy cap and a wry smile, with the Syrian flag billowing behind him. It conjured a sense of nostalgia for a bygone world—for your grandfather and mine—for the grandfather of all Syria, this sunny-looking dictator.

The otherworldly ambiance was undiminished inside the mausoleum. Asad's grave lay in a shallow octagonal depression in the floor, beneath the main dome. The casket, draped in a rich green cloth, was surrounded by a wreath of fresh flowers, and a second band of green satin sheets. To the left was the grave of Basel, the dauphin of the house of Asad who died tragically in 1994 (after crashing his Mercedes on the airport road outside Damascus, for which he is remembered as a *shahid*, or martyr). There were other empty graves in the building, presumably awaiting the deaths of other Asad family members—including Hafez's widow Aniseh and their son Bashar, who took over the family business in 2000.

Tomb of Hafez al-Asad, Qardaha, Latakia Province

The mausoleum of Hafez al-Asad was more of a cultic site than a grave. Here, 'Alawi security officers dutifully tended the tomb when not oiling their pistols or sipping tea, and piles of flowers left by dignitaries and pilgrims lay strewn outside. It looked like the mourning had never ended. There was a strange dignity to the place: it was a memorial to a man of ferocious but incredible ambition, as well as to a community that had managed to emancipate itself from its mountain miseries and take center stage in modern Syrian history. The story of Hafez al-Asad—the Alawi peasant who would become king—has no parallel in its particulars across this country. But in its generalities, it sums up the experience of many minorities over the past hundred years. It is the story of the outsider made insider, of the particular who managed to carve out a place for himself by redefining the universal.

The Demography of Diversity

As we saw in chapter one, Sunni Muslims form an overwhelming majority in Syria (as throughout the Middle East except Lebanon and Israel), around 75% of a population of 22 million. Sunnis are spread throughout the country, from the large agro-cities of the west (Aleppo, Hama, Homs, Damascus) through the eastern deserts and beyond. But Syria is also home to a wide variety of other sects, Muslim and non-Muslim alike, each with its own geographic and cultural hub.[3]

The next largest group are the 'Alawis, also known as Nusayris, who make up around 12% of the population, or a little over two million. Historically, they were concentrated in the highlands of Syria's northwest, but in the twentieth century, they spread into the coastal cities of Latakia and Tartus, as well as certain neighborhoods in and around Hama, Homs and Damascus. The 'Alawis practice a small and poorly understood form of Shi'ism. Like most Shi'is, the 'Alawis believe that leadership of the Muslim community was originally entrusted to the descendants of the Prophet Muhammad, beginning with his cousin and son-in-law, 'Ali. Where the 'Alawis break with mainstream Shi'is is their belief that 'Ali was not merely the chosen deputy of Muhammad, but in fact God incarnate. Besides this there are other beliefs that put the 'Alawis at odds with most Muslims, Sunni and Shi'i alike, including the reincarnation of souls, as well as various practices adopted from Christianity and Gnosticism, especially the veneration of saints. We will return to the origins of the 'Alawi community in the following pages.

There are also the Christians of Syria—whom we met in chapter two—who form a dwindling 5 to 10% of the population. The largest denomination are the Greek Orthodox, followed by smaller communities of Greek Catholics, Syrian Orthodox, Armenian Orthodox, Maronites, and others. They are settled throughout the country, though they tend to congregate in cities and certain rural pockets, such as Wadi al-Nasara (the Valley of the Christians), just north of the Lebanese border. Members of the Druze sect, another branch of Shi'ism, which traces its origins to a Fatimid caliph in Egypt in the eleventh century, are concentrated in the southern district of Suweida and make up roughly 3% of Syria's population. The Isma'ilis, another Shi'i group (of which the Aga Khan is the global head) form a tiny but important sliver—not more than 1% of the population—concentrated in an agricultural belt near the city of Hama, in the districts of Salamiyya and Masyaf. There are also small communities of Twelver Shi'is (the largest branch of Shi'ism worldwide, whose members predominate in Iran, Iraq, and parts of Lebanon, Pakistan, and India) in a handful of villages in the west, around Damascus, the northwest, and far east of the country. There also used to be a sizeable Jewish community in Syria, but as in other parts of the Middle East, it has disappeared over the course of the twentieth century, drained by emigration to Europe, the United States, and Israel.

Religion is not the only kind of diversity in Syria. Ethnic and tribal identities form equally important cleavages, overlapping with—sometimes even eclipsing—sectarian loyalties, as do ties of region and class. Nonetheless, this book is interested in how religion shapes politics, and in turn, how politics shapes religion. To that end, we will have to gloss over many of the other fascinating dynamics that have molded Syrian society in their own profound ways.

Finally, as we discuss religious diversity, it's worth explaining a related concept, "sectarianism," and what I mean by it. Finding a precise definition for the term can be as controversial as the phenomenon itself. In recent years, scholars of the modern Middle East have favored a definition which reflects the specific social and political circumstances of the nineteenth and twentieth centuries, when according to some, sectarianism first emerged as a potent force in the history of the region.[4] Under this light, "sectarianism" comes to refer to the elevation of religious difference to the most fundamental element of political life, used to organize society and its relationship with the state. Furthermore, "sectarianism" refers to the process whereby the polity comes to be thought of as a corporative entity, in which each confessional community (Muslim and non-Muslim alike) receives representation according to its proper demographic weight (as in modern Lebanon). As a result, some come to be defined as numerical majorities and others as numerical minorities.

Sectarianism undoubtedly encompasses these characteristics, but what I refer to here is something broader, whose roots long antedate the collapse of the Ottoman Empire. For me sectarianism—both medieval and modern—is the activation of religious identity as one of the main principles of social and political life. It exists in the context of mixed societies in which, very often, different confessional groups live side by side and share many cultural practices, even beliefs. Therefore, it is an instrument of differentiation, powering identity formation in times of peace, though especially in times of conflict with the social and religious "other."

Sectarianism and religious belief are different things: although religious diversity is the stuff of sectarian conflict (that is, sectarianism cannot arise in religiously homogenous societies), religious diversity does not *per se* generate sectarianism. The existence of confessional distinctions (in Syria, for example) does not necessarily mean that violence between groups is inevitable—far from it.

My point here is simple: although sectarianism took on important political valences in modern times, especially with the rise of the nation states, this does not mean that there was no sectarianism before the modern period. Nor is it hard to find in many pre-modern texts from the Middle East the notion that one's religious affiliation mattered deeply for one's political predilections.[5] Indeed, from the early Islamic period forward, an individual's religious affiliation *was* the basis of his political affiliation.[6] We must keep this always in mind, while at the same time remembering that the phenomenon of "sectarianism" changes across centuries and places. There is no single "sectarianism" stretching through the ages, merely—as in any society around the world—recurring themes that provoke useful comparisons between past and present.

An Ancient Outpost on the Euphrates

Syria's religious diversity today is largely a product of developments in the medieval and modern period, namely, the rise and splintering of the Muslim faith. But religious diversity *per se* has been a fact of Syrian history for far, far longer. Take, for instance, Dura Europos, an ancient settlement that overlooks the banks of the Euphrates River, about three hundred miles northeast of Damascus in the middle of the desert. I roamed around the site for several hours one summer morning in 2009, arriving before the sun had a chance to make its cruel midday circuit.

A planned city since the second century BC, Dura Europos was prized for its strategic location on the frontiers between the Greco-Roman and Persian worlds.[7] Like a star planted firmly between two galaxies, Dura drew energy and influence from its larger neighbors, as reflected in its hybrid art, architecture, and religion. The most important ruins at Dura Europos date from the period of Roman occupation, especially the second and third centuries AD, when it was home to an important garrison of the Roman army. On the eastern, river-facing side of the city, where the army and administration were once housed, I came across the remains of a stately *agora*, grid-like streets, a bathhouse, and several temples dedicated to Roman gods, including Jupiter and Diana. Although many of these had been reduced to rubble, that the Romans had managed to transplant the essential elements of their orderly, disciplined life to this sun-scorched waste was to me remarkable.

Dura Europos incorporated many features of urban and religious life that once existed throughout the Roman Empire, but it also contained elements you were unlikely to find outside of Syria. I encountered four most unexpected religious buildings cramped beside the western wall of the city: a house church, a synagogue, a *mithraeum* (a temple of the god Mithras; this was one of the "mystery religions" of late antiquity that spread thanks to its popularity among the Roman legions), and a temple of the Semitic god Bel, all of them dating to the late-second and third centuries. They formed a peripheral, almost forgotten neighborhood in Dura Europos, as far from the downtown and its stately colonnades as possible without actually leaving the confines of the city.

Though they were far away from civic officialdom, these buildings were by no means marginal: they provided a window into the startling religious diversity of pre-modern Syria, a place where traditional pagan cults—themselves chimeric blends of Greco-Roman, Persian, and Syrian traditions—vied for attention with (and increasingly lost ground to) upstart faiths such as Christianity, Judaism, and Mithraism.

What is more, Dura Europos showed this ancient religious culture at a moment of dramatic transition. The house church—whose wall paintings now hang at the Gallery of Fine Arts at Yale University—and synagogue—whose stunning frescoes are housed in the National Museum in Damascus—represented an inflection point when the spiritual energies of the ancient world began coalescing firmly behind belief in the One God rather than His manifold competitors.[8] At Dura Europos in the third century, this belief may have been culturally and physically marginal, exiled to the outer reaches of the city. But within a few generations, this novel idea called "monotheism" would muscle its way into the imagination of Roman emperors, ushering in a religious epoch that endures to this day.

Dura Europos can tell us a lot about religious competition in ancient times, but it also reveals something about religious culture in Syria across the centuries. This was a world in which old faiths begat new ones, in which competing congregations set up shop beside one another—engaging in a boisterous parry of insults that blurred lines as much as sharpened them. Indeed, the proximity of different religious groups to one another catalyzed both assimilation and differentiation. Religious tension was not an uncommon phenomenon of life in ancient Syria, as it became in the Middle

Ages, and so remains today, even as the actors and circumstances changed dramatically from one age to another.

Religion and Community on a Back-country Road

The old religions of Syria have all but melted away. They have been replaced, however, by new faiths whose diversity mirrors the range of belief found on the back streets of Dura Europos. On another summer weekend, this time in 2010, I spent a few days driving around the hill country of the Orontes River valley, northwest of Damascus. There, I came across a string of villages each with its own confessional color: one predominantly Christian, the other Sunni, and the other 'Alawi. I knew the region was a melting pot, but nothing could have prepared me for the encounter of clashing faiths and lifestyles I would find along that narrow stretch of country road.

The most pronounced differences I saw on that summer day were between the Sunni and 'Alawi villages. In the Sunni village, a modest mosque dominated the dusty downtown. It was a Friday afternoon when I drove through, not long after the communal prayers had let out, and most of the locals were still lingering in the streets. Men and women kept to themselves in small groups, some women (fewer in number than the men) with long black *abayas* that concealed everything save for their faces.

By contrast, further down the road, in the 'Alawi village, young men and women congregated near a grimy corner shop. It looked like a motorcycle rally, with tough-looking *shabab* (young men) circling the intersection as young women straddled the backs of their bikes, whispering flirtatiously into their ears.

As we have seen, the 'Alawis practice a form of Shi'i Islam that varies considerably from the beliefs of most mainstream Shi'a today.[9] Their religion traces its roots to mid-ninth century Baghdad and a man named Muhammad Ibn al-Nusayr al-Namiri (whence we get the term "Nusayris," common in the pre-modern period, though now considered derogatory by many 'Alawis). Ibn al-Nusayr was a confidant of the tenth and eleventh imams of Shi'i tradition, and considered himself a mediator of divine revelation.

In those early years, 'Alawi belief was very fluid, not easily distinguished from those of competing Shi'i sects, such as the Isma'ilis. Indeed, the movement gained ground in areas of the Middle East where it was in direct competition with other emergent strands of Shi'ism, most especially in northern Syria. It was here that its unconventional teachings about saint worship, the coming apocalypse, and the transmigration of souls proved very popular among recently settled Bedouin populations and other marginal groups. In the eleventh century the movement began to win converts in the mountainous highlands abutting the Mediterranean, in an area that has ever since been the historic homeland of the 'Alawis. This was thanks to the efforts of the Banu Tanukh, an important tribe in the area, who served as governors of the city of Maarat al-Nu'man.

The 'Alawi religion is often said to be secretive, because as in other Muslim sects from the period—especially the Druze—only a small group of men are supposed to be initiated into full comprehension of the community's beliefs. In practice, this means that many 'Alawis today are fairly secular, and their everyday pieties (including the veneration of saints) are somewhat disconnected from the doctrines of the initiated class of religious leaders (called *sheikh*s). While villages like the one I visited usually had a shrine or meeting house, few attended services in them. Indeed, on that particular afternoon, the young men and women of the 'Alawi village seemed to have little idea that their Sunni counterparts a few miles away were just then streaming out of the mosque. There was a palpable contrast between the two places.

We often think of sectarianism as a clash of theologies, but in these villages I realized that sectarianism was also as a clash of lifestyles: of different visions of the culture and values of the nation. It is no wonder that since the start of the Syrian uprising in March 2011, some of the worst violence between the regime and the opposition has engulfed the Orontes Valley, a place where Sunnis and 'Alawis live in uncomfortably close proximity to one another.

In hindsight, I had witnessed the same scene play out in Damascus countless times over the preceding years. The capital was a microcosm of this rural world, a place to which people from across Syria migrated. It created a Babel of stunning diversity, where instead of living miles apart on back country roads, Sunnis, 'Alawis, Christians, and Druze shared neighborhoods, restaurants, sidewalks, and other intimate spaces. The most personal forms of contact were often the most banal, especially on the public bus. Here, I was often reminded that dress can be a most unreliable marker of religiosity in the Middle East—much less of sect. It is nearly impossible to tell men of different religions apart. As for women, it can be easier, but also extremely tricky: a Greek Orthodox nun can look a lot like a Muslim woman in a hijab, and a religious Christian mother can dress more daringly than a non-practicing Sunni teenager with the veil. Still, appearance can signal culture, and in a place like Syria where sectarianism is communicated through a constellation of subtle symbols and cues, one realizes that appearance is both everything and nothing at all. What matters is identity, and the ways in which one conveys that to the people around you.

Such are some of the social habits of sectarianism in Syria. But how do these identities play out in the arena of politics?

The Conflicting Consequences of Reform

The dilemma facing minorities in Syria over the past century has been the experience of living between particularism and universalism. It is the dilemma of belonging to communities of dissent, which fall outside the religious "mainstream" of Sunni Islam, while at the same time, supporting ideologies and parties that urge integration and equality. It is a tension that has affected practically every minority group, from the 'Alawis and Christians to the Druze, Ismailis, and Shi'is. It has also shaped major political developments in Syria for decades.

To understand the roots of this tension, we must return to the early nineteenth century, when Syria, still a province of the Ottoman Empire, was caught up in the modernizing fervor of the age. The last great Muslim power in world history, the Ottoman Empire stretched from the Balkans to Iraq and from the Caucasus to the Hijaz. With such a geographic sweep, its population invariably included large numbers of religious minorities—both Muslim minorities, like Shiʻis, ʻAlawis, Yazidis, and Druze, as well as non-Muslim minorities, such as Christians and Jews. Under Islamic law, non-Muslims were traditionally regarded as *dhimmi*s, or "people of the covenant." As such, they were subject to special taxes and restrictions different from those of their Muslim neighbors (such as the poll tax known as the *jizya*, mentioned above). In theory, they profited from the full protection of the state, and according to many historians, Ottoman *dhimmi*s enjoyed greater prosperity and security than their minority counterparts in Europe.[10] Despite this, most non-Muslims lived under a system that was, by contemporary standards, rather unequal. The very notion of a *dhimmi* reflected a two-tiered vision of subjecthood, with "orthodox" Muslims enjoying a fuller suite of rights and opportunities than their Jewish and Christian neighbors.

In the early nineteenth century, this began to change. A continent away, the Enlightenment was popularizing the notion of equality before the law. Before long, this idea had permeated the Ottoman court, and along with it, concepts such as individual rights, respect for private property, and the market economy. The buzz generated a flood of liberal, secularizing reforms, affecting everything from the organization of the army to taxation, state bureaucracy, and the law. These reforms were referred to collectively as the *Tanzimat*.[11]

There were two important factors that spurred the change. The first was a growing sense among Ottoman bureaucrats that the empire was lagging behind its imperial peers by failing to step fully into the modern world. Related to this, many feared that unless they embraced European norms of statecraft, the Ottomans' sovereignty, territory, and finances would be subject increasingly to interference from outside. Despite their best efforts, however, European meddling only increased during the course of the *Tanzimat* period, such that by the end of the nineteenth century, Europeans were even more involved in managing the economy, debt, and political decisions of the court than at any other time before the reforms began. These considerations—partly internal, partly external—can help us understand the urgency with which reformers approached their task during that crucial half-century.

To understand the origins of the *Tanzimat*, we must situate ourselves in the place where they began: Gülhane Park, a haven of towering trees and rose bushes that once formed the outer perimeter of Topkapi Palace in Istanbul, the residence of the Ottoman sultan. It was here—in the shadow of the Byzantine church of Hagia Sophia, converted into a mosque after the Turkish conquest of 1453—that Ottoman reformers would change the lives of Christians, Jews, and other minorities forever. In 1839, they promulgated a short document known as the *Hatt-i Sharif*, or Gülhane Decree. Widely regarded as the opening salvo of the *Tanzimat*, the decree included one very important but rather opaque reference to the rights of non-Muslims: "The Muslim and non-Muslim subjects of our lofty sultanate shall, without exception, enjoy our imperial concessions."[12] Though this was widely interpreted as granting the subjects of the subjects of the empire equal rights regardless of religion, it took another seventeen years for the reformers to spell out explicitly what they meant by this. The follow-up decree of 1856, known as the *Islahat Fermani*, outlined in great detail the full rights of non-Muslims, nearly all of them positive from the perspective of the minorities except for the new requirement of compulsory military service, which mirrored the longstanding obligation of Muslims to serve in the army.[13] Henceforth, at least in theory, Christians and Jews would enjoy the same basic rights as Muslims, overturning a centuries-old legal consensus in Islam, which regarded non-Muslims as second-class citizens.[14]

Although the changes initiated at Gülhane Park in the mid-nineteenth century are often remembered for advancing the status of minorities, reformers were motivated by numerous strategic considerations, not all of them altruistic and many of them contradictory to their wider goals of modernization. The most important of these was a desire to promote *Osmanlilik*, or Ottomanism. It was the notion that the subjects of the empire should share a common political and cultural identity—one that transcended the divisive ties of religion, region, and race which were seen by reformers as fragmenting society. In the view of these men, the empire was more a mosaic of semi-autonomous groups than a confraternity of citizens—certainly in contrast to the nation-states of Europe, which the *cognoscenti* looked upon as models of progress and unity. There is much to critique in this view of a fractured and weak

Ottoman Empire—not to mention the reformers' dream-like vision of European societies. That said, the *Tanzimat* did promote equality among Muslims and non-Muslims, an equality that only deepened thanks to the expanding European influence inside Ottoman lands. Indeed, seen from another direction, these reforms made official a still longer-term process of advancement among Christians and Jews in the Middle East. In many cities, European powers came to rely on *dhimmi*s as middlemen, representing their interests as consuls and agents for businesses.[15] These provided a wealth of new opportunities to non-Muslims, especially in Arab lands, where they profited from a quasi-independent political status, as well as education in foreign-run schools, especially those established by Catholic and Protestant missionaries.[16]

Although the *Tanzimat* expanded the political horizons of minorities, they were by no means a resounding success. Despite the stated desire to create a universal identity for all subjects in the empire, neither Muslims nor Christians were altogether pleased with these efforts. Many Ottoman Muslims, for example, looked upon the reforms as a kind of perfidious foreign intervention, reflecting the agenda of the sultan's European puppet masters. There was much truth to this: certain reforms were signed specifically to assuage European diplomats, including the great *Islahat Fermani* of 1856, which Sultan Abdülmecid issued only after prompting by the British ambassador, Viscount Stratford de Redcliffe (as part of a larger spat between England and Russia that would lead directly to the Crimean War). Ottoman Muslims also looked with special skepticism on clauses that expanded economic privileges for Christians, who had quickly seized on their new rights and wealth to build opulent churches, dress in lavish clothes, and behave in a manner which many Muslims in mixed cities regarded as "uppity." For their part, too, Christians and Jews resented the imposition of new duties that came with the revised notion of subjecthood. In particular, they protested having to fulfill the military service from which they had been exempt in exchange for paying a tax. What is more, Christians and Jews had enjoyed a certain degree of legal autonomy under the *ancien régime*, thanks to the *millet* system, in which non-Muslim communities were left to govern themselves under a chief rabbi or patriarch appointed with the consent of the sultan.[17] All this stood to disappear in a world that exalted the universal over the particular, a world that had begun back at Gülhane Park.

Finally, for some Christians, the *Tanzimat* were dismissed as an unsatisfactory vessel for achieving the kind of long-term political goals they truly desired. In their judgment, legal equality under an Islamic regime was a way station en route to a bigger prize, namely, full independence. The path to equality, they believed, ran through nationalist revolution—much as the Greeks had accomplished through their war of independence, which ended in 1832, seven years before the promulgation of the Gülhane Decree.

Religion and Citizenship at the End of the Ottoman Empire

These problems compounded over time, such that by the late nineteenth century, the *Tanzimat* ended up reinforcing the very concept of religious particularism they had set out to erase. Certain indicators of the failure of the reforms are well known, such as the waves of sectarian violence that swept through the Middle East in the mid-nineteenth century. Indeed, fighting between Muslims and Christians erupted in places as diverse as Aleppo in 1850, Mosul in 1854, Nablus in 1856, and most famously, Mt Lebanon and Damascus in 1860.[18] The causes of these conflicts were manifold, and in many instances, reflected long-simmering local tensions that had little to do with Christianity and Islam, much less the politics of the Ottoman court. In other respects, as some scholars have noted, they can also be seen as backlashes against the reforms themselves, particularly the blatant overturning of Islamic law, which had long maintained a clear hierarchy between Muslims and non-Muslims. Whatever the case may be, these sectarian events struck a discordant note at a time when the *Tanzimat* were—at least notionally—working to improve the conditions of non-Muslims in the empire, not make them worse.

Another reason for the failure of the *Tanzimat* was inherent in the idea of Ottomanism itself, one of several forms of political identity that tended to compete with one another inside the empire until its demise after World War I.[19] The impulse behind Ottomanism was to fashion a new Ottoman identity capacious enough to embrace Sunni Muslims as well as the various sectarian communities of the empire. But the vocabulary available for framing such Ottomanism was surprisingly thin. It was circumscribed by the very Islamic carapace that had for centuries given Ottoman society its internal coherence, its cultural binding. Thus, with an eye trained on universalism, at times, the reformers ended up promoting a remarkably narrow notion of the universal: to be a good Ottoman was to be a good Muslim, and what is more, a good Sunni Muslim of the state-sponsored Hanafi *madhhab*, or school of law. It was universal only in the sense that this identity coincided with that of the empire's ruling elites. It would become a top-town, aspirational form of universalism—ideologically pure and honoring the sultan's role as the defender of Islam—but it left many subjects out in the cold—either those who did not fit the description or those who had little desire to conform to it.

The religious coloring of Ottomanism became apparent during the reign of the sultan Abdülhamid II (r. 1876–1909).[20] His years in power are regarded as a conservative reaction to the liberal overreach of the *Tanzimat*. Indeed, it was under Abdülhamid that the Ottoman constitution—the signature achievement of the era of reform—was revoked and replaced by traditional absolute monarchy (only to be revoked yet again at the end of his reign in response to the revolution of the Young Turks). When it came to religion, Abdülhamid was a staunch pan-Islamist. He sought to enhance the Islamic character of the state by emphasizing the sacredness of his own imperial office. He lavished money on religious scholars, mosques, and pious endowments (*awqaf*), and even sought to standardize the practice of Islam through new institutions such as the Commission for the Inspection of Qurans.

The minorities of the Ottoman Empire bore the brunt of this change in policy. One way the state attempted to promote Islamic universalism was by sending missionaries into the provinces to tame "wayward" religious groups.[21] From 1891 to 1892, for example, the state tried to convert large numbers of Yazidis to Sunni Islam. A Kurdish ethno-religious minority concentrated in northern

Iraq, the Yazidis followed a religion that blended elements of Zoroastrianism, Christianity, and Islam, and as such, earned a false reputation as "devil worshippers." There were several reasons for the state's newfound evangelical fervor, foremost among them a desire to reverse the Yazidis' longstanding exemption from military service and to draft members of the community into the army. That said, another important factor was a deep anxiety over unorthodoxy in Abdülhamid's pan-Islamic society. The state was not entirely successful in this; indeed, so heavy-handed were Ottoman efforts to convert the Yazidis that they contacted the French consul in Mosul in northern Iraq, offering to convert to Christianity if he could protect them from the Turks.

Ottoman attitudes towards the Yazidis exemplify their views of other minorities throughout the empire, whom—in the words of historian Selim Deringil—they "wanted to convert ideologically so that they could be utilized as reliable members of the population."[22] The campaign for conformity also touched Bedouin tribes in Syria; 'Alawis in Aleppo; and "wayward" Muslims in Anatolia suspected of flirting with Christianity.

Whatever the truth of these anxieties, the state initiated aggressive campaigns of proselytization. Education reform, in particular, was a favored means of inculcating Hamidian values in the children of minority groups. There were special schools and scholarships set up for Shi'i boys from Iraq, Arab tribesmen from Syria, and Yazidis (in certain instances, their religious shrines were even transformed into Sunni madrasas).

The Ottoman Empire may have collapsed after World War I, but the era of the *Tanzimat*, as well as the conservative reaction of the sultan Abdülhamid, changed the status of minorities forever. On the one hand, the nineteenth century had empowered Jews, Christians, and heterodox Muslims by emphasizing Ottomanism over sectarian particularism. On the other hand, what the empire understood by the term "Ottomanism" was increasingly pregnant with religious connotations. It was a quixotic wager, and ultimately, the minorities found themselves stranded in a treacherous no-man's land between belonging and exile, between the universal impulses of nineteenth century reform and the particularism of sect and creed. Let's move ahead to the twentieth century to see how Syria's minorities negotiated this balance in a post-Ottoman world.

Taking Sectarianism Seriously: Plural Identities in a Plural Society

As we explore religion and identity in the Middle East, it's important to pause and remember that for many in the region—today, as in the nineteenth century—religion is one of many forms of identity. Indeed, just as in the United States or Europe, identity in many Middle Eastern societies is plural: identities grounded in citizenship or political affiliation exist alongside identities based in class, sect, region, or level of education. One identity does not predominate over the others, but rather, they shift, rise, and fall in accordance with the various pressures exerted by the outside world.

I learned this first hand in the spring of 2013 during a meeting of academics and Syrian opposition activists who had gathered to discuss the ongoing crisis in the country. At the beginning of the conference, the participants were invited to help draw up an agenda for the coming days. The usual litany of concerns came up: chemical weapons, foreign intervention, the treatment of refugees, etc. After nearly twenty minutes, no one had broached one of the most important yet highly disputed aspects of the conflict, namely sectarianism, which was then on the media's radar throughout the United States and Europe. So, a colleague—an American—raised his hand and proposed that the group devote some time to unpacking the religious dimensions of the war and what could be done to ameliorate them.

Almost immediately, in a tone at once condescending and weary, one activist turned to the questioner and said: "*Please* do not tell us about sectarianism in our country. Do not buy into the way this war is being depicted on television and on the internet. Take it from the Syrians assembled around this table that religion plays no role in what's going on. We come from different religious communities, but these have no bearing on our political stances. Don't tell us about sectarianism."

I was mildly shocked by the reaction of this woman: at first glance, hers was a studied denial of the reality of the war, which had turned dangerously confessional since its relatively un-confessional start in March 2011. How could someone so deeply involved in the war not see it—the constant threats of retribution by Salafi sheikhs against "godless" 'Alawis? The influx of Shi'i soldiers from places like Lebanon, Iraq, and Iran? The careful targeting of religious sites by both sides in order to fan the flames of war? If these did not count as the signposts of sectarianism, I wasn't sure what did.

But on further reflection, I began to appreciate what lay behind the woman's reprimand. Indeed, for all the talk of Sunni and Shi'i axes in the revolution, the small group of activists seated at the table that day challenged casual assumptions about the allegedly immutable tie between sect and politics. Most of the activists present were Sunnis, as was to be expected, but some of the senior participants were Christians and 'Alawis—members of minority communities usually seen as resolute supporters of Bashar al-Asad. In this, the woman had the ultimate trump card against those who would dare indulge in stereotypes: there were always exceptions to so-called rules.

Lurking beneath her castigation of my colleague, however, I sensed a deeper fear: that by treating sectarianism as a politically and strategically salient dimension of the conflict, we would somehow give credence to it, legitimize it, and normalize it through discussion. Yet as the woman had informed us so unambiguously, sectarianism was not something "real" in Syrian society. It was an accident of the war, a pernicious creation of belligerents who wanted to rally their troops by demonizing the "other". Worst of all, one suspects she feared casting a monolithic net over the followers of different faiths, thereby assuming an absolute and essential connection between creed and politics. It was to assume that nothing mattered more to a person than the kind of God he or she worshipped.

In this sense, the woman's rebuke was a healthy reminder that even in the most tense of times, identity is plural. Whether in Syria or any other country, a person cannot be reduced to merely one aspect of his or her life. The question at hand was thus not whether sectarianism existed—for it surely did—but how much weight to assign it given that sect always exists in a messy matrix of loyalties.

In a sense, the exchange between the woman and my colleague was an echo of a wider debate that has been raging since the time of the *Tanzimat*: to what extent can people configure forms of identity that aspire toward the universal, while at the same time adhering to forms of identity that reinforce the particular?

The Rise of Arab Nationalism

So far, we have discussed the ways in which Ottomanism attempted to create new forms of identity in the nineteenth century. Of course, the Ottoman Empire would fall apart after World War I, and with it, all possibility of reconfiguring the Middle East along the lines envisioned by the reformers. It would be replaced, however, by an ideology of equal daring, and with its own record of mixed success.

Arab nationalism (*al-Qawmiyya al-'Arabiyya*) called for the creation of a pan-Arab identity grounded in the cultural and intellectual achievements of Arabic speakers. It owed its inspiration to a group of nineteenth-century writers in Tunisia, Egypt, Lebanon, and Syria. These were the trailblazers of the *Nahda*, the Arabic literary "awakening" centered principally on Egypt and the Levant, which harnessed the power of the printing press to disseminate novel ideas about citizenship, religion, technology, and progress.[23] Many of the leading lights of the *Nahda* were Christians—men like Butrus al-Bustani and Ahmad Faris Shidyaq (who later converted to Islam), both from what is now Lebanon. They profited from education in Western institutions (many of them run by Christian missionaries, Catholic and Protestant alike) and emboldened by the reforms of the *Tanzimat*, they offered new narratives of identity for the communities of the region. Arab nationalism—one of the great contributions of *Nahda*-era thinkers—was a brilliant compromise between the universal and the particular. On the one hand, it offered a deeper and more meaningful form of identity than the weak recipe of Ottomanism provided, but on the other, it aimed to transcend historic cleavages among Arabic speakers. Henceforth, Arabism would embrace peoples as far flung as Morocco and Iraq, whether they prayed in Sunni or Shi'i mosques, in Christian churches, 'Alawi shrines, or even Jewish synagogues. Of course, Arabism was from the beginning tied closely to Islamic culture. As the majority religion in the Middle East, Sunni Islam was seen as the great guardian of Arabism, and many Sunni thinkers played important roles in popularizing the ideology. That said, Arab nationalism offered a new identity that aspired to embrace certain universals (ethnicity, language) and transcend certain particulars (religion).

The philosophy of Arab nationalism was incubated first among Christians and Sunni Muslims, but when it came to political activism it sprang to life through the efforts of a relatively obscure community living in the grain fields of southern Syria: the Druze, like the 'Alawis another offshoot of Shi'i Islam.

Follow the Grain: Minorities and Revolution in the Interwar Period

To understand this turn of events, we must return to Damascus, to the district known as Midan, which stretches south of the city along the perimeter of an old Roman hippodrome. When in Damascus, I visited Midan almost daily. It was a fascinating neighborhood, far from where most foreigners tended to congregate. Midan was the heart of traditional Damascus. It was here, throughout medieval and Ottoman times, that the governor of the city would meet the pilgrim caravan before accompanying it south to the holy cities of Mecca and Medina, banners unfurled. The provision of the pilgrimage caravan became an important part of the local economy, and to this day, the streets of Midan shelter one of Damascus' most famous *souqs*, a vast open space best enjoyed in the early evening cool, when bakers would display enormous round trays of flaky sweets, grocers would assemble small mountains of peaches and watermelons, and butchers would hang chickens, lamb shanks, and sheep's heads for buyers to peruse. Nearby, my Syrian teachers shared a flat with a group of students from Chad, who spoke beautiful classical Arabic (their own Chadian dialect was virtually unintelligible to the students who lodged with them). It was here during a lesson that I also had my one and only encounter with the feared *mukhabarat* (the Syrian secret police), who had been monitoring the apartment after one summer tenant—a flamboyant Colombian student who worked as a hairdresser aboard cruise ships—brought home one too many local men, arousing the suspicions of his conservative neighbors.

Midan had grown wealthy over the years as a hub of the regional grain trade. As scholar Michael Provence has shown, the grain came largely from the Druze tribes of southeastern Syria, a region known as Suweida.[24] The soil in this region, part of a larger area known as the Hawran, was excellent for farming, enriched by dark volcanic stone that had once provided sturdy masonry for Roman builders (the city of Bosra, mentioned in the previous chapter, was not far away). In the nineteenth century, Druze farmers established commercial ties with these Sunni merchants in Midan: grain was cultivated in the south, then transported north to Damascus, where it would be sold to urban buyers. It brought wealth and stability to Syria's agricultural fringe, and more importantly, it established an economic and political axis between the Druze countryside and the Sunni metropole.

Around the same time, the Ottoman authorities established military academies to train and fill the ranks of the professional officer corps. By and large, the traditional urban elites of Syria scorned these institutions, looking upon military service as a relatively undignified calling.[25] They preferred to pay to train their sons in schools of the Ottoman civil service, from which they would return to administer the affairs of the Arab provinces. By contrast, heavily subsidized military training was the only kind of education available to the sons of Syria's outsiders, including minority groups like the Druze. Not only was it among the few forms of advanced education open to them, but in a more general sense, it was also among the only paths of social advancement for a community that had stood on the margins of Syrian society through much of history. Needless to say, it was a boon to the Druze, and on the eve of World War I, the system inadvertently created two elite constituencies in Ottoman Syria: first, Sunni Muslims, who dominated the ranks of the civil service and commerce, and second, the Druze, who enjoyed disproportionate representation in the upper echelons of the military.

After the end of World War I, Syria fell under the control of a French mandate. Despite pretensions the post-Ottoman Middle

East, the mandate was perceived as little more than colonialism in disguise, and many of the Sunni elites who had facilitated Ottoman rule prior to the war now found themselves serving European masters in the same capacities. Although some Sunni elites profited from the French presence, which for them preserved the status quo ante, many others—from the cities to the countryside—reviled it as simply another form of foreign despotism. Ironically, the very elites best positioned to challenge colonial rule had been co-opted by it. What is more, there was at that time little organized opposition to the French: many of the most fervent nationalists from the war years had either been exiled from Syria or voluntarily fled it, such as the leaders of the People's Party of Damascus.

This left behind a single group in Syria with the ability and determination to challenge French rule: the Druze officers. As traditional outsiders to Syrian society, they stood to profit little from new colonial arrangements that perpetuated the Ottoman ones of old; furthermore, unlike the urban notables, the Druze had the military and organizational know-how to launch a successful insurgency.

Thus, in 1925, Druze rebels ignited what would become the longest anti-colonial revolt of the inter-war period in the Middle East. Its success owed to the long-standing commercial contacts between the Druze sheikhs of the south and their Sunni partners in the Midan quarter of Damascus. Although members of the city's Sunni majority, these merchants formed a class of urban "outsiders" who did not enjoy the same traditional power and influence as the notables—namely, access to the civil service. The axis of the revolt followed the grain trade—a commercial corridor connecting city to countryside, ensuring that the insurrection would find support well outside its two initial and rather narrow constituencies. The French failed to appreciate the importance of this axis, an oversight that allowed the revolt to smolder well into 1927, when its leaders were finally defeated and sent into exile.

The French depicted the revolt as the insurrection of a small religious minority. But for the Druze who led the revolt, the goals of the insurrection were strictly nationalistic. The rebels considered themselves to be part of a larger Syrian nation, and as such, felt obliged to liberate the country from foreign occupation. Their greater Syria would be one united by Arab culture and language, a society that transcended the narrow confines of sect and region. In this, they rejected the governing strategy of the French mandatory governors which had attempted to control Syria by dividing it into sectarian "cantons," coinciding roughly with the historic territory of various religious groups.

Although the revolt failed, it had profound long-term consequences for Syria: it signaled the onset of a new struggle between the old landed elites, who had cooperated with the French authorities, and a new class of rural elites, who had cut their teeth in Ottoman military academies. It also established the Druze—historical outsiders to the dreams of Syria's cities—as the standard-bearers of Syrian nationalism, an ideology that not only rejected colonial rule, but also attempted to move beyond divisive religious cleavages. The rise of the Druze rebels foreshadowed the emergence of even more successful nationalists after them—especially men like future president Hafez al-Asad, who began as a member of another sectarian community, but who, through military training and commitment to the nationalist cause, managed to catapult himself into the upper echelons of the power elite.

Michel 'Aflaq: An Arab Christian and his Muslim Prophet

As we've seen, the Midan quarter of Damascus was a hotbed of revolutionary activity. A conservative place with a knack for disobedience, it kept its reputation alive well after the end of the Druze revolt. Indeed, in the course of the present war in Syria, it has witnessed some of the fiercest anti-government resistance in the capital.

In 1910, an event took place in Midan of even greater long-term consequence for Syria than the Druze revolt: the birth of Michel 'Aflaq.[26] The son of a Greek Orthodox merchant family involved in trading in cereals, 'Aflaq showed himself to be a talented student, and in 1929, was sent abroad to study at the Sorbonne. There, he met another ambitious young Damascene—Salah al-Din Bitar, a Sunni Muslim whose father was also involved in the grain trade in Midan—and together they began dreaming up a new political ideology, blending elements of the socialist and nationalist movements

Michel 'Aflaq, 1910–1989

then in vogue throughout Europe. The team returned to Damascus in 1934, assuming teaching positions at the Tahjiz al-'Ula, one of Syria's most prestigious secondary schools. At first in secret, they founded a new political party they called the Arab Baath Movement (*baath*, meaning "resurrection," or "rising"), which disseminated its views through pamphleteering and student activism. Its goals were straightforward: to facilitate the creation of a pan-Arab state, relying on the revolutionary activities of a secretive political minority (much like the "vanguard of the proletariat" envisioned in the writings of Vladimir Lenin).

From its beginnings, Baathism showed curious attitudes toward religion. On the one hand, it promoted a vision of Arab identity that transcended conventional sectarian cleavages among Arabic speakers. Henceforth, there would be no distinctions among Sunnis, Shi'is, Christians or Jews, or among the particular denominations within these larger groups. Yet at the same time, as a matter of historical reflection, it was undeniable that Islam had played a special role in the creation and spread of Arab culture. That the Prophet Muhammad had received his revelation in Arabic, that the armies of Islam were responsible for conveying this Arab culture across the Middle East and beyond gave the religion a special place in an otherwise avowedly secular worldview.

The paradoxes inherent in this were evident in many early speeches given by Baathist leaders. Perhaps the most famous was one delivered by 'Aflaq at the University of Damascus in 1943 on the anniversary of the Prophet Muhammad's birth.[27] It was a fascinating and forceful expression of the civilizational potency of Islam—even for those who technically did not belong to it, like the Christian 'Aflaq.

At the start of the speech, 'Aflaq lamented the decline of the Arab nation, especially the growing chasm between its "glorious past" and its "shameful present." The Arabs—asphyxiated by centuries of Turkish rule, then subjugated by French colonialism—had to recover a sense of pride in themselves, to return to a moment of grandeur in their ancient past. For 'Aflaq, this meant one thing, the dawn of Islam. For just as Islam had rescued the Arabs from the shackles of paganism in the seventh century, so would Arabism retrieve the Arabs from their present political and cultural malaise. For 'Aflaq, the Prophet embodied all that was essential about Arabness ('uruba). Through him, the Arabs had "conquered their souls, plumbed their depths, and come to know their inner selves; and before they governed the nations, they governed themselves, controlled their passions, and mastered their desires."

From all reports, 'Aflaq was not a very religious man. But according to the authorities in Iraq, where 'Aflaq lived for the final decades of his life after falling out with the Baath Party in Syria, he eventually converted to Islam. In 1995, six years after his death, 'Aflaq's son contacted Saddam Hussein about the matter, providing "proof" of his father's conversion. According to the original letter, dated 1980 and discovered in 'Aflaq's private copy of the Quran, the Baath Party founder wrote: "If an accident were to occur to me, then I will die under the religion of Islam and I bear witness that there is no god but God and Muhammad is His prophet."[28] The letter was signed: "Ahmad Michel Aflaq." The Christian Michel had become the Muslim Ahmad.

There is some dispute as to whether 'Aflaq truly converted in his final years, or if the Iraqi Baath engineered it as a publicity stunt. Whatever the case may be, it would seem that at the end of his life, the Christian school teacher of Damascus had come to see Islam as something greater than simply another form of Arab patriotism.

The Rise of the 'Alawis: From the Margins to the Mainstream

So far, we have seen the ways in which Arab nationalism generally, as well as Baathism specifically, appealed to Syria's minority communities. By emphasizing the centrality of Arab language and culture, they reshaped the frontiers of the majority, supplying communities that had stood warily on the sidelines of history with a sense of belonging. Of course, the rise of Baathism since the 1960s has been associated with one minority community above the rest: the 'Alawis. Indeed, the 'Alawi sect furnished an important early ideologue of the Baath in the writer Zaki Arsuzi, who was a contemporary and rival of Michel 'Aflaq and Salah al-Din Bitar. The 'Alawis would also give Baathism its two greatest political leaders:

the long-serving president Hafez al-Asad and his son, the current president of Syria, Bashar al-Asad.

Under the post-war mandate, the French had attempted to rule Syria by dividing it into sectarian statelets. There were the vast and predominantly Sunni provinces of Aleppo and Damascus, which stretched east beyond the Euphrates River. There were also the smaller cantons of Jabal al-Duruz in the south, carved out for the Druze community; Greater Lebanon on the Mediterranean coast, established mainly for France's Maronite Christian clients; and an 'Alawi state directly to the north, centered on the mountainous area above Tartus and Latakia.

For centuries, the 'Alawis had subsisted on the margins of Syrian society. In a country filled with religious dissidents, the 'Alawis were the most despised of them all—impoverished practitioners of a secretive Shi'i sect that sampled from the beliefs of Islam, Christianity, and Gnosticism. In light of this, the foundation of a semi-autonomous 'Alawi statelet in 1920 was a boon to the community. True, some 'Alawis had participated in a revolt against the French in 1919, and many 'Alawis remained tepid toward the French mandatory power after World War I.[29] But as the mandate wore on, enthusiasm for the French only warmed; indeed, by the time of the Druze rebellion in 1925, most 'Alawis elected to stay on the sidelines, content with the quasi-autonomy they enjoyed under their European masters.

In 1936, as part of an agreement with the surging Syrian nationalists, France agreed to transfer custody of the 'Alawi state to Damascus. In protest, 'Alawi notables petitioned the governor in Latakia to establish a permanent 'Alawi state for them. As minorities, they argued, they risked subjugation at the hands of Syria's Sunni Muslim majority. Furthermore, like the Jews of Palestine, they argued that the only way to secure their safety was to grant them sovereignty. Unfortunately, their petition fell on deaf ears, and the delegation returned home, resigned to an uncertain future. Among the petitioners was none other than the father of future president Hafez al-Asad. The territory again became autonomous in 1939, but was incorporated into Syria once and for all in 1942.[30]

For Hafez al-Asad and his generation, the lessons of French colonialism were simple: if the 'Alawis could not achieve autonomy

Mountains of northwestern Syria, with Mediterranean Sea, near Baniyas, Tartus Province

through the creation of a special canton, they would will themselves to power by becoming the standard-bearers of the Arab mainstream. The French had prepared the way for this. Throughout their twenty-year rule of Syria, the French authorities installed 'Alawis and other minorities, including Christians and Circassians, as members of the *troupes spéciales du Levant*—military units designed for deployment to troubled hot-spots under French control. This was part of a wider strategy of "divide and rule" intended to keep the Sunni Muslim majority in check. Indeed, by winning the loyalty of the 'Alawis and other minorities, the French hoped to weaken any possibility of resistance in their colonial backyard. It was a ruthless but effective tactic. From Mt Lebanon to the 'Alawi heartlands, the French managed to weave an overlapping network of sectarian constituents who prized half-hearted autonomy under the French more than outright independence under what many feared would become a threatening Sunni majority. In this, the French continued a long tradition of cultivating minorities as middlemen, a practice whose roots go back centuries—to the time when European powers relied on Christians as representative of their political and economic interests in the area. The minorities became a wedge, foiling aspirations for true freedom by insisting on special treatment through outside protection.

In 1946, the Republic of Syria became an independent state. From northern Mesopotamia to the northern stretches of Transjordan, Syria would henceforth constitute an integral geographic and political unit. Many of Syria's minorities acquiesced quietly to the end of French rule, recognizing that their fate lay with the Sunni Muslims whether they liked it or not. Many of Syria's minorities learned to overcome their skepticism by enthusiastically muscling their way into the mainstream. Specifically, when it became clear that they would no longer profit by clinging to the dream of separatism, the 'Alawis began flooding the ranks of the most robustly Arab nationalist group on the scene: the Baath Party, especially its military wing. Thus, the very community that stuck out by dint of its "heretical beliefs" and geographic isolation became the leaders of a movement that claimed adamantly to transcend sectarianism in the name of "Arabness."[31] Armed with this new raison d'être, and paired with a long tradition of military service, 'Alawis became the defenders of 'Aflaq's "eternal Arab message."

The 'Alawis in the Baath Party may have earned political credibility as the guardians of Arabness, but the regime established by Hafez al-Asad in 1970 never managed to distance itself from a perceived attachment to its original sectarian milieu. Indeed, despite its pretensions to embrace all Syrians and to incorporate individuals from a range of backgrounds into the party leadership, many continued to look upon Baathism as the ideological façade for a much narrower agenda of 'Alawi rule. For allies and opponents of the regime alike, all roads led back to the mountain villages of Jabal Ansariyya, from which Asad recruited many members of his inner circle and the powerful security services.

Many Sunnis in Syria were dismayed by this turn of events. It was not only unjust (many landowners lost significant wealth as a result of the Baath Party's aggressive land reforms), but in their eyes also embarrassing: Syria—the great bastion of Islamic culture and sophistication—had been hijacked by a cabal of country bumpkins. Old Damascenes spoke derisively of the influx of 'Alawis into the capital after the Baath Party coup of 1963, and after the second coup that brought then-defense minister Hafez al-Asad to power seven years later. They referred it an invasion of the *qaf*, given the tendency of 'Alawis from the northwest to pronounce the Arabic *q* with bracing clarity—unlike the softer Arabic accent of Damascus, in which the *qaf* disappears into a glottal stop.[32]

A friend once reported to me a joke that had been relayed to him about the 'Alawi "invasion" of the city during the 1960s and 1970s. "Did you ever notice that the 'Alawis all have the same shaped head?" I confessed I had not, so he explained further: "Well, if you look at a picture of Hafez al-Asad, or you drive around Baniyas or Latakia, you'll see that lots of 'Alawis have the same shaped head: wide and very flat in the back, like a pancake." I knew the punch-line was coming, so obliging, I asked why their heads looked like pancakes: "Well," he said, "when an 'Alawi woman gives birth to a son, the first thing she does is to smack him in the back of the head, and exhort him, 'Get to Damascus, get to Damascus!'" As ethnic or religious jokes go, this one was harmless, but underlying it was a deeper sense that Syria's 'Alawi masters were undeserving of the power they possessed.

For a long time the regime, its non-'Alawi supporters, and outside observers downplayed the sectarian aspect of political life in Syria: "It's more complicated than just the 'Alawis," was their constant refrain, and indeed it was for a time, when the Baath Party relied on a wider spectrum of communities to maintain its grip on power.

Sadly, this has changed in the context of the present war, in which the fighting has become polarized over the issue of sect. On the one hand, we have seen the emergence of an ever more strident Sunni opposition, led by fearsome Islamist groups like Jabhat al-Nusra and the Islamic State financed by donors from conservative Gulf monarchies where fundamentalist ideologies are ascendant. On the other hand, the regime has come to rely ever more on its 'Alawi base, often organized into the fearsome militias known as *Shabiha*, along with outside support from Iran, Hezbollah, and Iraqi militias, who follow more mainstream Shi'ism. Despite their theological and historical differences (which we explored at the start of this chapter), the alliance of 'Alawi Shi'a and Twelver Shi'a has given the regime's cause a strongly confessional coloring.

As a result of all this, among the great tragedies of the Syrian uprising has been the disappearance of a notionally inclusive nationalist ideology. This, in turn, has exposed the raw flesh of old religious tensions, which pit a Sunni Muslim majority—especially members of the lower classes, asphyxiated by the failed land reforms of Hafez al-Asad, as well as the crony capitalism of his son—against the 'Alawi ruling clique. But as we saw on our visit to Qardaha at the beginning of this chapter, the 'Alawis have not profited uniformly from Baathist rule: far from it. Poverty has remained deeply entrenched throughout parts of the 'Alawi heartlands, prompting periodic revolts. Still, in an age in which Baathism has become the "religion" of many secularly-minded 'Alawis, who live in fear of sectarian reprisals by Sunni fighters, the future of the regime has become the fate of the whole community. Not all 'Alawis profited from the rise of the House of Asad, but many will suffer for its sins.

Moving on and Memories of a Massacre

Sadly, whatever the ambitions of Ottoman reformers, Druze revolutionaries, or Baathist ideologues, religion has remained a sensitive, often divisive element in Syrian society and politics. "We have no sectarianism here" was the refrain I heard from Syrians on the eve of the war. Even as I was writing this book, in the thick of the conflict, I was cautioned by friends not to overemphasize the issue, lest I give credence to what many are convinced is a phenomenon born of foreign interference and fear-mongering. True, the destructive sectarianism the world has witnessed in Syria recently is something new, but it seems clear that as a discourse and a practice, sectarianism is appealing precisely because it builds on pressures that have existed in Syria for a long time. To acknowledge this is not to celebrate them or to legitimize them. It is to confront them soberly in the interest of understanding them.

In the coming years, the political order in Syria will look very different—whether the rebellion prevails or not. In this future, it will fall to new groups to step into the leadership vacuum. As of now, based on trends in Syria and the wider Middle East, I would expect their ideology to include in whole or in part the traditions of political Islam that have been ascendant since the 1950s.

One plausible candidate for leadership in this world will be the Muslim Brotherhood. The Brotherhood first came to Syria in the late 1930s, but rose to prominence in the 1970s and 80s, during which it launched a bloody insurrection against the regime. Famously, the government succeeded in quashing the Islamist rebellion by flattening the Sunni stronghold of Hama, killing as many as 30,000 people in the process.[33] Since the 1980s, the Syrian Brotherhood has been licking its wounds in exile from abroad. Yet the war has given it reason to hope, and today, it represents one of the most influential elements in the opposition.

As the Brotherhood sees it, the revolution has provided a good opportunity to project an air of competence—in effect, to audition for the leadership of the country in a post-Asad age. To that end, in April 2012, the organization issued a remarkable statement, outlining its vision for post-war Syria. Entitled "The Pact and Covenant of the Association of the Muslim Brothers of Syria,"[34] the document began by stating the group's commitment to "a modern secular state," democratic in its practices and respectful of the country's diverse peoples, regardless of "differences in their roots, religions, ideologies, and viewpoints." The pact also alleged to uphold human rights, as reflected in "the divine law as well as international agreements."

Overall, the pact promised that post-Asad Syria would be a nation built upon "conversation and cooperation," a place where people would exercise ultimate sovereignty in running the country. Significantly, it spoke of a post-revolutionary society in which there would be no place for revenge, "even [against] those whose hands are polluted with blood." Even they, the document stated, deserve justice.

I first discussed the Brotherhood's covenant in the company of a young Greek Orthodox woman from Aleppo named Nadia. In many ways, she exemplified the post-sectarian sensibilities of many well-educated Syrians, especially of the younger generation. She wasn't particularly religious and happily consented to wearing a hijab during her time teaching among the poor Sunni villages in the countryside of Aleppo.

We were discussing the document with several other friends, most of them foreigners, when Nadia asked whether we believed what the Brotherhood said about itself. A few chimed in that they did, expressing hope that they did actually want a secular state in Syria. Disappointed, Nadia proceeded to politely debunk what she regarded as their naïve interpretations and to point out what she felt was obvious evidence of Islamist ideology between the lines of the covenant—proof positive, in her opinion, that that Brotherhood had no desire for democracy, only for domination. As examples, she pointed out several Quranic verses in the text, references to the implementation of *shari'a*, and pledges to work on behalf of God first, and the people of Syria second.

Nadia was no conspiracy theorist. Yet at the same time, a lifetime spent in the soft sectarianism of Baathist Syria had taught her to distrust narrow religious groups alleging to speak on behalf of the whole. "I want to believe this document, I do," Nadia explained, "It describes the kind of country I would like to live in. Yet I cannot present this document to my family in Aleppo and tell them, 'Trust the Brotherhood; everything will be alright.'"

In June 1979, Nadia's father had been training at the Aleppo Military Academy when it was attacked by Islamist militants.[35] The attack was meant to target young 'Alawi recruits—who formed 260 of the 320 cadets enrolled (83 of them, all 'Alawis, were assassinated)—but it nearly killed Nadia's father, a Christian, as well. "There's no trust among the Christians. They have no special love for 'Alawis, but at the same time, after what happened between the government and the Brotherhood thirty years ago, how can I tell my family to forget what they did to our people? I cannot."

Herein lies the challenge of the Syrian revolution, as well as the longer-term failure of various Ottomanists, nationalists, and Baathists over the years: to fashion an identity for Syria that transcends the ties that bind and divide. If Nadia—a young woman who in every other respect was open to negotiation and compromise—could not overcome her distrust about the Brotherhood's declaration, what minority member could?

In the next chapter, we will continue the story of the state and society in Syria, exploring how everyday Syrians perceived their relationship to the government and to Western powers.

4

GUARDIANS OF THE HOMELAND

STATE AND SOCIETY IN SYRIA

The frontier town of Deir ez-Zor sits two hundred and fifty miles northeast of Damascus, a lonely hub of urban life in the midst of the desert. The Euphrates runs through the city like a green ribbon, bringing life and purpose to the rocky wastes. The area around Deir ez-Zor is the historic homeland of Syria's Bedouin, and to this day, the tribal sheikhs play an important role in mediating power between the government and the strong-headed communities of the desert fringe. Here, far away from the metropoles of western Syria, life is shaped by a sense of separation from state and society.

In 2009, I came to Deir ez-Zor for a weekend of sightseeing: the city and the area around it contain some of the finest archaeological treasures in the country, including prehistoric human settlements, Byzantine churches,[1] and Umayyad castles.[2] Deir ez-Zor itself was unremarkable, a concrete boom town with an unruly market, memorials of fallen Baathist leaders, and several suspension bridges spanning the river.

At sunset a friend and I decided to take a pre-dinner stroll along one of these bridges. Peering out over the Euphrates, I became lost in my thoughts, imagining a distant age when the beating heart of the world's ancient civilizations lay along these banks. Then, as now, water was liquid gold, a guarantor of prosperity in a world shaken routinely by drought and famine. It was the self-assured current of the river that created room for more civilized pursuits in those distant times—the cultivation of politics, science, art and literature, especially.

My dreams of ancient Mesopotamia came to a sudden halt as I detected a new presence tugging at my shirt sleeve. Turning around, I found a boy of seven or eight with messy black hair and charcoal eyes, who leaned on a rusted bike as old as Hammurabi himself. The boy presented his open palm: *baksheesh*, he repeated several times, "Give me a tip." My friend and I tried to ignore this little Oliver, but he followed us along the bridge, figuring that persistence would win us over.

He asked where we had come from. "The United States," I said in reply, prompting a furrowed, quizzical look. The boy seemed confused as to whether this lay upstream or downstream from Deir ez-Zor. We then asked him whether he liked Syria. "Very much," he replied with gusto, "It's the best."

He then said something strange. "You know, my father came to Syria from Tel Aviv." Incredulous at this, we pressed the boy further. "He was from Israel and then left. He was a soldier." There was no way this could have been true. For a child of his age, Tel Aviv might as well have been the Land of Oz, a distant and fantastical place. But unlike Oz, Tel Aviv was also an ominous place—an impression fed by TV news and Baathist schoolbooks that spoke menacingly of the "Zionist entity." But at the end of the day, especially for this boy, Tel Aviv was a faceless place.

Still wearing his poker face, the boy asked us, "Did you meet my father when you visited Israel?" The logic of the conversation became suddenly clear. Our friend was fishing for information, asking about a fictional Israeli father in order to provoke us—two foreign tourists—into reminiscing about our own supposed travels to the "land that must not be named" (according to law, anyone bearing an Israeli stamp in his or her passport may not enter Syria). Gazing down the bridge to the crowds of young men also watching the sunset, I sensed a bigger, badder maestro lurking behind the questions. None of the young men looked back in our direction, but it seemed clear that the boy had been sent as an emissary of someone else.

Sunset over the Euphrates River, Deir ez-Zor

Thankfully, our companion quickly lost interest in Israel. "Do you have swine flu?" he proceeded to ask out of the blue, as if ticking his questions off a government-issued checklist. If we weren't Israeli agents, the next worse scenario was that we were carriers of swine flu, which was then sweeping across Mexico and the United States. "I hope not," he said, preempting any reply, "because we don't have swine flu in this country."

To understand the boy's non-sequitur, one must realize that the Middle East had been paralyzed by fear of swine flu during much of 2009. Here was a real portent of the end times—a lethal disease born in America and conveyed via pigs—double trouble in a country skeptical of American influence and non-halal meats alike. On several occasions that summer, when I crossed the border into Syria after visits to Jordan and Lebanon, officials from the Ministry of Health plunged probes into my ears to make sure I would not communicate my foreign germs throughout their uninfected country. In his own way, this child shared their mania. Satisfied that we didn't have swine flu, the boy continued to his next question: "Also, there are only three people in Syria with AIDS. Do you have AIDS?" God knows whether he understood what this meant, either.

All the same, what struck me about the interrogation was not the absurdity of the questions. Rather, what interested me was the wider culture that had educated, indoctrinated, and frightened the boy into asking his questions in the first place. Here in Deir ez-Zor, a small child had managed to parrot some of the choicest propaganda his government had to spread: outsiders were suspect of being agents of foreign governments, and the homeland was a pristine garden under threat of Western contagion.

Anyone who has visited the Middle East knows that the *mu'amara*, or conspiracy, is a favorite topic of conversation around the dinner table. Whether it was Zionism, George Bush, or the pushy neighbor down the street, secret plots abounded. Here was a child preternaturally attuned to the conspiracy: to the threat of Israelis, swine flu, AIDS, and a whole host of other anxieties his questions never touched upon.

Bored with the dull foreigners standing before him, the boy departed on his rusting bike. On the return journey back to our hotel, we spied him bragging to a pack of older children. There he stood, leaning on the bike with a large lollypop hanging from his mouth like a fat cigarette. I wondered if this was his reward from that invisible patron for a job well done.

In a limited way, my encounter in Deir ez-Zor summed up one way the state had managed to shape the national consciousness in Syria. Through misinformation, it had cultivated nationalism and suspicion in equal parts. In the chapter that follows, we will explore the character of that state writ large, especially people's everyday experience of it and its impact on society.

The Red Tape State

Syria remains the last bastion of Soviet-style bureaucracy in the Middle East. During the Cold War, the Baathists learned from their Russian handlers the art of statecraft. To put a finer point on it, the Russians introduced to Syria's leaders the arts of obstructionism and pushing paper. Although these techniques slowed the pace of government service, as they did in the USSR, their real effect—and genius—was to disguise the channels of power and influence. Even as Communist Russia collapsed in 1989, Syria clung tenaciously to these Soviet-style procedures. The Baath Party knew there was much to be gained by employing vast teams of government workers in unnamed offices and commissions. This created the semblance of a strong state, concealing the fact that the president and his tight circle of deputies really ran the show.

As a foreigner in Syria, my contact with the state was limited. It was concerned mostly with matters of immigration and security. All the same, these experiences provided me with a sense of how many Syrians probably interacted with their government when seeking its help. I will never forget my first encounter with Syrian officialdom upon landing in Damascus in the summer of 2008. I had hoped to begin my studies at the University of Damascus soon after arriving, but was told that I couldn't enroll at the university unless I completed a government-mandated AIDS test. At American universities, students are required to complete exams for meningitis and other diseases that predominate in college dorms. But here,

Syria's flagship university was worried about a foreigner's alleged loose morality and its epidemiological impact.

I don't mean to be flippant about AIDS or the health crisis it has created. It's just that Syria, like many Arab nations, had among the lowest rates of AIDS infections in the world. What is more, there was a clear assumption on the part of the university administration that foreign students were natural carriers of the illness. For the university and the Ministry of Health, it seemed obvious that outsiders were likely more to convey the disease, whether because they were also more likely to sleep around, more likely to use drugs, or simply more determined to intentionally infect other people.

I obliged the bureaucrats and headed to a testing center on the other side of the city. There, I waited in a hot lobby for nearly an hour before being summoned to meet a large woman surrounded by a bucket of needles (think Nurse Ratched in a hijab). She seized my arm, wound it tight with a tourniquet and stuck me hard. Barely hitting her mark, she drew a generous syringe of blood, and with a grunt ushered me toward the door. I returned two days later to collect a stack of papers bearing an impressive collection of stamps and signatures, assuring me, the university, and the state that I was—praise God—at no risk of infecting anyone.

The next place in which I encountered real bureaucracy was in the office which granted the residency permit, known as the *iqama*. According to the rules, American and other visitors usually received a two-month visa to remain in Syria. That said, within two weeks of arriving, one had to register one's presence with the state. There were two offices in Damascus where foreigners "checked in". The first was a tidy, antiseptic place where you could leave your passport overnight and collect it the next morning. The other was a chaotic grey tower down the street from Marja Square, a dilapidated neighborhood with many cheap motels, where the presence of the immigration office had spawned a virtual sub-economy of photocopiers, notaries, and scribes to help grease the way for the uninitiated.

The *iqama* office had an immediate leveling effect. As I entered, I was surrounded by swarms of Iraqi refugees, Sudanese students, and Palestinian businessmen, like me, begging for the continued hospitality of the state. There were no signs or instructions posted on the wall. Trial by error indicated that visitors had to collect their first round of signatures in a tiny office on the second floor of the building. Inside, I found twenty people crowded into a space no bigger than ten feet long by fifteen feet wide, all jostling for the attention of a single on-duty officer, who seemed far more interested in sipping his off-brand Coca Cola with his off-duty friends—three or four of whom sat around doing nothing—than in addressing the swelling crowd. The room was filled with stacks of antique paper registries. There were no computers, indeed, one wondered how the feared *mukhabarat*—the secret police—would ever manage to track you down in the records of this mess of tinder (that is, if a stray cigarette didn't incinerate it first). I seemed to be the only one confused by the process. The other petitioners—especially the Arabs—knew the drill all too well. They were masters of navigating the bureaucratic disorder found in government offices across the Middle East.

After a while, I collected my signature, and with a nod, a soldier pointed me to the next room. The process continued in this manner for nearly an hour. At each office, a bored official would add to my petition another indecipherable signature—all in black pen. Eventually, I was invited to go up to see the *mudir al-maktab*, the presiding officer. Like a vintage Nintendo game in which the hero confronts his nastiest, most formidable foe on the final stage of his journey, I was invited to stand before this taciturn officer as he reviewed my papers and assessed me with a bored stare. Once satisfied that I had collected enough scribbles from his underlings down below, he removed a red pen from his chest pocket and added his own name. His throne room was a surreal sight: around him stood wedding-style bouquets, framed portraits of Bashar al-Asad, and trays of oriental sweets. In the corner, a stooge—still padded with baby fat and dressed in a cheap polyester suit and pointy dress shoes—fiddled with his flip phone. The *mudir* summarily dismissed me from his court.

A Culture of Secrecy

If suspicion and obstructionism were my initial introductions to Syrian bureaucracy, I would learn quickly about a still more sinister side of the Soviet legacy: the internal security services, known as the *mukhabarat*. Syria has long been considered the most ferocious police state in the Middle East—and given the competition, that's saying a lot. The Baath Party managed to remain in power for decades thanks to a deep and loyal network of security services whose job was to constantly monitor the public, crushing criminality and freedom (depending on one's perspective) long before they had the chance to flourish.

When I lived in the country, uniformed police officers constituted a relatively small portion of the overall security presence. Instead, the majority slinked around in plain clothes, mixing anonymously with the population. They formed a vast para-state that was both everywhere and nowhere. Some Syrian friends claimed to have been able to recognize a *mukhabarat* agent in disguise: "Look for the expensive shoes, the sunglasses, and the look of attentive uninterest. He's watching everything," advised a friend. Perhaps a lifetime living under the scrutiny of these sentinels gave one a knack for picking them out, but I had trouble doing so. For all intents and purposes, they were invisible to me.

The most egregious crimes of the *mukhabarat* are well known: their fetid prisons, constant surveillance, and creative acts of torture. Indeed, at the start of the war, it was the security services and certain elite army units that were the principal guarantors of President Asad's rule, materializing in vast numbers to crush demonstrations before they had a chance to assemble. As one friend living in Damascus said to me: "At times, you feel there are more plainclothes police on the streets than civilians." For the thousands who have disappeared into the custody of the *mukhabarat* since the start of the Arab Spring, they face a grim fate. Stories leaking out of Syria have described prisons like meat lockers, where opponents of the regime are left to rot, butchered and brutalized.

Such are the obvious crimes of Syria's internal security services. At a still deeper level, however, the presence of *mukhabarat* had a worse effect on the national psyche: breeding distrust among normal people. Because the man sitting next to you on the bus, weighing your produce, or giving you a lift in his taxi might be a member of state intelligence, you quickly learned to keep quiet. Real opinions were for friends and family members only, and even then, distrust could pervade the most intimate kinds of relationships.

Like many Syrians, I learned to speak in half-truths during my time in the country. Political opinions shouted too loudly were strictly *verboten*. At least in public, talk of one's personal life and the United States was ill-advised, as was the biggest taboo of them all, discussion of Israel, which some foreigners learned to call "Disneyland" to avoid unwanted attention.

If the *mukhabarat* made life inconvenient for a law-abiding American in Damascus, they had a far deeper, more insidious effect on locals. Their presence created a culture of distrust, stoking fear that one's neighbors, co-workers, and even relatives might be passing information to unmarked government offices. As in the Soviet Union, where secret police compiled thick dossiers on the perceived enemies of the state, the *mukhabarat* patrolled society with ruthless vigilance. Theirs was a subtle despotism that imprisoned Syria in a cloud of half-truths. Open conversation on matters of substance was a forgotten luxury, and those deserving of real trust tended to be family members, perhaps one's friends or members of a religious community. But even those kinds of relationships had their limits. I witnessed this first-hand among friends in Syria, who would speak freely with me on personal, non-political matters, but who refused to discuss anything of deeper consequence: better to speak elliptically and pledge one's loyalty to Bashar than to risk a foreigner with loose lips spreading your opinions around the streets.

The collateral damage caused by this system showed up in unexpected ways. A young American woman I met after leaving Syria, who had spent several years in Damascus as well, once explained to me her experience of dating Syrian men. An accomplished Arabic speaker and NGO worker, she was not easily intimidated and certainly no complainer. All the same, she had failed to forge successful relationships in Damascus. She found the young men untrusting, prone to jejune bouts of jealousy, and unable to communicate openly and directly. As she explained to me: "After all these relationships, I figured out what was happening. They come from a country where many live in fear of being monitored and arrested. You learn to trust only the ones you need to trust, and everyone else—even your girlfriend—you learn to keep at arm's length. A lot of these guys are not able to trust—trust is a luxury."

What my friend was describing was the most tragic side-effect of Syria's security state: the decay of civil society, of the invisible bonds that create an *esprit de corps* among a people. This is not to say that Syrians lacked national unity or were unable to build friendships among themselves or with outsiders—far from it. But in comparison to the relatively unencumbered life we enjoy in the United States and Europe, the presence of the *mukhabarat* in Syria created a prison in which people could not be themselves in public as fully as they could be in private. It was a form of intellectual and spiritual incarceration.

The Long Shadow of Bashar

If the intelligence services were the most important branch of the Syrian government, then there was only one person in that regime who really mattered: the president. Of course, he had to cope with a thick bureaucracy beneath him, as well as the ill-defined web of family and sectarian interests. But as in many despotic regimes around the world, the leader in Syria was everything.

Bashar al-Asad is an unlikely dictator. Born in 1965, he was the fifth of seven children and the second of four boys. In childhood, he was overshadowed by his older, more charismatic brother Basel, whom their father—President Hafez al-Asad—had decided to groom as his successor, giving him starring roles in the Syrian military and party politics. Aside from considerations of age, one suspects that the father also realized that Bashar was ill-suited to the job. Tall, lanky, and cursed by a receding chin, Bashar moved with an awkward gait and spoke with an endearing if un-commanding lisp. The prominence of his brother Basel allowed him to cultivate interests outside of politics. He chose to become an eye doctor, serving for a time as a physician in the Syrian Army before decamping to London where he trained at a well-known eye hospital. But in 1994, only a few months into his stay in Britain, Bashar was summoned back to Damascus. Basel, the dauphin, had wrapped his black Mercedes around a pole along the airport road. Hafez al-

Billboard with President Asad, outside the Souq al-Hamidiyya, Damascus

Asad's succession plans were thrown into disarray, and thanks to an aggressive propaganda campaign and rapid promotion in the army, Bashar was transformed into a seemingly acceptable substitute overnight. But no matter how many murals of Bashar appeared on the sides of buildings throughout Syria, or how many empty medals were pinned to his chest, he remained his father's second choice. Thus, when Hafez al-Asad died in 2000, and the Syrian constitution was amended to facilitate the accession of his 34-year-old heir, the world watched and waited: would Bashar succeed in consolidating control as his father had done so effectively and ruthlessly before?

Bashar's first year in power is often called the "Damascus Spring." Politically inexperienced and eager to distance himself from his father's long and gloomy reign, Bashar spoke of liberalizing the economy, freeing political prisoners, and even removing crusty old Baathists from power. But the entrenched order smothered the young president, and soon things were back to normal. The system was too entrenched and the new leader too weak to effect real change, whether he desired it sincerely or not. Above all, one suspects that Bashar knew that ruthlessness would be his most faithful friend. A vast and impressive public relations machine would sell to the outside world the story of a Western-educated leader, his handsome British-Syrian wife, and their impossible desire to reform this traditional society. All the while, beyond the photo spreads and shopping sprees in Europe, Bashar would continue to play the long game of single-party autocratic rule. In hindsight, few meaningful things changed in Syria after 2000; the regime simply became better at disguising itself to its critics, giving its Western admirers enough reason to hope for reform, while at the same time strengthening its reliance on the *mukhabarat*, its 'Alawi partisans, its cronies in the business community, and foreign allies such as Iran and Hezbollah.

During my time living in Syria, Bashar sometimes felt like the distant relative I had never met. Everywhere I went, official portraits of the president stared down at me from the walls of friends' homes, from behind cash registers, from billboards along the side of the road, and even from certain mosques and churches.[3] The most popular of these portraits was taken around the time of Bashar's accession in 2000. They show a youthful man with a thin wisp of a mustache, dreamy blue eyes, and a calm, collected look. Here was a man made to appear comfortable bearing your troubles and mine, a king who projected confidence in a world rife with instability. His was an invitation to believe.

In ancient Rome, the emperors were revered as gods. They claimed to rule by divine right, exploiting this as the basis of a brutal form of dictatorship. Among the ways they promoted the imperial cult was by spreading images of themselves throughout the empire.[4] Temples dedicated to the emperor and his family sprang up in cities across the Mediterranean, along with marble statues, painted portraits, and coins bearing his face. The likeness of the emperor was impossible to avoid, a form of public propaganda that constantly maintained the proper distance between the god-king on high and his tiny subjects down below.

The imperial cult is preserved in our cultural memory thanks to the tales of early Christian martyrs. These were men and women who would often die for refusing to sacrifice before statues of the emperor. They were punished fiercely for their disobedience: according to their biographies, thrown to the lions, torn to pieces, and burned alive. To sacrifice to the image of the emperor was to acknowledge one's place in a vast network of political and social interests converging on the person of the ruler. It was to accept subordination, to accept that all of society belonged in the pocket of one man. The Roman martyrs may have died long ago, but the logic of their tormenters lived on in Bashar's Syria. As in the Roman Empire, his ubiquitous image was a justification for autocratic rule, and above all, a reminder to would-be dissenters to remain silent or face the Colosseum.

In Syria, sovereignty was attached directly to the person of the ruler. The country's entire political system was anchored by a single individual and the ruling clique around him. In the event of a power vacuum—say, the sudden assassination of the president or a succession crisis—the system risked disintegrating. This was among the main reasons for the strange cult of personality surrounding Bashar al-Asad: power in Syria was deeply personal, and the ubiquitous portraiture existed to remind the public of who stood at the apex of this power.

The system I've described was characteristic of many other states in the late twentieth-century Middle East: Egypt under Hosni Mubarak, Tunis under Zayn al-'Abidin Ben 'Ali, and Yemen under 'Ali 'Abdallah Saleh—all of them swept from power due to the events of the so-called Arab Spring. What is also characteristic of these states is that they disguised autocratic, highly personal systems of rule with the language of republicanism. Indeed, according to the constitution of Syria, the president has to compete in elections every four years to preserve his office. On each occasion, of course, he would win 97% of the vote. The figure was not the result of assiduous campaigning or debate among opposing candidates. Article VIII of the Syrian Constitutions recognizes the Baath as the ruling party, and the Asads admitted no competitors. Rather, "democratic" victory was an elaborate ritual designed to obscure the essentially authoritarian nature of the Syrian regime. It gave a patina of respectability to an eminently undemocratic system, thereby preempting Syria's critics at home and abroad.

Syria and the Outside World: The Two Faces of Damascus

But who actually believed that Syria was a genuine republic, or that its president was a democratically elected leader? During my time in Damascus, I befriended a young Christian woman named Antoinette, who helped shed light on the situation. Fluent in English and enamored of Oprah, hers was the face of a new generation of Syrians from the cities who lived Western-oriented, fairly secular lives. She admired Michelle Obama, decried the sins of Abu Ghraib, and hoped to study in France once she had finished her education in Damascus.

Antoinette was a friend of my Arabic teacher and would sometimes cover his lessons on busy days. On one occasion, I came to her office to find her deeply upset. She had just finished a lesson with several feisty Spanish students, who had used their limited Arabic to critique the state of politics in her country. The conversation had turned into a tense debate, and I had to deal with the bitter backwash. Antoinette explained: "They kept saying to me that the elections here aren't real. But *we* elected Bashar! So many Westerners criticize our government for these things [censorship, human rights abuses, etc.], but we have freedom in Syria, we can speak openly about our politics. The police make us safe."

Antoinette was not naïve: not so deep down, one suspects, she agreed with the Spaniards. Even as a middle-class Christian who supported the government, how could she ignore the facts? The charade-like elections, the political prisoners, the secret police? Whatever the realities on the ground, however, Antoinette and her family were emblematic of a whole class of citizens whose lives had improved under the Asads. They were not exactly partisans of the 'Alawi clique that controlled the country. But at the same time, they were grateful that it had kept the Muslim Brotherhood at bay and ensured a secular order friendly to minorities. At a personal level, Antoinette had profited from the slow opening of the economy and took pride in watching Bashar and his wife hobnob with Carla Bruni on the Champs Élysées, a scene we watched on television together that summer. Yet hers was a studied denial of reality.

Syrians like Antoinette were not the only ones who pretended as if everything was normal.[5] Before the start of the revolution, streams of Western dignitaries heaped praise on Asad as a credible partner in reform. Among US politicians, then-Senator John Kerry was a frequent guest in Damascus, engaging in sensitive high-level talks, often in person with Bashar. Even after the uprisings began in March 2011, Hillary Clinton assured the American public on CBS News that the president was a "reformer" (citing the opinion of lawmakers in Congress).[6] Among the foreign policy *cognoscenti*, it was common to hear about "the Syria track" of the Middle East peace process—the notion that all roads to Jerusalem ran through Damascus, that Bashar could be a credible partner in dealing with Israelis and Palestinians alike—if only he was given a chance. These were false hopes.

Like my friend Antoinette, the *cognoscenti* cannot be blamed entirely for being misled. They were driven by a conviction that if only Syria's opponents tried hard enough to understand Asad and his system—battered as it was by US sanctions and international rebuke—they might make an ally of a longstanding foe. In the process, the believers turned a blind eye to the atrocities of this "misunderstood" dictator: the torture of his opponents, the single-party rule, the arms shipments to foes of the United States and Europe. The onus was on Western countries to compromise and meet him half-way.

An acquaintance who worked for the US government and who followed Syria closely during the 2000s once put it to me this way: "Syria has a whole class of what I like to call 'barbarian handlers': people whose job it is to mollify and soothe the worries of politicians from the West. They speak English, talk of reform, and seem to resemble us. But then there's another class of person who works for the regime who doesn't look like this. These are the people Bashar uses to ferry *mujahideen* from the Damascus airport to the Iraqi border to kill US soldiers, these are the people who electrocute dissidents, these are the people who arm Hezbollah."

My acquaintance was touching on the Janus-faced character of the leadership in Syria: a group of people who paid just enough lip service to liberality to win the hearts of politicians in Washington and Brussels, yet at the same time oversaw a deeply inhuman system at home.

I once had the chance to meet among the most prominent of Syria's "barbarian handlers"—a woman named Bouthaina Shaaban, a senior political and media adviser to Bashar al-Asad. Born in Homs and educated in Britain, Shaaban rose to prominence as a professor of English literature at the University of Damascus and served as an interpreter for Hafez al-Asad. Under Bashar, she was named minister for expatriates and soon became a trusted member of his inner circle, responsible for dealing with foreign diplomats, Western media, and political strategy. At the time, I was part of a research team from Princeton that had come to Syria to study its relations with the United States, and Shaaban met us near her office.

Little of that meeting was memorable in terms of content. Shaaban was a shrewd operator, adept at dodging difficult questions from the delegation and at displacing blame for various missteps onto the United States. Her message resembled that of Americans back home who, in wishing to engage with the regime, became apologists for it: "If only America gave us a chance, we could work with you!" It was nearly believable. With her fluency in English and stylish clothes, Shaaban personified the kind of liberal-minded Syrian whom Americans hoped to cultivate—forward-looking, open to the West and to reform.

Of course, Shaaban was a very carefully chosen representative—useful for dealing with foreign groups like ours. Many in the Western media, in particular, happily publicized the stories of Westernized elites, whom they depicted as heroes trying to rescue their country from a state of backwardness. Perhaps the most egregious example of this was a February 2011 article in *Vogue* entitled, "A Rose in the Desert," which profiled the first lady of Syria, Asma al-Asad.[7] Published immediately after Egyptians had deposed Hosni Mubarak in Tahrir Square, the article gushed about the lithe and stylish Asma—known as "Emma" to her friends back in London, where she had grown up and worked for J.P. Morgan until marrying Bashar al-Asad in 2000. As critics at the time noted, the article (now completely scrubbed from the internet) seemed more concerned with the flash of her red-soled Christian Louboutin heels than what all that "grace" and "killer IQ" concealed—namely, complicity in the actions of a vast police state. Anna Wintour, editor of *Vogue*, took a shellacking for publishing the piece, but in the end, the Asads had won. Even as popular revolution spread across the country—the first protests in the city of Dera'a erupted a month after the article was published—here was a woman and a nation who belied expectations. "If only we gave them a chance."

The Axis of Resistance

At the end of our meeting with Bouthaina Shaaban, each of us received a media packet containing a sampling of her best English-language writing. On the flight back to New York, I opened the pack and was surprised to discover, not policy papers or op-eds, but rather, movie reviews. One discussed the science-fiction blockbuster *Avatar*, which follows the rape of a resource-rich planet called Pandora, as well as the brave Navi people who rise up in rebellion against it.[8] In a poorly written piece for the left-leaning American newsletter *CounterPunch*, Shaaban explained that the movie was a morality tale about Western imperialism, especially the tendency of colonial powers to exploit native groups. As she wrote: "The movie needs only the Navi natives of planet Pandora to raise the Palestinian flag and the invaders to carry the Israeli flag to become a detailed reading of the Israeli settlement of Palestine with modern cinematic techniques, but also with symbolic nuance that illustrates the nature of this conflict." Shaaban even proposed using Avatar to spread the word about the struggle for Palestinian statehood: "I suggest that demonstrators against Israeli occupation wear the blue shirts of the Navi tribe in order to make it easier for westerners to understand their cause."

The shallow essay exemplified another important characteristic of the regime in Damascus: its focus on the Palestinian cause and the defeat of Israel.

In this, Syria was not alone. The Palestinians were a favorite hobby horse of autocratic regimes across the Middle East. As these police states tortured, taxed, and terrified their own people, they claimed to champion the rights of oppressed Palestinians in Israel, Gaza, and the West Bank. For leaders like Hafez and Bashar al-Asad, this was a matter of shrewd politics. Acting as defenders of the Palestinians burnished their pan-Arab credentials. What is more, they realized that the cause of Palestinian statehood could help to channel the rage of Syria's own oppressed people to problems outside their borders.

A perfect example of this came in July 2011, several months after the start of the Syrian revolution, when the regime allowed streams of pro-Palestinians demonstrators to mass at the Israeli border in the Golan Heights.[9] They were commemorating what Arabs call Naksa Day, which marks the "disaster" of 1967 (known to most in Europe and the United States as the Six-Day War), when Israel captured the Golan Heights, the West Bank, the Sinai Peninsula and the Gaza Strip.[10] The absurdity of the situation was lost on no one: here were swarms of young Syrians and Palestinian refugees allowed to protest against a foreign enemy, while at the very same time, other protesters in Damascus, Homs, and Dera'a were being shot and beaten for speaking out against the regime.

Shi'i Mosque of Sayyida Zeinab, Damascus

In many ways, Syria's opposition to Israel was a rhetorical charade. Despite the bluster, the border between the two countries was among the most peaceful in the entire Middle East. Indeed, a favorite weekend excursion of Western students in Damascus was to head to the city of Quneitra in the Golan Heights. There, accompanied by a guide from the security services, they would drive through the bombed-out remnants of this once-prosperous town which had succumbed to neglect since the 1967 war. As part of the visit, the agent would lead visitors to the frontier where they could gaze out onto a fence and strip of landmines that separated Syria and Israel. This was intended to summon feelings of outrage at the Israelis and their imperialism. But what the officials did not seem to realize was that just beyond this field, the Israelis were waging their own propaganda campaign against the Syrians. Having seen the concrete husk of Quneitra, visitors could look beyond the demilitarized zone to green fields on the Israeli side: among them, a vineyard owned jointly by several local *kibbutzim*. This wasn't Arcadia exactly, but the message was clear. Israel may have seized these lands through war, but it didn't matter—they were here to stay.

Quneitra was part of a constellation of images, monuments, and memorials which the regime created in an effort to present itself as a regional bulwark against Western influence. Whereas countries like Egypt or Jordan had sold their souls to obtain US foreign aid (which they received on the basis of upholding unpopular peace agreements with Israel), Syria had remained uncorrupted by the meddling of the West. This was reflected in the iconography of the streets of Damascus, where it was once common to see portraits of Bashar al-Asad alongside Mahmoud Ahmadinejad, the former president of Iran, and Hassan Nasrallah, the secretary-general of Hezbollah in Lebanon. They made for curious bedfellows: the secular leader of Baathist Syria besides two great partisans of Iranian revolutionary ideology. In the context of the current war, their alliance has been explained as an alignment of Shi'i sectarian interests; but this overestimates the confessional unity between Syria's 'Alawis and the Twelver Shi'a of Iran and Hezbollah, and at the same time, underestimates their shared strategic and political concerns. Indeed, the "three amigos" were united by a sense of common purpose, of resisting Israel and her handlers to the end. Such was the identity of the regime in Damascus in the years before the war.

Queen Zenobia: An Arab Nationalist before her Time

The Syrian state's self-understanding as the final bastion of resistance against the West extended to its interpretation of ancient history. Nowhere was this more apparent than at the Roman ruins of Palmyra, situated on the edge of an oasis one hundred and fifty miles northwest of Damascus.[11] Known to romantics as "the Bride of the Desert," Palmyra was a patchwork of stone monuments—including the Temple of Bel, where animal sacrifice once took place, a stately colonnade designed to accommodate camel traffic, and clusters of tower-tombs on the edge of the city. Throughout my time in Syria, Palmyra was a favorite spot to visit.

First settled in the third millennium BC, the city made its fortunes as a trading depot for silk and other goods from the Far East.[12] These goods began their westward journey at the Indian port of Barbaricon, passing by boat to Seleucia and Babylon, before traveling by caravan to Palmyra, and then on to the Mediterranean. Palmyra's importance also depended on its strategic location between the two greatest powers of the ancient world: Rome and Persia. Recognizing this, the emperor Tiberius, who reigned from 14 to 37 AD, transformed Palmyra into a client state and a buffer against his eastern rivals.

Despite its formal submission to Rome, Palmyra retained a measure of autonomy. Its society was dominated by a small clique of ruling families who met in a local senate. In 252, as Rome lost control over the region, one of these families established itself a royal dynasty under its first king, Odenathus. Though Odenathus may have founded the kingdom of Palmyra, memory of the city lives on thanks to his wife and successor, the queen Zenobia. Ruling between 267 and 274, she came to power as Rome was reeling from a string of military coups and provincial rebellions known to scholars as the "Crisis of the Third Century." No longer content to play the lapdog, Zenobia dispatched her troops throughout the Roman Near East, establishing a short-lived domain that

Roman colonnade, Palmyra, Homs Province

stretched from Asia Minor to Egypt. It did not take long for Rome to notice what had happened. In 274, the emperor Aurelian retaliated, marching 40,000 of his men and local Arab allies into the desert to subdue this "new Cleopatra." Zenobia was captured and brought to Rome in golden chains—a melancholy trophy from a failed revolt.

Though Palmyra's imperial ambitions were short-lived, memory of the provincial coup has endured. In modern times, Zenobia has become a patriotic symbol in Syria—an Arab nationalist *avant la lettre* who threw off the yoke of imperialism and Western tyranny.[13] Her image appears on Syrian bank notes and she starred in a thinly veiled television mini-series about the Arab-Israeli conflict, in which the struggle for a Palmyrene kingdom was made to symbolize the Palestinian struggle for self-determination. Zenobia was even the subject of a glowing biography—actually, a heavy-handed treatise on power politics—by Gen. Mustafa Tlass, who served as Syria's defense minister for thirty years and was among the most prominent Sunnis at the top of Baathist regime.[14]

As with many historical symbols in modern Syria, there was a certain ambiguity in the regime's promotion of Zenobia. Not far from where the queen once fought for her "Arab kingdom," there stands Tadmor Prison. It is among the hated relics of the reign of Hafez al-Asad, a place where political prisoners used to languish in dank terror. In 1980, following an assassination attempt against Asad, Syrian commandos rushed there by helicopter and massacred hundreds of inmates. Many of these were members of the Muslim Brotherhood and other Islamist groups that had launched a fierce insurgency against Asad, and others were political prisoners, victims of a ruthless system that was altogether more "Roman" in spirit than "Palmyrene."

Hafez al-Asad's Religion Problem

At several points in the course of this book, we have heard about the conflict between the government and Islamist guerillas which raged between June 1979, when gunmen killed dozens of 'Alawi cadets at the Aleppo Military Academy, and February 1982, when Hafez al-

Asad managed to crush the revolt, massacring as many as 30,000 people in the process—most of them civilians—in the city of Homs. In many ways, those tumultuous years marked one of the great linchpins of recent Syrian history, and investigating them is crucial for grasping relations between Syrians and their government today.

To understand these events, we must return to 1970–71, when then-minister of defense Hafez al-Asad launched a successful coup and installed himself as president. Religiously observant elements in Syrian society looked warily upon these changes:[15] not only was Asad—an 'Alawi—the first non-Sunni Muslim to serve as president, but he was also champion of an avowedly secular, even atheistic ideology—Baathism (according to a notorious article in a 1967 Baathist military magazine, religion was to be exiled "in the museum of history"). At first, Asad managed to soothe these anxieties through carefully orchestrated public gestures, such as praying with prominent Sunni clergymen on important holidays and increasing the expenditures of the Ministry of Awqaf (religious endowments). Still, the objections of many conservative Sunni Muslims did not abate. These were brought to a boil by Asad's intervention in the Lebanese Civil War in 1976 on the side of the Maronite Christians. Suddenly, it seemed that Asad the 'Alawi was working to undermine Sunnis throughout the region by building alliances with other powerful minorities. This was unacceptable. Things came to a head in 1976 with the arrest of Marwan Hadid, a popular preacher affiliated with the Brotherhood, who spoke forcefully against the regime. Hadid staged a hunger strike in prison and eventually died, and the Brotherhood held the government accountable for his "murder." Islamist elements in the country began to organize and arm, and three years later, they launched their insurgency with the attack against the 'Alawi cadets in Aleppo. This inaugurated a period of turmoil that would change Syria dramatically.

After much effort, Asad emerged the victor in the civil war, managing to banish the Brotherhood and its allies from the country. Still, although it was clear that the regime needed to quash all remaining manifestations of threatening religious activism, Asad realized that he also suffered from a major gap in legitimacy among observant Sunni Muslims. Something had to be done to beef up the regime in the eyes of the very people who opposed it most vigorously.

136

The process of building legitimacy had actually begun years before the insurgency. With the rise of Hafez al-Asad, Syria's 'Alawi religious leaders felt pressure to present their faith as simply a variation of orthodox Twelver Shi'ism (the mainstream form of Shi'ism practiced in Iran, along with parts of Iraq, Lebanon, Bahrain, Pakistan, and India).[16] This was to counter the view of many Sunnis that 'Alawis were not Muslims, and therefore were unfit to govern Syria. Attempts to conflate 'Alawi and Twelver Shi'ism at the time were theologically problematic, even more so given that it was the 'Alawi sheikhs who were pressing the cause, not more mainstream Muslim leaders from outside their community. And so, in 1973, Musa al-Sadr, the charismatic Shi'i leader in Lebanon, was enlisted to recognize the 'Alawis as members of his Shi'i community; in return, Sadr earned goodwill and protection from Asad's regime. At least symbolically, Sadr's move robbed Asad's critics of their most basic line of attack, namely that Syria's president was a *kafir*, or heretic, and unfit to lead the country (though one suspects these critics continued to view Asad as illegitimate, regardless of what Sadr and the Lebanese clergy said).

After the Islamist uprising in Syria ended in 1982, the government attempted to improve its image among observant Sunni Muslims by financing religious institutions whose brand of Islam was deemed to be politically unthreatening. These included a network of institutes bearing the name of Hafez al-Asad committed to the study of the Quran, among other religious subjects. Again, one suspects that Asad cared little for these religious sciences, but the gesture of rapprochement was important nonetheless.

The regime also worked assiduously to cultivate members of the Sunni clergy in an effort to shore up its reputation.[17] In general, the regime was remarkably successful in this, creating a base of credible but loyal religious leaders who could help fortify a pro-Baathist current among Syrian Sunnis. At the same time, it is noteworthy that the regime never managed—or even tried—to fully co-opt these Sunni clergymen, as Nasser had managed to do in Egypt decades before among the scholars of al-Azhar. Rather, the regime sought individuals who had independent standing as religious scholars and who could approve certain political positions precisely because they operated outside the conventional centers of power and influence.[18] Put differently, the clerics the regime cultivated were not mere stooges: they were useful because they had a measure of independence beyond the hands of the state. A good case in point is Sheikh Muhammad Sa'id Ramadan al-Bouti, the most prominent Sunni scholar in Syria over the past thirty years, whom I heard preach several times at the Umayyad Mosque in Damascus. He was assassinated under mysterious circumstances in March 2013, another victim of the civil war.[19]

Bouti was the son of a respected Kurdish imam who had settled in Damascus following clashes with Kemalist forces in Turkey in the 1930s. His son followed in his path, earning a reputation as an accessible writer and preacher. In particular, he became well known for speaking against the evils of Marxism and nationalism, and indeed, his opposition to these fundamental elements in Baathist ideology at first made him an unlikely ally of the regime. Despite disagreements over Marxism and nationalism, however, there were certain concerns that drew them together. Specifically, Bouti shared with Asad's government a fierce enmity toward the Muslim Brotherhood and the Salafis, as well as a desire to keep men of religion out of political dealings. Thus did he famously go on television in June of 1979 to condemn the attack against the 'Alawi cadets in Aleppo. This endeared him to Asad, who would consult with the sheikh for hours on end for years to come—striking for a president who usually dealt briskly with visitors to his office, including members of his own family.

What did Bouti get in return? After all, by the end of his life, despite his best efforts to depict himself as an impartial mediator between the regime and the people, he was seen by many as a lickspittle of the Asads. Well, Bouti not only received privileged access to the halls of power (though this access initially dwindled after Hafez died), he also earned the right to speak more freely in public settings than a typical scholar would. He eventually became the director of the Umayyad Mosque in Damascus, a symbolic but influential position that helped him broadcast his views to a wider audience. Above all, he managed to wring from the government concessions that advanced his own religious agenda, including a crackdown on women's rights and the formation of a higher Islamic council of Muslim scholars.

In Bouti, we see how the notionally secular regime had to seek help from and in certain instances enact the policies of conservative religious leaders. As scholar Thomas Pierret argues in a recent book on Syria's religious scholars, such cooperation flies in the face of easy stereotypes of the regime as a bastion of secularism amidst a sea of conservative Islam. Indeed, as a matter of political expedience, the Baath Party cooperated with religious elements in society to a far greater extent than most people realize.

Syria, America, and Islam

Despite these efforts, the regime never succeeded in completely overcoming memories of its brutal crackdowns against the Islamists. As we have seen, its legitimacy gap was most pronounced among observant Sunnis, who remained incensed by the government's ideology and actions, and among Syria's poorer ranks, by the failed economic and political reforms of the preceding decades. Several of my friends in Damascus fit this description well. They were not impoverished, exactly, but in other respects they had been sidelined in an economy that prized the interference of the *wasta*—or middleman—to grease the way to success. They were also alienated by the secular values of the state that notionally represented them. I introduced one of these friends in an earlier chapter, my teacher Muhammad, who lived with his wife and young children in a tiny apartment in the Ghouta, a suburb on the northern side of Damascus famed for its orchards (and where notorious chemical weapon attacks would take place years later in August 2013).

Muhammad was in his mid-thirties and had completed his compulsory military service before we met, having been stationed with an army battalion in then-occupied Lebanon. Deeply religious and with a love for the great texts of Islamic culture, he decided to become an Arabic teacher upon his return to civilian life. Early stints with local students gave way to more lucrative posts tutoring foreigners. Muhammad was not well educated in the formal sense, but as a man raised in the shadow of mosques and religious schools, he was deeply literate. To teach Arabic was for him a religious duty. It was to share the language of divine revelation, to enter into fourteen hundred years of cultural achievement through poetry, historical texts, and philosophy. Muhammad taught because he had to, yet it was for him a form of *da'wa*, or religious outreach.

Despite our friendship, Muhammad often made clear his distaste for the United States and its role in the world. He had a traditional pedagogical philosophy, which authorized him as the teacher to lecture me about his political views, and me as his (paying) pupil to sit and absorb them. At the start of our friendship, in particular, he would pontificate on the sins of my country for half an hour each day: "Iraq, Afghanistan, Saudi Arabia, Egypt," he would count on his fingers, "America's influence is corrupting Muslim countries. And for what? For the sake of oil, for Israel, fear of terrorists, to spread its own culture?" Muhammad probably saw in our lessons an opportunity to educate me, to shape the views of a young American he hoped would acquire influence one day back home. This was his idea of "soft diplomacy," and the message was clear: America's was the contradiction of political power and cultural naïveté, of the will to dominate unmoored from the humility of understanding.

What really worried Muhammad was not Israel, the American military, or 9/11—though these were favorite bugaboos he liked to discuss. Rather, what worried Muhammad was America's cultural hegemony in the region. Geopolitics for him concealed a much deeper and more insidious agenda, namely, the overturning of traditional Muslim societies and their replacement with cultures of libertine commercialism.

In this, Muhammad was not alone. His criticism followed in the footsteps of famous thinkers like Sayyid Qutb, the Egyptian intellectual who became one of the greatest ideologues of political Islam in the twentieth century.[20] Qutb—who was executed for conspiracy by President Gamal 'Abdelnasser in 1966—came to loathe the West after studying in the United States in the late 1940s and early 1950s. What provoked his outrage was not the politics of the West toward the Middle East *per se*. Indeed, at that point in history, America was still a relative newcomer to the affairs of the Arab world. Rather, what truly repelled Qutb was what he perceived as America's moral decadence

Qutb's experiences in the United States inspired a wider critique of the "anything goes" lifestyle he feared was spreading from the West into Muslim societies. He called it a mentality of *jahiliyya*, or ignorance, a new form of paganism not unlike the old one the Prophet had confronted in Arabia. Qutb's solution was to assemble a vanguard of pious Muslims who would reverse the decline, using violence if necessary to implement their vision.

Qutb was a member of the Muslim Brotherhood, and despite his death—indeed, perhaps because of it—he became an important influence on more radical groups like al-Qaeda and al-Takfir wa'l-Hijra. In Syria, the Brotherhood was outlawed following the 1979–82 war, but that didn't stop people like Muhammad from being sympathizers. Though he was not active politically, Muhammad shared Qutb's worldview, believing that the political decline of Muslim countries was tied inextricably to the infiltration of un-Islamic values from without. The West had accomplished this by feeding Muslims a steady diet of pernicious foods—free sex, irreligion, alcohol, dance clubs, consumerism, according to Muhammad and Qutb. In the process, the West had destroyed the ability of Muslims to assert themselves politically. For my teacher, the desperate poverty of the Gaza Strip, the humiliations of Abu Ghraib, and the cozy relationships between American presidents and Arab dictators were symptoms of a wider problem: "You give us your culture, we give you our obedience."

Needless to say, despite constantly boasting that he understood it so well, Muhammad had a rather simplistic view of Western culture. He had little appreciation for the positive features of a free society, especially how, in a place like the United States or Western Europe, the excesses he decried were challenged and tempered by elements that called for restraint and a sense of public decency not far from Muhammad's own. He also showed little appreciation for the right of choice—for the right to select one's religion, political ideology, or lifestyle. Muhammad operated in a political system that afforded him almost no choices, personal, economic, or otherwise, and he couldn't imagine it any other way.

Although I disagreed with much of what my friend had to say, I could see where he was coming from, at least from the perspective of his own society, which sometimes seemed caught in a tug of war between different sets of values. A good case in point was an Italian acquaintance I made in Damascus who had been dating a Syrian medical student. Her boyfriend was urbane and handsome, spoke some English, and longed to work in Europe or the United States. Ideal dating material for a foreign woman living in Syria, right? Well, as the two spent more time together, my friend learned about his family and their different way of life. It turned that out the medic had several sisters, all of whom were *muhajibat* (veiled) and cloistered in their family apartment. They were forbidden from working or studying outside the home. My Italian friend would urge her boyfriend to bring his sisters along for dinner dates or movies. "That is not a good idea," he explained. "My sisters are Muslim girls. They must remain at home, as they are waiting to find husbands. This will not help them do so."

My acquaintance was bewildered by this apparent contradiction: on the one hand, her boyfriend was so concerned with protecting the honor of his sisters that he would not countenance their leaving home. But on the other, this same character spent most of his free time romancing Western girls. It was as if his sisters and his girlfriend belonged to two different categories.

How to explain these divergent views? The young medic clearly had a double standard when it came to the conduct of women. As my Italian acquaintance explained, her boyfriend perceived her as a species all her own—not deserving of the same respect as a man, but to be treated differently from his Syrian sisters, cousins, neighbors, or even a local on the street. One wonders what led him to view the Italian girl so differently. Was it the Western media, whose films, TV shows, and music—beamed constantly into Syria—created the false expectation that Western women were somehow easy or loose? Or was it rooted in a common disrespect for women, which expressed itself in the cloistering of his sisters and the dogged pursuit of European girls? Were these in fact two sides of the same coin? It is hard to say, but in the young Syrian medic the cultural confusion that so troubled my friend Muhammad was on clear display.

Views of the West: Of Love and Disgust

In the immediate aftermath of 9/11, many Americans surmised that the country's attackers had been unsophisticated farmers from the hills of Yemen. How else to explain such intense hatred of the West except by sheer ignorance of it? What many were surprised to learn, however, was that these individuals were far from country hicks. Like Osama Bin Laden—the son of a wealthy construction magnate in Saudi Arabia—the attackers were generally well educated, some with a command of European languages, others with degrees from Western institutions, and a taste for foreign culture. Strangely, their hatred of the West was born of a deep, almost prurient fascination with it. It was not a crime of ignorance, as the pundits imagined at the outset. It was a crime of passion gone awry, of dislocation between traditional Islamic values and the liberal zeitgeist of a globalized age.

As many Syrians reminded me during my time in Damascus, not a single one of their countrymen was among the 9/11 hijackers. Indeed, Syria did not breed extremists like Saudi Arabia, which had furnished the lion's share of the attackers despite its cozy ties to Washington. Syrians would tell me theirs was a more sophisticated country, a land of poets and statesmen, not fighters and ideologues. There were, of course, exceptions. A friend from Princeton who was also living in Damascus recounted to me a conversation with a Syrian taxi driver, who upon learning that his rider was an American, announced that he had just returned from fighting the Americans in Iraq. My friend gripped the door of the taxi for the remainder of the ride, ready to escape at a moment's notice, but the gregarious driver kept chatting, asking him about life in the US, and even refusing his money at the end of the trip. It was unclear whether this was a gesture of schizophrenic generosity, or of disgust at the prospect of receiving a tip from an American.

At a deeper level, I observed friends in Syria who seemed caught in the same tug of war that had driven the hijackers to perform those terrific feats of violence. These friends were not tempted by militancy—they were peace-loving—but I observed in them the same sense of inner conflict now familiar to the armchair psychologists of the post-9/11 world: an interest in, even obsession with the

143

West and her freedoms paired with an equally deep hatred of her policies and appetites.

A good example was my friend 'Abdallah, whom we met in an earlier chapter. 'Abdallah was a gifted linguist, and his fluency in English was one part of a much wider fascination with Western culture. He loved all things American, and thanks to foreign television and movies, as well as interaction with many foreign pupils, he had become a walking dictionary of American slang. Such was his mastery of colloquial English that he would occasionally drop words that even a native speaker would not know. Unfortunately, like anyone learning a second language, he was sometimes prone to using these words out of context (thus would he call Obama a "nigger" or Elton John a "fag," not realizing the full weight of these words when uttered back home).

Despite 'Abdallah's fascination with all things American, he loathed the country politically. In a way that was still sharper and more bitter than my friend Muhammad, 'Abdallah railed against America's attacks against Muslim countries, its perceived subjugation of Palestinians and its exploitation of Arab oil. Against, against, against: it was as if 'Abdallah were two separate people— one, a charming aficionado of all things "made in the USA," and the other, a bitter casualty of American imperialism. His split personality matched his view of America itself—on the one hand, a land of opportunity and freedom, but on the other, a source of what he regarded as deep injustice in the world.

'Abdallah was a gentle and open-minded person, but also susceptible to worrying ideologies. Indeed, the many hours he spent pounding the punching bags at the local boxing club in Damascus seemed to be his way of exhausting a pent-up energy deep inside— energy, creativity, and talent that went untapped in a system that imprisoned its citizens, refused them steady employment, and ignored their many gifts. It was for these reasons that I worried about 'Abdallah once the war got underway.

In the end, 'Abdallah fared well enough. Several months after the start of the revolution, I discovered that he had married a girl from Western Europe and departed the country safely. His future, at least, was bright, but what of the many other 'Abdallahs who remained in Syria, and came from much harder-luck backgrounds? They have risen up in rebellion against the government, and now die in droves every day. What will come of them once the fighting ends? What will come of their romance with the West and its culture? If Asad goes, will they build a government that provides people opportunities denied to them under the old system? Or will they build a regime as vengeful and narrow as the one it replaced? We will turn to these and other questions in the final chapter: where is Syria headed?

5

A VIEW FROM THE EDGE

WAR IN SYRIA

There is a maxim in the study of history: from the inside, every institution seems destined to carry on forever—that is, until it meets its end. Thus it was for the Roman Empire, the Umayyad caliphate, and according to some doomsday prophets, the United States, as well. To concede otherwise would be to admit the existence of weakness inside the system, and empires are rarely so introspective.

As it was, too, for more than forty years inside Baathist Syria. The house of Asad was convinced that its system of single-party rule would not only succeed in governing the country indefinitely, but would also reap rewards for the entire population by satisfying the needs of a relatively narrow clique at the top of the heap. But underlying this dream was a deep sense of insecurity. At some level, as we have seen throughout this book, Syria's rulers knew that the system they had created was deeply repressive. They had turned an entire country into their personal fiefdom, one tilled by vast teams of human mules who, in many respects, did not enjoy the fruits of their labors.

That this was a fragile arrangement was clear to everyone inside and outside the country. How else to explain the elaborate security apparatus the regime had installed to keep its citizens in check: the secret police, the hidden prisons, the wiretaps, the informants? The people of Syria were frightened of their rulers, to be sure. But this thick web of control underscored the fact that Syria's rulers were also frightened of their own people. The only way to forestall revolt was to instill in the masses even greater fear of the elites than the elites harbored towards the masses.

As a foreigner in Syria, I would be asked by friends and family back in the United States: "Will this system come to an end?" It seemed obvious to me that it would collapse someday. As we have seen at different points in this book, the system and its abundant constraints on freedom were unsustainable. At the same time, authoritarian rule in Syria had weathered many storms over the decades—the loss of the Golan Heights, civil war with the Muslim Brotherhood, and the invasion of neighboring Iraq—and on each occasion, it had proved surprisingly resilient. The iconography of authoritarianism—the ubiquitous images of the president, the Baathist memorials in town squares, etc.—gave the impression of solidity, of permanence. Inertia, too, made the prospect of change seem unreal. The longer the Asads remained in power, the will for resistance seemed to deteriorate among the people. Indeed, one sensed that many Syrians were so bullied by the unjust system in which they lived in that they had lost the ability to change it. How could they, when the regime's fist was clenched so tightly?

Thus, the collapse of the system was at once inevitable and impossible. It had to happen someday, of course, but that day would never be tomorrow, or the next, or the day after that.

Change did come to Syria eventually, and what a change it has been. The popular uprising that ignited in the southern city of Dera'a in March 2011 has claimed thousands and thousands of lives. It has also sparked a wider sectarian struggle between different elements inside Syria, as well as the broader Middle East. Along the way, civil society, to say nothing of the physical infrastructure of the country, has been devastated. Syria's economy is in a shambles; priceless cultural treasures have been destroyed; oceans of refugees churn along the country's borders; and entire communities have fled, perhaps never to return.

In January 2011, before all this began, Bashar al-Asad gave a rare interview to *The Wall Street Journal*, in which he claimed that

Syria would withstand the kinds of popular demonstrations that had already toppled authoritarian regimes in Tunisia and Egypt.[1] It would be another six weeks before the Arab Spring spread to his own backyard, and the president was feeling upbeat. As he told the reporters, his government was fundamentally different from others in the Middle East, because unlike them, he ruled with a mandate from the citizens: "Syria is stable. Why? [...] Because you have to be very closely linked to the beliefs of the people. This is the core issue. When there is divergence [...] you will have this vacuum that creates disturbances."

In hindsight, the interview reads like a litany of untruths—lies Bashar told the people of Syria to keep them in check, and more importantly, lies he told himself to look past reality. True, the regime had resisted civil war in the past, and Bashar rarely kowtowed to the Western consensus, which earned him adulation among Syrians and Arabs generally. Still, to imagine the Arab Spring in those early months as anything but a movement against oppressive governments and sluggish economies was to misunderstand the moment. And misunderstand it Bashar surely did.

The last time I visited Syria was in November 2010, a few months before the outbreak of fighting. I was then planning to return to Syria for a full year of research, and had sent off an application to a well-regarded research institute in Damascus. By late summer of 2011, I had been accepted, but with every passing week, the prospect of living in Syria grew dimmer. What had once been a local conflict isolated among the miserable *banlieues* of Syria's poorest cities now threatened to engulf more respectable parts of the country, including Damascus. Thus, by August the institute's directors judged it prudent to move their operations across the border to Beirut, a town with its own acquaintance with civil war. As a skeptical relative said to me before I departed: "Who the hell goes to Beirut because it's the only safe place in the Middle East?"

I was deeply disappointed by this move. I had harbored naïve hopes of watching the revolution up close from the comforts of Damascus, which was then insulated from the worst of the fighting. There were stories to hear, people to visit, history to witness. But as the year dragged on and Syria descended into bedlam, I was not only grateful for the relative security of Beirut, I also realized that in my Lebanese surroundings I had much to learn about the conflict across the border. The revolution touched me and my adopted home in ways I could not have imagined when I arrived: not only because I came to know the plight of many Syrians living in Beirut, but also because Lebanon offered a prism for understanding the course of the conflict exploding nearby. Above all, it provided clues as to what might become of Syria once the war was over. In the chapter that follows, I will peer into Syria from the edge. My goal is to gauge what might come to pass there based on the experiences of a remarkably similar tragedy that scarred Lebanon thirty years ago, and to assess the society that rose up from its ashes.

Lebanon and Syria: A View from the Mountains

A good place to contemplate the connections between Syria and Lebanon is in the mountainous lands of the north. Specifically, it is found by heading to the Lebanese villages of Bcharré and Ehden, where rainclouds roll lazily between jagged peaks and snow fields linger deep into spring. Rough stone churches pepper the landscape, evoking a bygone era when the region was not a weekend retreat from the cities for wealthy Christians, as it is today, but base camp for a thriving Maronite world. Indeed, it was among the hardy Maronite villages of the mountains that the idea for the state of Lebanon was first born, and with it, a sense of separation from surrounding Syria.

In many ways, Syria and Lebanon have always been a single unit, with a shared culture, economy, and demography. Carved out of the coastal littoral of Syria, the Republic of Lebanon is both physically and notionally engulfed by its larger neighbor. Eighteen times the size of Lebanon, and with a population five times greater, Syria has played an important role in managing the affairs of tiny Lebanon—sometimes safeguarding its political order, at other times intervening to disrupt it.

Throughout most of history, there were few meaningful distinctions between the two lands. Indeed, until the French created the state of Lebanon for their Maronite Christian clients in 1926, most

View of Wadi Qannoubine, northern Lebanon

people in the region considered "Lebanon" (a term that applied principally to the specific region of Mt Lebanon) just another part of *Bilad al-Sham* (Arabic for the "Lands of Damascus"). In Ottoman times, the territories coinciding with the modern Lebanese state were divided among several different administrative districts: Tripoli in the north, Sidon in the south, and Damascus inland. A new administrative capital centered on Beirut appeared in the late nineteenth century, but Beirut was the Johnny-come-lately of these Syrian metropoles. It had been an important center for the study of law in Roman times, but its star faded with the coming of Islam and remained relatively dim until its revival as a commercial and intellectual hub in the late Ottoman period.[2]

The creation of the Republic of Lebanon in 1926 was fraught with controversy. As we saw in Chapter 3, among the ways the European powers inserted themselves in Ottoman affairs was by patronizing minority groups, upon whom they relied as commercial and political middlemen. This was true of Christians throughout the region, though perhaps especially in Lebanon. The Maronite Church—a Syriac denomination whose homelands encompassed the coastal mountains north of Beirut, and which gradually spread to include the mountain ranges around the capital and to the south—was France's most important ally.[3]

There were obvious reasons for this. Despite their isolation, the Maronites claimed to have never fallen out of communion with the pope of Rome, and along with him, the Catholic Church based in Western Europe, especially in France. Soon this alliance, hitherto religious and political, flowered into a full-blown cultural romance. During the nineteenth century, French religious orders established schools throughout Lebanon, teaching Maronite boys to behave and speak like respectable Frenchmen. Many Maronites came to see themselves as French citizens abroad, owing their principal loyalty not to the sultan in Istanbul, but to the République in Paris.

During the nineteenth and early twentieth centuries, the special relationship between the French and the Maronites nurtured in them a sense of exceptionalism.[4] The Maronites came to see themselves as an island of Christianity and European respectability in a menacing sea of Islam and Arab culture. Cultural exceptionalism, in turn, encouraged dreams of a Maronite nation, a homeland carved from these mountain havens that would protect the Maronites' identity, interests, and natural connections to the West for years to come.

There were two problems inherent in this: first, few in the Middle East agreed that Mt Lebanon formed a distinctive geographic or cultural entity, certainly not enough to justify its separation from the rest of Syria, to say nothing of its transformation into an independent state. Mt Lebanon—like the 'Alawi territories further up the coast—had always been part of greater Syria.

Second, the Maronites were not content to create a state based solely on their historic homelands. The Alpine peaks of Mt Lebanon, along with the Metn and Shouf ranges, were illsuited as bases for an independent country. Their dizzying heights and harsh winters had bred in the Maronites the very sense of separation that now compelled them to found their own country. But as a base for a state itself, these remote areas left much to be desired. Thus did the Maronites convince the French to include in their statelet some of the choicest lands of the Mediterranean coast, including the wealthy trading cities of Tyre, Sidon, Beirut, and Tripoli, as well as the Beqaa Valley, a rich agricultural region to the east, between the coastal mountains where the Maronites predominated and the anti-Lebanon range, beyond which lay inland Syria. But by including these areas in their nascent state, the Maronites and their French partners brought into the country a mix of different communities. There were Sunnis along the coasts, Druze in the Shouf, Shi'a in the south and east, not to mention a dizzying variety of Christian denominations, including Greek Orthodox, Greek Catholics, Latin Catholics, Armenian Orthodox, Armenian Catholics, and Protestants scattered throughout. In sum, Maronite nationalism midwifed the birth of a nation whose borders encompassed the territory of many minority groups, not just the ones who were trying to steer the bark. The Maronites were a demographic plurality among these communities, and thus held the lion's share of the power. But the nationalist ambitions of one sect came to define the character and identity of the entire country. This would have disastrous consequences for the Maronites and the rest of Lebanon in the decades that followed.

In 1943, newly independent from French colonial rule, Lebanon's political elites were forced to create a system that would balance the interests of these various communities. It fell to the Maronites and the Sunni Muslims, then the two largest and most influential groups, to devise a permanent power-sharing agreement. Given their slim plurality, the Maronites claimed the most important positions in the government: the presidency, the leadership of the army, and the majority of seats in the parliament. To the Sunnis went the next most important jobs, especially the office of prime minister. To the Shi'a, who constituted a distant third among Lebanon's sects—and historically among the most marginalized[5]—went the duties of speaker of the parliament. The remaining positions were doled out among these three sects, as well as the other smaller communities.

Lebanon at War

If we wish to understand the tragedy of late twentieth century Lebanon, we must leave the north and head south—to the deep south, in fact, to the city of Tyre. An ancient trading metropolis with imposing Roman ruins, Tyre has had the double misfortune in modern history of lying too far from the centers of power and influence in Beirut, on the one hand, and of sitting too close—a mere fourteen miles—to the volatile Israeli border, on the other. Tyre was a natural port of call for Palestinian refugees over the years. Today, their sprawling camps lie on the edge of town, no longer temporary shelters, but permanent neighborhoods of occasional misery, rocked by war, overcrowding, and poor infrastructure. All the same, Tyre is a refreshingly Arab place: a city whose food, sounds, and smells recall those of inland Syria, far more than many parts of Beirut and the mountains.

The power-sharing agreement of 1943 served Lebanon well for several decades. Yet as the demography of the country changed during the mid-twentieth century, it came under intense pressure. Specifically, the Lebanese political system was predicated on an outdated census conducted by French officials in 1932. At that time, Christians (of various denominations) enjoyed a slim majority over other groups. Yet due to emigration and declining birth rates, Christians

Roman triumphal arch, Tyre, southern Lebanon

were quickly losing their edge. In spite of these changes, the political system continued to reflect the realities of the old order, and the Maronites clung jealously to an authority that no longer matched their numerical stature. Meanwhile, other communities were growing—namely the Sunnis and the Shi'is—and they began clamoring for a power commensurate to their newfound size.

The Lebanese political system also came under intense stress in the 1960s and 1970s due to an influx of Palestinian refugees into the country. The creation of the state of Israel in 1948 had displaced thousands of Palestinians, who sought sanctuary in the West Bank and Gaza Strip, as well as in neighboring Arab lands.[6] The largest portion settled in Jordan, where they eventually received full rights of citizenship, but many also flooded into places like Syria and Lebanon, where they carried on in legal limbo, neither citizens of their adoptive homelands nor welcome to go back to Israel and reclaim their property. In Lebanon, due to their large numbers and the sympathy of many Lebanese Muslims, Palestinian refugees managed to establish a quasi-independent state in the south, which went so far as to issue identity cards and license plates, and to provide other services to Palestinians outside the authority of the Lebanese central government. It was here that Yasser Arafat and the PLO set up shop in the early 1970s, and it was from here that Palestinian *fedayeen* launched numerous guerrilla attacks against Israel throughout the 1960s and 1970s. The area around Tyre was a center of this PLO microcosm, a slice of Palestine reconstituted a few miles up the coast from the real border.

Despite enjoying the support of certain segments of Lebanese society, the Palestinians did not endear themselves to one group in the country that really mattered: Lebanon's Christian elites. The Maronites looked warily upon the Palestinians, regarding them as rivals to their traditional monopoly on power. What is more, the Palestinians increased the demographic heft of the Maronites' main internal rivals, the Sunni Muslims (most Palestinians are Sunnis). Animosity between the communities festered for years, and in 1975, after a group of Christians gunned down a busload of Palestinians in the Beirut neighborhood of 'Ain al-Rummaneh, it became too much to contain. Thus began the Lebanese Civil War.[7]

Separated from Syria, Divided over Syria

As I mentioned above, many Syrians have historically looked upon Lebanon as an artificial entity, the pet project of European imperialists for their local Christian clients. In fact, many segments of the Lebanese public would probably agree with this: throughout my time in Beirut, I encountered countless portraits of Bashar al-Asad in homes, on billboards, monuments, and the sides of buildings. I remember one building in particular—an unmarked, menacing-looking grey block on the old "Green Line" just east of Beirut's glitzy downtown. The façade was papered over with images of Bashar and his father, Hafez. Further down the wall were pictures of their Lebanese allies, including Hassan Nasrallah, the secretary-general of Hezbollah, along with other prominent Shi'i clerics. I never found out who owned the building, but I smiled when I discovered a different kind of portrait a few hundred yards up the street, not far from the francophone Université Saint-Joseph: graffiti images of Bashar al-Asad sporting a Hitler-like mustache. Such was Beirut's ability to contain contradiction in a single city block.

Among the supporters of Syrian hegemony in Lebanon, many believed that the only people who had profited from the creation of Lebanon were the Maronites, who had woven a "bogus" tale of ancient exceptionalism to convince the French to create for them their own state. For those Lebanese who did not buy into the Maronites' particular form of nationalism, the dismemberment of greater Syria was seen as a tragedy. This was especially true of the Sunnis in the coastal cities, who harbored deep cultural and religious ties to the peoples of inland Syria, as well as some Greek Orthodox Christians, who (like Michel 'Aflaq, founder of the Baath Party) were great champions of Arab nationalism and saw Lebanon as a natural extension of its larger neighbor to the east. It was a Greek Orthodox Christian named Antun Saadeh who in 1932 founded the Syrian Social Nationalist Party (SSNP), a political movement in Lebanon whose goal was the eventual union of the two countries, as well as the lands of the southern Levant, into a single Syrian state.[8] Despite a troubled relationship with the Baath party in Damascus, members of the SSNP have for long worked as

157

agents and enforcers of Syria inside Lebanon. They are also well known for their brutality.

The notion that Lebanon and Syria are in fact one country has underlain much of the political jockeying between Damascus and Beirut over the past decades. For example, the Syrian army was among the major players in the Lebanese Civil War, intervening on behalf of Christian and Muslim factions at different points. In 1990, when the war came to an end, the international community allowed Syria to remain behind in Lebanon, allegedly to guarantee the stability of the new political order established by the famous Ta'if Agreement of 1989, but actually in part as a reward for its support of allied troops against Saddam Hussein in the first Gulf War. As a result, Syria came to treat Lebanon as its fiefdom, appointing and dissolving governments from its offices in the border town of 'Anjar (home to a large Armenian community and to the finest Umayyad ruins in the country). It was only in 2005, after the assassination of Prime Minister Rafiq al-Hariri—according to many, at the hands of Syrian intelligence operatives and their allies in Hezbollah[9]—that Syria was expelled from the country. Nonetheless, Syria has remained a major player in internal Lebanese politics. So profound has Syria's role in Lebanon been that the country's entire political system has been organized around pro- and anti-Syrian factions, with the Sunnis and a portion of the Christian bloc siding against the regime in Damascus, and with the Shi'a (including Hezbollah) and another portion of the Christian bloc supporting it.

A Quiet Spring: Beirut at a Time of Revolution

When I arrived in Beirut in September 2011, the country was remarkably quiet. Given the close ties between Syria and Lebanon, as well as Lebanon's reputation as a political tinderbox, many feared a spillover was inevitable. Yet to my surprise, and the surprise of most Lebanese, the conflict remained relatively distant, at least in those early months after the start of the conflict. This was for several reasons, the first of them political.

Despite the country's division between pro- and anti-Syrian parties, most everyone in Lebanon's political class realized that the spread of fighting would be in no one's near-term interest. Of course, many Lebanese groups were participating actively in the Syrian conflict, aiding and abetting government and opposition forces alike. But when it came to Lebanon itself, the *zu'ama'* (the political bosses) realized that the public was war-weary. Furthermore, they knew that the rivalries of internal Lebanese politics would be resolved eventually by the outcome of the Syrian war, regardless of whether fighting spread across the border. It was best to keep things quiet.

On a deeper level, the popular discontent then sweeping through the region seemed to breeze past tiny Lebanon. From Tunisia to Yemen, the so-called Arab Spring emerged as a reaction to the failures of Arab nationalist governments, which for decades had promised their peoples social and economic progress but had succeeded in delivering only corruption and sluggish growth. In other words, the protests were about big government gone horribly awry. Lebanon's political system was corrupt, but because of the deep divisions among the sects, the central government wielded remarkably little power of its own (most power resides in the individual parties, which in turn represent the interests of the different communities). Whole offices of the Lebanese state were the turf of one sect or another. The government paved roads, equipped the army, and gave its citizens a few hours of electricity per day, but not much else. As an American friend in Beirut used to say to me: "Lebanon is Ron Paul's libertarian paradise: the government's nonexistent, you can pay for everything in dollars, and everybody's got a gun." As a result of all this, the Arab Spring struck many Lebanese as a very distant reality. The closest statement of solidarity I saw during my time was a roadside billboard advertising cigarettes with an image of posh Beirutis hanging out in a nightclub. The label read: "The official lights of the Arab Spring." For a small number of Lebanese, at least, the revolution was an occasion for crass commercialism.

But there were deeper cultural reasons for Lebanon's notional distance from the Syrian crisis. The sense of detachment from the world was especially pronounced in the fancy cafés, nightclubs, and shopping malls of Beirut, which continued to hum along, seemingly oblivious to the fighting only two hours away. During their own civil war, many Lebanese had learned to forget the ravages of everyday life by pretending that nothing was wrong. This led to a great boom in boozy partying in certain neighborhoods of the city, as well as points north, like Jounieh, a port town known for its gambling and night clubs.

As a Lebanese friend explained to me one night while having drinks in Gemmayze, the historic district where Ferraris and Bentleys weave through narrow alleyways: "Lebanon's hard drinking culture really began during the war," he said, "Think about it: You would fight all day, and by the end of it, all you wanted to do was forget your life. So you'd head out and lose your mind. Though the fighting ended, this culture did not. Now people drink to forget the society they live in, the miserable government, the memories of the war."

What he said struck a chord. The press loves to crown Beirut "the party capital of the Middle East"[10] (and Beirut, in turn, revels in the accolades), but there was something melancholy underlying this carefree culture. Nothing said it more than the northern suburb of Beirut known as Karantina, where the priciest nightclubs are located. So called for the Ottoman-era quarantine that once stood here—where travelers would be "cleansed" of the diseases they had acquired in the Orient before heading back to Europe—the area was home to some of the fiercest fighting during the war, when Christian militias dismantled the predominantly Muslim shanty-towns that had sprung up here. Today, the shantytowns are gone, and instead, rich Beirutis dance the night away at flashy discos, pounding vodka and popping designer drugs (including at one sub-terranean club designed to mimic a coffin, in a macabre nod to the black history of the area).

Despite this, the sense of separation from the uprising in Syria was an illusion. In poorer parts of Lebanon, Syrian refugees were flooding in by the thousands. This was especially true in the Beqaa Valley, just across the border from the war-torn Syrian cities of Hama and Qusayr. Indigent Syrians roamed the streets of Beirut, begging to give a shoe-shine in exchange for a little help. Syrian workers, already a major segment of the labor force in Beirut, seemed to be present in especially large numbers: their forlorn outfits and thick country accents contrasting with the sophistication of the francophone neighborhoods in which they toiled.

There were other more ominous signs that the conflict was spreading. In the fall of 2011, when I arrived, newspapers were filled with reports of Syrian intelligence agents kidnapping enemies of the regime who were hiding out in Lebanon. Mosques I visited in the southern city of Sidon were filled with leaflets exhorting the faithful to send prayers, money, and arms to their Muslim brethren in Syria. Pockets of violence also erupted in Tripoli in the north, where the Syrian revolution played out on a smaller scale in the form of gun battles between rival Sunni and 'Alawi neighborhoods. There were even periodic bouts of violence in Beirut itself, particularly between Sunni supporters of the opposition and Shi'i partisans of the government of Bashar al-Asad. Among the most turbulent events of my time was when a group of Shi'a who were passing through Syria—allegedly pilgrims on their way home to Lebanon, but more likely Hezbollah operatives who had been participating in the conflict—were kidnapped, setting off a tense diplomatic row.[11] Their supporters in the predominantly Shi'i suburbs south of Beirut (in Arabic, the *Dahiyeh al-Janubiyeh*) blocked the main road to the airport and started burning cars and tires. I recall landing at Beirut International one night during the thick of the protests and having to pay the taxi driver double the normal fare to dash through crowds of angry protesters. That night, normally exuberant Beirut was eerily quiet, waiting for an explosion of violence that thankfully did not come.

By and large, I confess I succumbed to much the same amnesia about the Syrian conflict that seemed to affect many Lebanese. To be sure, I interacted with Syrians every day—whether it was the friendly 'Alawi baker from Tartus from whom I bought my sweets, the Sunni brothers from Dera'a who made my *manouche* (a Lebanese sandwich), or various acquaintances in the city. But they seemed uninterested or unwilling to talk about what was happening back home, and given the relative stability of life in Beirut, who could blame them? There in Beirut, they were engaging in their own form of forgetting.

A Lonely Journey: The Road from Damascus to Beirut

Although the conflict did not manifest itself so obviously in Beirut, it did impact me and my world in more subtle ways. I spent the year under the auspices of an Arabic language institute affiliated with the French embassy. The institute had operated in Damascus for a long time, and there, had developed a reputation as an intellectual watering hole for Western-educated Syrian intellectuals, who taught foreigners and had time for their own research and writing. Some of these professors were politically active, but the government seemed to tolerate their tiny island of dissent, putting up with the institute's liberally-minded lectures and film screenings because the audience consisted largely of outsiders and known activists.

When the program moved to Beirut, many members of the Syrian teaching staff came with it. They commuted back and forth, undertaking the two to three hour trip by taxi once a week. As the year wore on, however, the commute became harder. Not only did the trip itself become more perilous because of the fighting, but the experience of moving between melancholy Damascus and gay Beirut induced a kind of cultural whiplash. To enter Lebanon was to enter a world that understood the ravages of war, but which had grown too callous to sympathize with them. It was to spend many tedious hours in the company of students who could not understand the stresses of life across the border, but who persisted in chatting about weekend ski trips, nights out on the town, and other reminders of a carefree life that had all but disappeared in most parts of Syria. Above all, it was to watch a tragic history unfold from afar, and to know you had little power to change it.

In addition to the Syrian teachers at the institute, I got to know a number of other Damascenes who moved regularly between the two capitals for work. One was named Fadi, a handsome and dynamic Sunni Muslim man who traveled frequently to Beirut on banking business. Fadi had grown up in humble circumstances, but a foreign university education gave him entrée to high society and good wages. In many ways, Fadi was the face of a secular, forward-looking Syria: fluent in several languages and a frequent traveler abroad, he was a cosmopolitan success story in a country whose government, as we have seen, liked to highlight its sophistication and commitment to progress.

Over the course of my year in Beirut, the conflict in Syria took on an increasingly sectarian tone. What had begun as a struggle between the regime and the economically disenfranchised quickly transformed into a darker conflict between 'Alawis, Sunnis, and their respective regional allies. Many of the fiercest and most effective branches of the opposition were made up of Salafis, Sunni fundamentalists akin to some Wahhabi groups who predominate in Saudi Arabia. There were also the Muslim Brothers—exiled from Syria since the Islamist insurgency ended in the early 1980s—who were among the best organized parts of the resistance thanks to patronage from countries such as Qatar and Turkey.

For someone like Fadi, the rise of Islamist groups was a menacing harbinger of things to come. Whenever Bashar fell, as seemed inevitable at that early point, it would be religiously conservative rebels who took control, he said, not the secularists who were running the political wing of the opposition from Istanbul and who earned the fawning attention of foreign diplomats. When that day came, Fadi warned, Syria would change dramatically: "The goal is not the fall of the regime; the goal is the fall of Syria, all of it." It was the overturning of a secular order that had, in Fadi's judgment, brought sophistication and prosperity to his country. In human terms, it was an end to the high-end shopping malls where he could buy his sleek Italian loafers; to the bookstores where he could peruse foreign novels; to the restaurants and bars in the Old City of Damascus where he could mix with friends. There are countless millions in Syria who have suffered under the present regime, but in Fadi I realized there were millions more who stood to lose out in a Syria that suddenly became the playground of fundamentalists instead of impious Baathists. This is not to defend the regime—far from it. It is merely to point out that through Fadi I came to see the war less as a Manichean struggle between good and evil—the typical narrative advanced in many Western newspapers—and more as a winnerless battle over two visions of the future. Justice was on the side of those who hoped Syria would become a more conservative country after the war. But tragedy would befall those who, like Fadi, thrived in a Western-oriented, "open" place promised but rarely delivered by the Asads.

Another Syrian friend was Nour, a middle-aged Ismaili woman. Nour was heavily made up, and a lifetime of Marlboro Reds had given her voice a hoarse and smoky edge. Nour spent most of her week as a book editor in Damascus and would come to Beirut occasionally to finish her projects, usually laden with depressing stories about the situation on the other side of the border. These were not only about the rising cost of bread in Damascus, the spontaneous firefights and explosions, but also the human toll of the war and its effects on civil society. In particular, she would lament the suspicion with which she was greeted by friends and co-workers back home, who saw her—a member of a small but influential religious minority—as a loyal supporter of Bashar al-Asad (never mind that the Ismailis had been split in their attitudes to the regime since the start of the fighting). Nour was no partisan of the regime, but like Fadi, she was precisely the kind of Syrian who stood to lose out if radical elements took control of the country.

I once bumped into Nour wiping tears from her face. That week, colleagues back in Damascus had been whispering cruel insults behind her back—"*Sharmouta* (whore), you filthy Ismaili"—and the stress of it was getting to her. "What will happen when this ends? Will this become the normal way Syrians interact with each other, and if so, what does this mean for me? Do they forget that the Baathists killed Ismailis, too, forget about the Christians or the Druze?"

Much of Nour's family lived abroad. Despite these connections, she felt herself trapped in Syria. She lacked the fancy Western education of some of her colleagues, she could not speak any foreign languages, and she did not earn enough money to decamp to a nearby country and start over. Her only choice was to weather the storm, undertaking the cold and lonely commute between Damascus and Beirut, especially when things got too hot back home. The tragedy of her situation became real for me one day shortly before Christmas. I was preparing to return home to see family and friends and happened to bump into Nour and told her of my plans. She smiled politely, but winced when I asked about her plans for the Christmas and New Year holiday, always a festive time, even in Muslim neighborhoods of Damascus. "I'm staying at home," she said with heavy resignation, "I tried to get a visa to visit my sister in the Gulf, but the government there isn't issuing permits to Syrians, plus, I don't really have the money, and even if I did, I'd be worried someone would break into my house."

Immediately, I felt ashamed of my question. How foolish of me to describe dinners in New York City and trips to Washington, DC when Nour could not escape the living hell of Damascus in revolt. It was then I realized what it meant to live in a prison. My exposure to danger was neither proximate nor real. For better or worse, with a credit card and some determination, I could escape Beirut at a moment's notice. For Nour, there was no escape, no foreign patrons, and no money for flights. It made me feel grateful for being a foreigner in this unstable corner of the world, but also made me feel deeply sad for people like Nour, trapped by bad decisions an entire political system had made on her behalf.

The last of my Syrian acquaintances was Rashid, a writer with an interest in the history of the modern Middle East and contemporary Arab thought. Ideologically, he was something of a curiosity, a member of a dying breed of Nasserists whose fortunes had tumbled with the concomitant rise of the Islamists in recent decades. Nevertheless, Rashid carried on in his activism with dignity and grace. He was deeply learned and humble, a man whose easy-going demeanor disguised a fierce intelligence and strong political commitments.

Over the course of that year in Beirut, Rashid succumbed to fatigue. The deteriorating situation back home, not to mention the punishing journeys back and forth to Damascus, sapped him of his energy. Still, Rashid always became animated when the conversation turned to history, especially to one of his favorite topics, the *Nahda*, the Arab literary renaissance of the nineteenth and early twentieth centuries. As we have seen, one of its principal goals was to equip Arab societies with the tools—intellectual, cultural, religious, and political—to face the modern world, reconciling the traditions of the past with the intellectual and scientific progress of the present. It produced great intellectuals, many of them Syrians and Lebanese, who challenged their cultures to think seriously about matters like women's rights, the separation of religion and the state, and pan-Arab identity. To chat with Rashid about the great thinkers of the *Nahda* against the backdrop of the Arab Spring was to contemplate the success and legacy of this movement. In many ways, the regimes under threat today were intellectual heirs of those *Nahda*-era thinkers. They began on the promise of pan-Arab unity, of progress through economic development, and of citizenship grounded in secular codes of law. Yet they ended up flawed heirs of the *Nahda*, trading its bold ideas about progress for techniques of oppression and control.

In light of this, I once asked Rashid whether the *Nahda* had succeeded. After thinking for a moment, he replied that no, the *Nahda* had not succeeded in reforming and modernizing Arab society, but where it *had* succeeded had been in laying the groundwork for renewal at some future date. Like a bear that hibernates in the cold of winter, the revolutionary ideas of the *Nahda*, he believed, were waiting to be stirred and brought to life. For him, the ultimate legacy of those bold philosophers was not the secular states that had sprung up in the mid-twentieth century in the Arab world, and had failed tragically by the early twenty-first.[12] Rather, it was the ocean of philosophy that lay waiting to be tapped for *ressourcement* (French for "return to the sources") down the road.

I confess that I disagreed with Rashid's reading of the situation. Not only did the legacy of the *Nahda* seem to be fading, but it was being replaced by new and dynamic ideas about society and politics, namely, those of political Islam. It was telling how in a matter of months, the Syrian revolution, which had begun as a peaceful protest movement among individuals clamoring for *karama* (dignity), had become a violent insurrection powered in large part by religious fundamentalists. Much the same could be said of Egypt's initial experience of the Arab Spring, in which a youthful revolution fell into the laps of more numerous and better organized legions of Muslim Brothers and Salafis. In our conversations, Rashid challenged the tidy distinctions between modernity and Islamism. While they seemed at times to be diametrically opposed, Rashid saw in them products of the same modernizing impulse, the one avowedly secular in its language, the other avowedly religious, but both committed to a certain political egalitarianism that disrupted old hierarchies and institutions.

"And We Remain": Memories of Power, Memories of Loss

Up to now, I've focused on the plight of Syrians I met in Beirut. Friends, teachers, and strangers I encountered on the street, these Syrians helped me understand the travails of their country up-close, putting a human face on a conflict usually measured through impersonal statistics such as body counts or the rising cost of an AK-47. As I tried to make sense of the revolution, however, I realized that the streets of Beirut could furnish some insights of their own.

As we've seen, Lebanese politics is in many ways *sui generis*, and the particular circumstances surrounding the famous armistice that ended the civil war, signed in the city of Ta'if in Saudi Arabia in 1989, are even more so. That said, Lebanon and Syria share a common history and matrix of peoples. The war came to an end in Lebanon when these groups finally realized that they lacked the means to subjugate one another, and it was in their personal interest to make peace instead of fight. Sadly, the Syrian civil war has unfolded as more of a zero-sum game, a high-stakes dance in which the power of one community (the 'Alawis, allied with the regime of President Asad and supported by Russia and Iran) stands at odds with that of another (the predominantly Sunni opposition, supported by Turkey, Qatar, Saudi Arabia, and others). Despite this and other important differences, let's delve into Lebanon's past to try to derive some clues about Syria's future.

Memories of the civil war are still raw for many Lebanese, and it's not hard to see why. Both physically and notionally, the country continues to recover from the conflict that ended more than twenty years ago. After the war was over, investors poured money into rebuilding a glitzy and soulless downtown, trying to recover some of the magic of pre-war Beirut, when the city was hailed as "the Paris of the East." But as downtown has come to resemble a miniature Dubai, just beyond her precincts entire neighborhoods still bear the marks of machine-gun fire.

I spent a year in a lower middle-class Christian neighborhood in East Beirut near the French Hospital of Hôtel Dieu. The ghosts of

'The Yellow House,' Sodeco, Beirut; built ca. 1924, destroyed during the Civil War

the war were everywhere around me. Some men seemed to carry wounds connected to the fighting: missing fingers, winding scars, stubborn limps. They had been soldiers in their twenties and thirties, mostly for the right-wing Christian militias who controlled this part of the city. Politics may have moved on in Lebanon since then, but in certain ways, the lives of these men had not.

One such person was a friendly Shi'i grocer named 'Ali, from whom I bought my fruit and vegetables, and who seemed to be one of the only Muslims in my immediate area. He told me he had maintained his property during the course of the war, electing to stay in East Beirut at a time when most of its Muslim residents were fleeing. He would speak to me about the war in generalities, how far Lebanon had come since the fighting had ended, and how he was happy to remain there in the neighborhood. The war had been a painful experience not to be revisited, and certainly not to be shared in intimate terms with an outsider like me. Still, he would lift the veil from time to time and describe the horror that had engulfed our quiet street.

"The bullets fell on us like snow in winter," he said to me once, gesturing to the damaged façade of a building, which still had the texture of raw meat from the machine-gun fire after all these years still had the texture of raw meat from the machine-gun fire. "It was fierce, but praise God, we're still alive."

'Ali didn't need to narrate the gory details of the civil war for me to understand the tragedies that had taken place around us. An acquaintance in the United States once recalled a relative who had been working at a Beirut base belonging to the Phalange, the main Christian militia and one of Lebanon's main political parties. He described how one day, a Palestinian Christian approached his uncle and a group of fighters who were relaxing outside the base. The man greeted the soldiers as a fellow Christian, but the Phalange commander, standing up, ordered him to stop speaking. "A Palestinian is a Palestinian, Christian or not," he said. The soldier then tied the Palestinian to the bumper of his car and took him for a ride, dragging the poor man up the coastal highway. Needless to say, he did not survive.

In many ways, the Lebanese Civil War and the Syrian Revolution are both stories of embattled minorities trying to maintain their out-

Bashir Gemayel, political posters near Sassine Square, east Beirut

sized share of power. So it was for the Christians of Lebanon throughout the 1970s and 80s—onetime masters of the country thanks to French patronage, but powerless to shift a changing society in their favor—and so it is for the 'Alawis of Syria today. Old memories of Christian dominance fill the streets of East Beirut. In many places still loyal to the Phalange (and the Lebanese Forces, another Christian party), it is not uncommon to see hagiographic portraits of Bashir Gemayel—the Phalange commander who became president in 1982 in the thick of the war, but who was assassinated in a ferocious bombing shortly thereafter. Gemayel is a nostalgic figure for many Christians, the last representative of an imagined era in which Christians spoke with one voice (forgetting that he emerged as *primus inter pares* only after defeating his enemies from rival Christian groups), in contrast to recent times, when Christians have been split between pro- and anti-Syrian factions.

The iconography of Bashir Gemayel is fascinating.[13] In the streets, it is common to find photos of the slain commander bearing week-old stubble and carrying a Kalashnikov, looking like a Lebanese Che Guevara. There are also small, round portraits of Gemayel assembled in the form of crosses and stuck onto the side of buildings, drawing a not-so-subtle comparison between two martyrs, old and new. The most common imagery in my neighborhood was a heavily photoshopped poster of Gemayel, his hand raised in emphasis as he delivered an impassioned speech. The Arabic above him read *wa-nabqaa*—"and we remain"—a profession of resistance against a world that would seek to drive Christianity out of the country.

More than twenty years after civil war ended, many Christians hung on these fading words. *Wa-nabqaa* became a slogan of grievance, a way of mourning the lost days when Christians not only "remained" in Lebanon, but ruled it. It was also a statement of desperation about the circumstances of the present, when emigration and falling fertility rates have sapped the Christian community of its former influence. *Wa-nabqaa* becomes a reminder to Christians not to abandon their country to *shari'a* law, as many see it, permitting Lebanon to become a satellite of Saudi Arabia or Iran, depending on which side of the political aisle one sits, with the Sunnis or the Shi'is.

"One Man's Hero..."

Although a sense of loss pervades the worldview of many members of Lebanon's Maronite community, the tale of Christian decline is tinged with darker colors. Immediately after Bashir Gemayel was assassinated in September 1982, members of his Phalange militia—receiving cover from the Israeli Defense Forces, who were then occupying Beirut, and with whom they were allied—entered the impoverished Palestinian refugee camps of Sabra and Shatila.[14] With ruthless precision, the Christian soldiers executed around 2,000 men, women, and children. Many were shot at point-blank range, others had their throats slit, and some women were even raped as they were about to die. It was a singularly inhuman moment in a war of unspeakable tragedy.

The man who commanded the Phalange that night was Elie Hobeika, whose family had been among the hundreds of Christians massacred by Palestinian gunmen in the village of Damour, south of Beirut, in 1976 (one of the opening events of the war, itself in retaliation for the massacre of Palestinians in the slums of Karantina, north of Beirut, earlier that year). Sabra and Shatila were widely regarded as his act of revenge. After the war, Hobeika—like many prominent military leaders—joined the ranks of the country's political elite. He became a member of parliament, serving (ironically) as minister of displaced persons, social affairs and the handicapped, and ultimately, as minister of water and electricity. In 2001, due to an international suit filed against Ariel Sharon—the Israeli defense minister at the time of Sabra and Shatila, who was widely believed to have given the green light for the massacre—Hobeika was called to testify in Brussels, but was assassinated in Beirut before he could leave.[15] There is speculation that he had intended to reveal Sharon's role in the attack, but was never allowed to do so.

January 2012 marked the ten-year anniversary of Hobeika's death. Posters appeared suddenly throughout East Beirut commemorating the assassination of this "hero." As an outsider, there seemed to me something perverse about celebrating this butcher. All parties in the Lebanese Civil War had blood on their hands—Christian, Sunni, Shi'i, Druze, and Palestinian alike. Yet Hobeika's crimes were particularly appalling, which made his transformation into a martyr all the more shocking. Who knew that massacring thousands of civilians could put you on the fast-track to civic sainthood?

The commemoration of Hobeika in Beirut taught me two things: first, that memories of conflict are relative; second, that no matter what political settlement brings an end to such bitter fighting, the raw animosities that drove the conflict in the first place are always slow to die.

Along these lines, I recall a conversation I had with a young Christian businessman a few months after the anniversary of Hobeika's death during the course of a church event. We were chatting with a European who had professional dealings with the UN, and who was criticizing the organization's population control policies. According to him, the UN often called for the provision of abortion and contraceptive services to communities in the developing world. The Lebanese man balked at this, then began comparing this policy to the stance of the Lebanese state.

He explained that the state had failed to contain explosive growth among the country's Shi'a community, especially in the south and in the Beqaa Valley, where fertility rates were skyrocketing, while those of the Christians were plummeting. I knew this to be true generally, as worries about changing demography underlie many questions about the balance of political power in Lebanon. All the same, I was not expecting what came next: "I don't mean to get all *ta'ifi* (sectarian)," the young man said to us, "but I have no problem promoting abortion among the Muslims. As a Catholic, of course, I'm against this, but it's in these people's nature to be violent. I wouldn't want the U.N. to start promoting abortion among us Christians, but for the Muslims I have no problem. I mean, whether it's Hermel [a poor, predominantly Shi'i area in the north of the country] or in the Palestinian camps, we would do the world a service by stopping these kids from either starving because their parents have no money, or from going to fight for the Taliban."

By outward appearances, the young man wasn't a likely holder of vile opinions. Trilingual and well educated, he had recently returned from a silent retreat in preparation for Easter. Yet his self-professed double standard betrayed a deeper worldview, one that saw Muslims as "less than human," more prone to violence than his own comments suggested about him. In moments like these, the tensions of the civil war seemed shockingly close.

I have focused on the Maronites in this chapter mostly because they are the community I have come to know best. It's also a community I came to admire deeply. It's important to note that the views of this young man and the partisans of Elie Hobeika are not characteristic of all Maronites—indeed, for every individual like the young businessman I met, I encountered many others of profound compassion and kindness, who had no patience for the barbed sectarianism of the civil war.

Indeed, suspicion towards the "other" was a feeling not restricted to the Maronites. I recall another encounter while I was walking through an old graveyard in the predominantly Sunni neighborhood of Basta in Beirut. Not realizing the makeup of the area at first, I asked an old man inside the cemetery whether it was Sunni or Shi'i, to which he replied "Sunni." He then asked where I had come from, and upon hearing "the United States," he began a litany of complaints against the Shi'a (presuming that as an American, I would be an enemy of the Shi'a and their political parties, including Hezbollah, and he would be free to speak his mind). "They're shit," he said to me bluntly, "They pull Iran and China into our country and wreck it. Beirut belongs to the Sunnis—always has, and always will. The Christians—we can live with them, no problem. But the Shi'a, they have no ethics (*akhlaq*)."

The Arabic term *akhlaq* has a wider range of meaning than merely "ethics." It conveys a sense of decorum, of morality, of sophistication, which in the eyes of this old Sunni man, the Shi'a lacked desperately. He wasn't calling for the sterilization of his enemies like the young businessman I had met, but the same sense of hostility toward the other bubbled below the surface. The civil war wasn't over. The tensions that had caused it had merely been buried for the sake of greater goods, such as a fragile stability from which everyone in Lebanon could benefit.

Neighbors, Sectarianism, and Survival

It is not my intention to focus here on the tragic aspects of Lebanon's history and culture. God knows the country has received enough bad press to last a lifetime. I focus on it to highlight one aspect of what will inevitably come when the fighting ends in Syria. No matter the international agreements, reconstruction efforts, or pledges of sectarian solidarity after the revolution, "moving on" will be a very tough business. Creating a climate of trust will be especially challenging, a climate in which groups that once related to each other as "rulers" and "subjects" learn to interact with each other as "partners" and "peers."

There are promising signs that this is taking place in Lebanon. During my time in Beirut, I came to know a Sunni woman named Iman, who worked as a nurse in a local hospital. Iman was unveiled, and furthermore, belonged to an old Sunni family that had lived in an area known as Beydoun for generations. The neighborhood is a tiny enclave of Muslims in an otherwise Christian part of East Beirut, and Iman and I used to pass each other when I walked through it to reach the Maronite Church I attended for mass.

One afternoon, she kindly invited me to drink coffee with her. Inside her salon, Iman told me about her father, who had been a successful businessman who had insisted that all the children in his large family receive a proper education. It was a story—and an anxiety—I had heard before from Muslims in the city: looking upon the sudden squalor and misfortune of the Palestinians who had fled to Lebanon after 1948 and 1967, many parents of that generation were determined for their children to avoid the same fate if a similar tragedy ever befall Lebanon. For Iman's father, education was the ticket out of a conflict, and right he was. In addition to Iman, the family included several engineers, businessmen, and teachers (some of them living abroad). It seemed like the clan was thriving despite all that had happened to their country over the decades.

I was struck by the sensibilities of my hosts, which were typical of old Sunni families in Beirut (who along with the Greek Orthodox, formed a majority of the city's original inhabitants). Neither Iman nor her sister who joined us wore the veil, and in fact, they spoke in jest about the more conservative Sunni neighborhoods of the city. For them, Beirut was a city of *infitah* (openness), a salutary contrast with Damascus just across the border, which they looked upon as a place of intense religiosity and relative unsophistication.

I asked the sisters about relations between Muslims and Christians in their neighborhood. It was, after all, unusual to find the roles reversed in this day and age, to be members of a Muslim minority in a predominantly Christian area. They described peaceful relations between the two communities. Even during the worst periods of fighting, neighborly courtesies had carried on unencumbered—the sharing of highly prized fruits and sweets, marriages among members of different sects, even political cooperation. "Bashir Gemayel once visited our street," Iman told me, referring to the slain Phalange commander and president, whose authority extended over this Sunni neighborhood during the war. "He asked every family here, 'What do you need, how can we help?'—Christian and Muslim alike. This area was under his supervision."

It is easy for an outsider to feel surprise at such stories. But these stories underscore an important lesson about sectarianism in Lebanon and the region generally. On the one hand, such examples of co-existence among sects, organized around neighborly good practice and conviviality—known in Arabic as *'aysh mushtarak*—point to the utter irrelevance of religious identity in certain spheres of everyday life. Yet at the same time, the language of *'aysh mushtarak* does not so much question or discount the sectarian organization of society as it takes it for granted, all the while insisting upon the essential harmony among different groups.

In other words, depending on the angle from which you saw it, sectarianism was either pervasive or utterly unimportant. In its assertive and destructive forms it was the creation of political elites who divided and ruled more than it was of citizens who attended the same schools and shopped in the same stores. Iman was an admittedly exceptional example of this; she was molded by the sensibilities of an old-fashioned Beiruti culture that has all but disappeared in many parts of the city because of the war, as well as the presence of new communities recently arrived from rural areas where interaction with the religious "other" was less common. But in her story I discovered something that could apply to Lebanon and Syria alike: the possibility of civil society—of *'aysh mushtarak*—subsisting, even thriving in the face of terrible pressures that would tear it apart. In Iman—to say nothing of many other Lebanese friends who worked actively to counter the culture of sectarianism—I saw a model for post-conflict societies like Syria's to become stronger.

Martyrs' Square, Beirut: A Common Past, a Divided Future

Both Beirut and Damascus have large public spaces called "Martyrs' Square"—in Arabic, *Sahat al-Shuhada'*. The version in Damascus (also known as Marja Square) is located northwest of the Old City, not far from the chaotic visa office we visited earlier, while its counterpart in Beirut sits just north of the glitzy downtown. They share not only a common name, but also a common history.

In the summer of 2013 I sat in Martyr's Square for an hour one evening, mulling over this extroverted and melancholy place, as well as its sad sister fifty miles inland. More than two years had passed since revolts began smoldering throughout the Arab world, yet it was hard to tell from Beirut's mid-summer bustle that anything was burning nearby. For once in recent memory, stormy Lebanon was an oasis of calm in a very restive Middle East.

At first glance, it was hard to recognize Martyrs' Square as the nerve-center of the city. Known colloquially as the *Bourj* (tower), so-called for the fortifications that used to stand nearby, it was a vast expanse of asphalt and concrete—around 250 meters long and 50 meters wide—yawning on the edge of Beirut's posh shopping and administrative district. Save for the carousel of buses and taxis whipping around, the square that night was almost empty. Around its edge, I noticed a mix of totems both sacred and profane—the blue domes of the al-Amin mosque, a Virgin Megastore, a Dunkin Donuts, and even a Ferrari dealership in the distance. Parking lots filled the open spaces in between. Although it may have resembled an unfinished construction site, Martyrs' Square was hallowed ground.

The modern history of the square begins in May 1916, when the Ottoman governor Jamal Pasha (known to the Arabs as *al-Saffah*, "the butcher") executed fourteen men for conspiracy against the empire.[16] He executed another seven in Damascus on similar charges. Prior to World War I, these men—a mix of Muslims and Christians—had collaborated secretly with French and British

Martyrs' Memorial, Martyrs' Square, downtown Beirut

authorities in plans to overthrow Turkish rule and install an Arab nationalist regime. Eventually their plot was discovered, and after a series of military tribunals, they were hanged in the two squares, set up to face important Ottoman administrative buildings in both places. The dead were celebrated as martyrs of Lebanese and Syrian independence, as well as of Arab nationalism. In their honor, the squares in Damascus and Beirut were rechristened "Martyrs' Square" after the war.

In 1920, France assumed custody of Syria and Lebanon, and in Beirut it consented to the creation of a memorial to the martyrs. Though the Ottomans were long gone, the square conserved its historical charge, quickly becoming a focal point of resistance against the French Mandate, which many Lebanese resented as a form of neo-colonial rule. Most notably, it was to Martyrs' Square that Bechara al-Khoury and Riad al-Solh—the first president and prime minister of Lebanon—hurried to mark the foundation of an independent state after their release from prison on November 22nd, 1943 (whence came the famous power-sharing agreement between Maronites and Sunnis mentioned above).

In the 1950s, the old martyrs' memorial of Beirut was defaced by a vandal. It was decided that Lebanon needed a far grander statue to commemorate its heroes, and so an Italian sculptor, Marino Mazzacurati, was hired to create a new monument. In May 1960, his commission was unveiled—a bronze statue around 20 feet high modeled vaguely on the famous painting of Eugène Delacroix, *Liberty Leading the People*. The central figures were allegorical representations of Freedom and the Nation—a towering woman with a torch grasping the shoulder of a handsome youth, meant to resemble a Greek hero. At their feet lay two men who symbolized the martyrs of 1916, staring in fear at invisible tormenters as they struggled to stand up.

The statue received mixed reviews. Critics attacked the monument for being adamantly un-Lebanese, a foreign sculptor's pompous shrine to Classical art having little to do with Lebanon's own history and culture. There was also some evidence that Mazzacurati did not create the memorial specifically for Beirut, but rather, assembled it from pre-existing works in his studio.

Whatever the initial controversy, it subsided by 1976 as Lebanon slipped into civil war. Martyrs' Square marked the beginning of the so-called "Green Line" that divided predominantly Muslim West Beirut from Christian East Beirut. Throughout this conflict, the square was a virtual no-man's land, a sniper's paradise reclaimed by weeds and trees. As a result, Mazzacurati's statue sustained significant damage. The arms of the standing youth were blown clean off, and the rest of the figures were pock-marked by bullets and shrapnel. Still, the monument survived the fighting.

After the civil war ended in 1990, the statues were removed for restoration. Conservationists decided not to repair the wounds entirely. Rather, they preserved the gaping holes and jagged edges as a reminder of the bloody conflict that had once swallowed Martyrs' Square and the entire country. The statues returned to the Bourj in 2004.

In the post-war period, the square continued to play its historic role as the great stage of Lebanese politics. Notably, it was the site of huge protests—totaling nearly two million people over a two-week period in March 2005—following the assassination of Prime Minister Rafiq al-Hariri. Hariri's body was interred under a great tent on the southeast side of the square, where it remains today in a bold claim on the legacy of the martyrs of 1916.

The term "martyr" has powerful, if ambiguous purchase throughout Beirut. In practically every neighborhood of the city—whether Sunni, Christian, Shi'i, or Druze—one finds memorials to the heroic dead, men and women who died witnessing to their community's particular vision of political and religious truth. Despite the preponderance of martyrs, however, there is no consensus in Beirut on who counts as a saint. In this country of deep internal divisions, martyrs perform an essential role in reinforcing a sense of difference among the sects, allowing the great battles of the past to continue to fester deep into the present.

So it is today in Syria, where many victims of the conflict bear the title "martyr"—whether they are soldiers who died fighting for the regime, rebels who fell supporting the opposition, or civilians who found themselves trapped in the crossfire. In Syria, the bloody war will one day end, leaving behind a country that is divided along sectarian, ethnic and regional lines. It will fall to Syria's new leaders to repair these divisions, to recover a sense of a united Syria that is stronger than its constituent parts. In this world, "martyrs" represent both promise and peril. Can they be sources of strength for a new kind of society, like the martyrs of 1916 were for independent Syria and Lebanon after World War I? Or will they resemble the sectarian martyrs of modern Beirut, stubborn reminders of a contested past, memories of which ensure a divided future? For Syria's sake, let's hope the legacy of the martyrs of 1916 prevails.

EPILOGUE

AMONG THE RUINS

It feels premature to write a conclusion for this book. Conclusions are best left for a time when history has run its course, not when it is still frantically racing ahead.

Furthermore, it strikes me that conclusions are usually a good place to prognosticate about the future. But in the case of Syria, where the ledgers of war seem to flip-flop all too quickly, predictions are a fool's game at best. In any event, the purpose of this book was never to divine what may come to pass. Rather it was to reflect on the major historical themes that have shaped Syria's past, and which, in a general sense, have delivered the country to this present moment in time.

Therefore, I will resist the impulse to play the prophet, and allow readers to draw their own conclusions. I suspect they will have found in these pages many reasons to be pessimistic, at least in the near term. At the same time, I hope they will have found at least a few reasons to be hopeful, buoyed, perhaps, by a better understanding of Syria's history and its resilient people.

While a conventional conclusion is ill-advised, there are a few matters that have piqued my interest in the process of writing, and which merit discussion in these closing pages. The first is terminology.

As I look back on the past years of war, it is extremely difficult to assign a single label to all that's happened. Early on, I—like many Syria-watchers—preferred to see this as a manifestation of the "Arab Spring." It was a rosy term for a rosy time when in a terrific feat of seeming coordination, Arabic-speakers from Tunis to Yemen managed to rise up against autocratic leaders and claim a brighter future for themselves. Syria's "Arab Spring" harnessed this zeitgeist, especially in the early months of 2011 after protests first erupted in Dera'a.

But as time wore on, peaceful demonstrations gave way to bloody crackdowns, and protesters traded rhyming chants against Bashar for automatic weapons against his militias. Syria had descended into a brutal and brutalizing war, and the term "Arab Spring" no longer seemed to match the black mood of the moment. If anything, Syria—like many other states in the region, where the fallout of revolution proved more menacing than anyone could have imagined at the outset—seemed headed for a long winter.

While "Arab Spring" may have lost its utility, the alternatives were not much better. "The Syrian revolution"—a title favored by many American and European media outlets, as well as Arab satellite channels like al-Jazeera which championed the rebel cause—failed to acknowledge that for many Syrians, this was no noble fight. Rather, it was seen as an insidious effort to topple the country from within. "Revolution" seemed to impose a false sense of unanimity on the legitimacy and desirability of the war among the Syrian people. Revolutions are a matter of perspective, and perspective in Syria was deeply divided.

With "Arab Spring" and "Syrian Revolution" out for the count, "civil war" appeared to be an acceptable substitute (indeed, I have resorted to using "civil war" many times in this book). The term summed up the basic dynamic of the conflict in a neutral, rather straightforward way.

Yet "civil war" failed to account for the regional and global dimensions of the conflict, which took on increasing significance as 2011 gave way to 2012, 2012 to 2013, and 2013 to 2014. For in Syria, the local struggle between the regime and the opposition became a proxy war for wider conflicts between Iran and its allies, on the one hand, and Turkey and the conservative Gulf monarchies, on the other. To add fuel to the fire, the local and regional dimensions were overlaid with a renewed Cold War rivalry between Russia and China, on the one hand—implacable supporters of

President Asad—and the United States and the European Union, on the other—champions of the opposition (though rather tepid in their enthusiasm for sending weapons). Thus, the term "civil war" was simply too narrow to accurately describe the manifold actors and interests converging on Syria.

Debates about nomenclature may seem pedantic, but they are crucially important for understanding the shifting nature of the war. Indeed, it has been a marvel to witness the conflict change so much over so short a time. Where it will turn next remains unclear, but given the high stakes, even more fundamental transformations seem inevitable.

As we focus on the macro-level dimensions of the conflict, it can be difficult to keep alive the voices of individuals caught in the crossfire. They have had little say in the war, but they have borne the brunt of Syria's losses. One of these victims was my friend and teacher Muhammad, whom we met several times in the preceding pages—a young father who loved the Arabic language and looked skeptically on the United States and its role in the world. His fate since 2011 has made the tragedy of Syria's disintegration more real for me than any newspaper headline.

After leaving Damascus three years ago, I fell out of touch with Muhammad. But a steady stream of bad news from the Ghouta—the suburb of the capital where he lived, famous for its lush orchards—prompted me to write. An email from Muhammad in October 2012 included the following information:

The situation here is very, very difficult. I'm currently trying to find a new place to live, but in reality, there's no quiet place for us. We're searching for something that's a little better. God willing, there won't be a civil war [...] We're looking for food for the children and nothing more.

Muhammad was well educated, but he had little money and few foreign contacts that could help him escape. Of course, despite what he said, civil war had come to Syria long before, but with no ability to get out, the only form of comfort left to him was to deny reality and hope for the best.

My next correspondence with Muhammad came in the early summer of 2013. By then, his situation had improved slightly, as he and his family had managed to sell some jewelry and flee to Egypt:

Thank God, recently I left the country with my wife and children. The regime has destroyed everything. They struck my house and everything beautiful: the schools and the hospitals, the mosques and even the churches. Everything—it's been a terrible act of vengeance against the people. There we were, constantly between life and death.

There are many wealthy Syrians who have escaped their country and picked up more or less where they left off, renting large homes in Beirut or Amman, enrolling their children in good schools, and finding work in new companies. These are the lucky few. There are many more who have not been so fortunate—who toil in vast tent cities on the borders of their burning country, carrying on in squalor and uncertainty as resources and the patience of their host nations run dry.

Muhammad fell somewhere between these groups. He and his family had managed to scrounge enough money to head to distant Cairo, thereby avoiding the grim fate of the refugee camps. At the same time, upon arriving in Egypt, with no further financial resources and terrific medical problems, it became clear that they had simply traded one living hell for another. Although Egypt was a relative success story in contrast to Syria's violent "Arab Spring," a sluggish economy, collapsing security, and ferocious political rivalries had turned their new country into a tinderbox. This became especially apparent during the summer of 2013, when President Muhammad Morsi was deposed by the Egyptian army, unleashing waves of unrest throughout the country. Muhammad and his family enjoyed more security in Cairo than they would in Damascus, to be sure, but given Egypt's own growing pains and the trenchant discrimination faced by foreign refugees, their future was not exactly bright.

As we corresponded, I thought often of Muhammad's children. I thought especially of his daughter, Zeina, who used to interrupt our Arabic lessons back in Damascus with tiny fits of laughter and "secrets" she would whisper into my ear. I would ask whether she wanted to come back with me to New York, whether she could fit into my luggage on the plane, questions that always elicited further rounds of giggles.

Zeina is older now, perhaps eight or nine, and like Syrians of all ages, she has been sobered by the experience of war. I wonder what she understands of her family's sad change in fortunes. I wonder whether she expects to ever return home. I wonder if she can imagine a permanent life for herself in the precarious world of the refugees of Cairo. Sadly, I fear that she is but one of millions of a new "lost generation" that will never know normalcy. Even if she manages to return to the Ghouta, the neighborhood of Damascus where she grew up, she will find it a changed place. It was in the Ghouta in late August 2013 that the regime detonated a series of chemical weapons, killing around 1,400 people according to US intelligence estimates. In response, under pressure from American and Russian diplomats, President Asad consented to dismantle his entire chemical arsenal, but the Ghouta—a neighborhood I knew from the many hours I spent there with Muhammad and his children—will never be the same.

I have written these final pages of the book in Beirut. Throughout the past century, tiny Lebanon's fate has been tied to that of its larger neighbor. Now, despite civil war simmering across the border and sometimes spilling over, Lebanon can seem strangely aloof from the crisis. Its beaches are still packed with bronzed bodies, seasonal workers still pick grapes for the fall vintage, and Ramadan decorations festoon village squares throughout the country.

That said, you don't have to dig far to sense the terrible danger Lebanon faces because of events in Syria. There are many more Syrian refugees in Beirut than what I remember from last year. Some are children—ragged and hungry—though the most melancholy are the elderly men and women who hawk boxes of Chiclets at polluted intersections throughout the city. The experience of every Syrian refugee is tragic, though one suspects that for these old people, life is never destined to get better.

The summer of 2013 witnessed a string of Syria-related violence inside Lebanon. In early June, for example, Ahmad al-Assir, a Salafi preacher in the southern city of Sidon, known for his fiery sermons against Bashar al-Asad and Hezbollah, engaged in a bloody stand-off with the Lebanese Army. Between Assir's men and the Lebanese soldiers, dozens were killed and over a hundred were injured. A few weeks later, a great car bomb exploded in the southern suburbs of

Beirut where Hezbollah holds sway, apparently an act of retaliation for the group's aggressive interventions on the side of the regime. After each crisis, Lebanon managed to return to an uneasy calm, but it was undeniable that with each attack, the temperature in the country climbed a few degrees and refused to go down. That this would spark a wider conflagration at some point down the road seemed inevitable.

More than actual events in Lebanon, it has been the changing iconography of Beirut's streets that has signaled that Syria's fight has become Lebanon's as well. In Sassine Square, the heart of Christian East Beirut, there hung a great banner pleading for the release of two Christian bishops who were abducted from their car in Aleppo in April 2013. In Basta al-Tahta, a run-down predominantly Shi'i neighborhood not far from downtown, winding alleyways are plastered with portraits of young Hezbollah fighters "martyred" in Syria, sent there to protect the great Shi'i shrine of Sayyida Zeinab (which we encountered earlier). Further south, in Ras al-Nabaa, a mixed Sunni and Shi'i area, there are images of the Syrian cleric Sa'id Ramadan al-Bouti (whom we met in a previous chapter) glued to the walls, a stalwart supporter of the Asads until his assassination in Damascus in March 2013. In death, the martyred Bouti continues to rebuff the West and to confer legitimacy on the Baathist regime, his closing words printed in red: "Islam as the Quran has commanded, not as America has decreed!"

Then there are the Syrians I knew living in Beirut: I ran into one of them, a Christian named Tony, who owned a small shop not far from Sassine Square. He came to Beirut years ago from Tartus, a coastal city twenty miles north of the Lebanese border with a mixed population of Christians, 'Alawis, and Sunnis. Two years previously, when I first met Tony, he was cautiously optimistic that the fighting would end and a brokered peace would emerge. This, he said, would produce a better future for all Syrians—Muslim and Christian alike.

But as time wore on, all sense of optimism in Tony's voice disappeared. As with many Christians, his support for Bashar had not been absolute, especially at the start of the uprising. But as the conflict dragged on, Tony faced a stark choice between the dictator he knew and the devil he did not: what the opposition wanted was no longer to overturn Asad's crony capitalism and smash his secret prisons, he said. The opposition—increasingly dominated by Islamists—wanted to establish a Muslim state in Syria. This, Tony feared, would restrict many basic Christian freedoms, whether the right to build churches, to purchase pork and alcohol, or to carry on unmolested in the streets. This was in contrast to other Arab countries like Egypt where Christians had faced deep discrimination for years.

Tony told me he had seen the Islamist threat coming years ago during his time as a conscript in the Syrian army. One day, a fellow soldier—a Sunni Muslim from Deir ez-Zor—started calling Tony a *kafir*, or "unbeliever." The commanding officer of their unit—an 'Alawi—caught wind of this and had the man jailed and flogged before the assembled cadets. "There is no Christian, Sunni, or 'Alawi in this army," the officer told them, "we are all Syrians." Tony's message to me was clear: in a world in which there are no 'Alawi strongmen to flog the religious extremists, everyone in Syria—though most especially the Christians—are destined to suffer. The fates of the two communities—'Alawis and Christians—were bound together.

If this book has accomplished anything, I hope it has convinced readers that the deep past exerts a powerful influence on the present. In this sense, Syria is no different from any other country where past and present mingle to configure a powerful sense of identity. In the context of the Syrian civil war, we are witnessing not only the culmination of certain long-term historical trends, but also a contest over how to properly interpret these trends and their relationship to the present. Is Syria's a history of unity arising amidst diversity, or unity destroyed by cleavage and division?

Nowhere is this more apparent than in the destruction of Syria's historical treasures. Since the start of the fighting, countless Roman temples, Byzantine churches, medieval mosques, and other sites have fallen victim to shelling and gunfire. The collapse of security in other areas has opened the floodgates of theft and pillaging, often on a massive, industrial scale. The loss of this cultural heritage is a tragedy not only in absolute terms. It is also robbing Syria of its connection to a multi-faceted and diverse past. Indeed, when you destroy a people's monuments and their material record, you destroy the people themselves. How much harder to rebuild a country when its most important symbols are gone forever?

I do not wish to end this book on a melancholy note. There has been much sorrow to swallow in the preceding pages, and in any event, I *do* believe there is reason for hope, even if the situation seems bleak. In the preface, I wrote that Syria is a "dynamic and diverse place, shaped and renewed by the very changes that in the near term can seem so destructive." One suspects that the country is in the throes of another one of these changes, and like a phoenix, it shall rise again once the fighting is over. I do not mean to suggest that bloodshed and destruction are the justified price of renewal in Syria—far from it. Rather, I believe that the rocky road ahead will lead to changes both positive and negative, changes that we cannot even imagine right now, but which are destined to be profound.

NOTES

PREFACE

1. These include: Sahner, Christian C., "Crac des Chevaliers: A Medieval Castle in the Middle East," *The Wall Street Journal*, 31 January 2009, accessible online: http://online.wsj.com/article/SB12333539820573 4847.html; idem, "The Umayyad Mosque of Damascus: A Glittering Crossroads," *The Wall Street Journal*, 17 July 2010, accessible online: http://online.wsj.com/article/SB1000142405274870357170457534085 33854939358.html; idem, "The Temple of Bel at Palmyra: Temple of the Bride of the Desert," *The Wall Street Journal*, 27 August 2011, accessible online: http://online.wsj.com/article/SB10001424052702304 52130457644786299989934.html; and in Jordan: idem, "Qusayr 'Amra: Snapshot of a Civilization in the Making," *The Wall Street Journal*, 27 November 2010, accessible online: http://online.wsj.com/article/SB10001424052748704141104575588302922407126.html

2. These include: Tabler, Andrew, *In the Lion's Den: An Eyewitness Account of Washington's Battle with Syria*, Chicago: Lawrence Hill Books, 2011; Ajami, Fouad, *The Syrian Rebellion*, Stanford, CA: Hoover Institution Press, 2012; Starr, Stephen, *Revolt in Syria: Eye-Witness to the Uprising*, London: Hurst, 2012; Lesch, David, *Syria: The Fall of the House of Assad*, New Haven: Yale University Press, 2012.

1. THE IMPERIAL MOMENT: ISLAM IN SYRIA

1. For good overviews of the history of Damascus across ancient, medieval, and modern times, see: Burns, Ross, *Damascus: A History*, London: Routledge, 2005; Degeorge, Gérard, *Damas: Des Ottomans à nos jours*, Paris: L'Harmattan, 1994; idem, *Damas: Des origines aux*

Mamluks, Paris: L'Harmattan, 1997. For a classic travelogue of life in Damascus in the 1960s, see: Thubron, Colin, *Mirror to Damascus*, London: Heinemann, 1967. On the geography of *Bilad al-Sham* and its political implications in the modern period see Rabinovich, Itmar, *The View from Damascus: State, Political Community and Foreign Relations in Modern and Contemporary Syria*, 2nd edn, London: Vallentine Mitchell, 2011, pp. 7–18.

2. For a helpful introduction to current scholarly debates about Syria in the early Islamic period, see various essays in Haldon, John F., ed., *Money, Power and Politics in Early Islamic Syria*, Farnham: Ashgate, 2010, especially the introduction: Haldon, "Greater Syria in the Seventh Century: Context and Background," pp. 1–20. Along these same lines, see the older collection of essays: Canivet, Pierre and Jean-Paul Rey-Coquais, eds, *La Syrie de Byzance à l'Islam VIIe-VIIIe siècles: Actes du Colloque international, Lyon-Maison de l'Orient Méditerranéen, Paris-Institut du Monde Arabe, 11–15 Septembre 1990*, Damascus: Institut Français de Damas, 1992. Also: Humphreys, R. Stephen, "Syria," *The New Cambridge History of Islam. Volume 1: The Formation of the Islamic World, Sixth to Eleventh Centuries*, Chase F. Robinson, ed., Cambridge: Cambridge University Press, 2010, pp. 506–40.

3. For a concise introduction to the Islamic conquests, see: Donner, Fred, *Muhammad and the Believers: At the Origins of Islam*, Cambridge, MA: The Belknap Press of Harvard University Press, 2010, pp. 92–133; and in greater detail: idem, *Early Islamic Conquests*, Princeton: Princeton University Press, 1981.

4. Humphreys, R. Stephen, *Mu'awiya Ibn Abi Sufyan: From Arabia to Empire*, Oxford: Oneworld, 2006; on the topic of governance: Foss, Clive, "Mu'āwiya's State," *Money, Power and Politics in Early Islamic Syria*, Haldon, ed., pp. 75–96.

5. For a brisk introduction to the Umayyad period and its rulers, see: Hawting, Gerald R., *First Dynasty of Islam: The Umayyad Caliphate AD 661–750*, London: Routledge, 2000; Cobb, Paul M., "The Empire in Syria, 705–763," *The New Cambridge History of Islam. Volume 1*, pp. 226–69.

6. Blankinship, Khalid Yahya, *The End of the Jihâd State: The Reign of Hishâm Ibn 'Abd al-Malik and the Collapse of the Umayyads*, Albany: State University of New York Press, 1994, pp. 49–50.

7. On the archaeology of early Islamic Syria, see the overview of the field: Walmsley, Alan, *Early Islamic Syria: An Archaeological Assessment*,

London: Duckworth, 2007; Schick, Robert, *The Christian Communities of Palestine from Byzantine to Islamic Rule: A Historical and Archaeological Study*, Princeton: Darwin Press, 1995; Morony, Michael G., "Economic Boundaries: Late Antiquity and Early Islam," *Journal of the Economic and Social History of the Orient* 47 (2004), pp. 166–94; also: Haldon, "Greater Syria," pp. 8–9; and for urbanism in the early period, an article whose importance has endured despite the many subsequent challenges to its thesis: Kennedy, Hugh, "From Polis to Madina: Urban Change in Late Antique and Early Islamic Syria," *Past and Present* 106 (1985), pp. 3–27; and a more recent review of the issue: Avni, Gideon, "'From Polis to Madina' Revisited—Urban Change in Byzantine and early Islamic Palestine," *Journal of the Royal Asiatic Society*, Third Series, 21 (2011), pp. 301–29.

8. On the makeup of the Syrian elites before and after the Arab conquests, see: Kennedy, Hugh, "Syrian Elites from Byzantium to Islam: Survival or Extinction," *Money, Power and Politics in Early Islamic Syria*, Haldon, ed., pp. 181–200.

9. There were several exceptions: Walmsley, *Early Islamic Syria*, p. 105.

10. For translation and discussion of the blocked doorway, see: Burns, Ross, *Monuments of Syria: An Historical Guide*, London: I.B. Tauris, 1999, p. 84.

11. Dussaud, René, "Le temple de Jupiter Damascénien et ses transformations aux époques chrétienne et musulmane," *Syria* 3 (1922), pp. 219–50.

12. Nasrallah, Joseph, "De la cathédrale de Damas à la mosquée omayyade," *La Syrie de Byzance à l'Islam VIIe-VIIIe siècles*, Canivet and Rey-Coquais, eds, pp. 139–44.

13. The anecdote is cited in Khalek, Nancy, *Damascus after the Muslim Conquest: Text and Image in Early Islam*, New York: Oxford University Press, 2011, p. 48.

14. On the cult of St John the Baptist in Damascus, see: Khalek, *Damascus after the Muslim Conquest*, pp. 85–134; for the discovery of the head: pp. 113–14.

15. On the history of the mosque generally, and its decorative elements, specifically: Flood, Finbarr Barry, *The Great Mosque of Damascus: Studies on the Makings of an Umayyad Visual Culture*, Boston: Brill, 2000.

16. Byron, Robert, *The Road to Oxiana*, with a new preface by Rory Stewart, Oxford: Oxford University Press, 2007, p. 39.

17. A famous palimpsest from the period is an early medieval Bible from

Mt Sinai, which preserves layers of writing in Arabic, Greek, and Syriac throughout the manuscript, a testament to linguistic change as much as to cultural change at the time: Evans, Helen C., ed., with Brandie Ratliff, *Byzantium and Islam: Age of Transition, 7th-9th Century*, New York: Metropolitan Museum of Art, with Yale University Press, 2012, p. 61.

18. On the early history of Shi'ism, and its roots among the Companions of the Prophet: Madelung, Wilferd, *The Succession to Muḥammad: A Study of the Early Caliphate*, New York: Cambridge University Press, 1997; Dakake, Maria, *The Charismatic Community: Shi'ite Identity in Early Islam*, Albany: State University of New York Press, 2007; as well as the seminal article, which continues to spark debate among scholars: Hodgson, Marshall, "How did the Early Shī'a Become Sectarian?" *Journal of the American Oriental Society* 75 (1955), pp. 1–13.

19. On the spiritual and political authority of the Umayyad caliphs, who styled themselves "caliphs of God," see: Crone, Patricia and Martin Hinds, *God's Caliph: Religious Authority in the First Centuries of Islam*, Cambridge: Cambridge University Press, 1986.

20. On contemporary tensions surrounding this place, as well as the growing presence of the Shi'a in Syria in recent decades: Pierret, Thomas, "Karbala in the Umayyad Mosque: Sunni Panic at the 'Shiitization' of Syria," *The Dynamics of Sunni-Shia Relationships: Doctrines, Transnationalism, Intellectuals and the Media*, Brigitte Maréchal and Sami Zemni, eds, Hurst: London, 2013, pp. 99–116.

21. For more on the celebration of 'Ashura in modern Lebanon, see: Weiss, Max, *In the Shadow of Sectarianism: Law, Shi'ism, and the Making of Modern Lebanon*, Cambridge, MA: Harvard University Press, 2010, pp. 61–91.

22. For general description: Burns, *The Monuments of Syria*, pp. 99–100; Sourdel-Thomine, Janine, "Les anciens lieux de pèlerinage damascains d'après les sources arabes," *Bulletin d'études orientales* 14 (1952–54), pp. 65–85, here: 77–9. Regarding the construction of the present shrines in the late Ottoman period, now: Mulder, Stephennie. "Abdülhamid and the 'Alids: Ottoman Patronage of 'Shi'i' Shrines in the Cemetery of Bāb al-Ṣaghīr in Damascus," *Studia Islamica* 108 (2013), pp. 16–47.

23. My analysis draws on the insights of: Fowden, Garth, *Quṣayr 'Amra: Art and the Umayyad Elite in Late Antique Syria*, Berkeley: University of California Press, 2004.

24. Given that many of the historical sources used to reconstruct Umayyad history were written by 'Abbasid authors, who did not smile on their predecessors, scholars have taken recently to studying how the Umayyads were depicted in hindsight, as opposed to how they actually lived and operated; for example, see: Borrut, Antoine, *Entre mémoire et pouvoir: L'espace syrien sous les derniers Omeyyades et les premiers Abbasides (v. 72–193/692–809)*, Leiden: Brill, 2011; and the related collection of essays: Borrut, Antoine and Paul M. Cobb, eds, *Umayyad Legacies: Medieval Memories from Syria to Spain*, Leiden: Brill, 2010.

25. Crone and Hinds, *God's Caliph*, p. 39.

26. On divisions among the early Islamic elite and competing visions of leadership, see: Hinds, Martin, "Kûfan Political Alignments," *International Journal of Middle East Studies* 2 (1971), pp. 346–67; idem, "The Murder of the Caliph 'Uthmân," *International Journal of Middle East Studies* 3 (1972), pp. 450–69; and a helpful overview of these and other alignments: Kennedy, Hugh, *The Prophet and the Age of the Caliphates: The Islamic Near East from the Sixth to the Eleventh Century*, Harlow: Longman, 2004, pp. 50–81.

27. For more on the Arab character of the dynasty, see the classic study: Wellhausen, Julius, *The Arab Kingdom and its Fall*, Margaret Graham Weir, trans., London: Routledge, 2000 (published originally as: *Arabische Reich und sein Sturz*, Berlin: Reimer, 1902). For an important article on the intertribal rivalries that plagued the Umayyad caliphs: Crone, Patricia, "Were the Qays and Yemen of the Umayyad Period Political Parties?," *Der Islam* 71 (1994), pp. 1–57.

28. For good introductory material on the 'Abbasid revolution, see: Kennedy, *The Prophet and the Age of the Caliphates*, pp. 112–32; Sharon, Moshe, *Black Banners from the East: The Establishment of the 'Abbāsid State: Incubation of a Revolt*, Jerusalem: Magnes Press, Hebrew University with Brill, 1983. On the early 'Abbasid caliphate generally: El Hibri, Tayeb, "The Empire in Iraq, 763–861," *The New Cambridge History of Islam. Volume 1*, pp. 269–304.

29. See the famous article: Moscati, Sabatino, "Le massacre des Umayyades dans l'histoire et dans les fragments poétiques," *Archiv orientální* 18 (1950), pp. 88–115.

30. Cobb, Paul M., *White Banners: Contention in 'Abbāsid Syria, 750–880*, Albany: State University of New York Press, 2001.

2. ONCE "OUR LAND": CHRISTIANITY IN SYRIA

1. The Arab conquests spurred the production of Christian apocalyptic texts in greater Syria, the most famous of which was the Apocalypse of Pseudo-Methodius, written in Syriac around the turn of the eighth century. Text and German translation: Reinink, G.J., ed., *Die syrische Apokalypse des Pseudo-Methodius*, 2 vols, Louvain: Peeters, 1993; idem, "Pseudo-Methodius: A Concept of History in Response to the Rise of Islam," *The Byzantine and Early Islamic Near East: Vol. 1: Problems in the Literary Source Material*, A. Cameron and L.I. Conrad, eds, Princeton: The Darwin Press, 1992, pp. 149–87. Soon after its composition, the Apocalypse was translated into Greek and Latin, an edn of which has recently appeared: Garstad, Benjamin, trans., *Apocalypse: An Alexandrian World Chronicle*, Cambridge, MA: Harvard University Press, 2012.

2. Scholars have proposed various theories for the date of the text. According to the first study of the document, it came from the eighth century: Violet, Bruno, "Ein zweispachiges Psalmfragment aus Damascus," *Orientalistische Literaturzeitung* 10 and 11 (1901), pp. 384–423, 425–88. Subsequent studies argued for no later than 710 AD: Haddad, Rachid, "La phonétique de l'arabe chrétien vers 700," *La Syrie de Byzance à l'Islam*, Canivet and Rey-Coquais, eds, pp. 159–64. The late ninth or early tenth century: Mavroudi, Maria, "Arabic Words in Greek Letters: The Violet Fragment and More," *Proceedings of the First International Symposium on Middle Arabic and Mixed Arabic Throughout History, Louvain-la-Neuve 11–14 May 2004*, J. Grand'Henry and J. Lentin eds, Louvain: Peeters, 2008, pp. 321–54. And most recently, to as early as the fourth or fifth century AD: Al-Jallad, Ahmad M., *Ancient Levantine Arabic: A Reconstruction Based on the Earliest Sources and the Modern Dialects* (forthcoming); I thank Ahmad Al-Jallad for providing me with an advance copy of his chapter on the Psalm fragment.

3. Burns, *Monuments of Syria*, p. 97.

4. Doran, Robert, trans., *The Life of Symeon Stylites*, Kalamazoo, MI: Cistercian Publications, 1992, p. 76–7; discussion MacMullen, Ramsay, *Christianizing the Roman Empire (A.D. 100–400)*, New Haven: Yale University Press, 1984, pp. 1–2.

5. The study of "holy men" like Symeon has been among the most productive fields of research in the history of late antiquity. See the following foundational articles: Brown, Peter R.L., "The Rise and Function of the Holy Man in Late Antiquity," *Journal of Roman Studies* 61

(1971), pp. 80–101; idem, "The Rise and Function of the Holy Man in Late Antiquity, 1971–1997," *Journal of Early Christian Studies* 6 (1998), pp. 353–76.

6. For more on the church of St Symeon, see: Krautheimer, Richard with Slobodan Ćurčić, *Early Christian and Byzantine Architecture*, 2ⁿᵈ edn, New Haven: Yale University Press, 1986, pp. 137–56. For a famous archaeological survey of the region and its many Byzantine remains, see: Tchalenko, Georges, *Villages antiques de la Syrie du Nord: Le massif du Bélus à l'époque romaine*, 3 vols, Paris: Geuthner, 1953–58; more recently: Wickham, Chris, *Framing the Early Middle Ages: Europe and the Mediterranean, 400–800*, Oxford: Oxford University Press, 2005, pp. 443–59.

7. Wilkinson, John, trans., *Egeria's Travels: Newly Translated (from the Latin) with Supporting Documents and Notes*, London: S.P.C.K., 1971, p. 137.

8. My thinking here has been influenced by: Fowden, Garth, *From Empire to Commonwealth: The Consequences of Monotheism in Late Antiquity*, Princeton: Princeton University Press, 1993.

9. For excellent overviews of the Arian controversy and the Council of Nicaea: Hanson, R.P.C., *The Search for the Christian Doctrine of God: The Arian Controversy, 318–381*, Edinburgh: T. & T. Clark, 1988; Chadwick, Henry, *Early Church*, London: Penguin Books, 1967, pp. 125–51. Very little of the Arians' own theological writings survives; scholars are left to reconstruct them based largely on the descriptions of their opponents, the most important of which is the *De Incarnatione* of Athanasius of Alexandria (d. 373), accessible English translation: Saint Athanasius, *On the Incarnation*, Cestwood, NY: St Vladimir's Seminary Press, 2012.

10. For one of the best introductions to this complex subject, see: Chadwick, Henry, "Eucharist and Christology in the Nestorian Controversy," *Journal of Theological Studies*, New Series 2 (1951), pp. 145–64. The canons of the Council of Chalcedon are now available in an excellent English translation: Price, Richard and Michael Gaddis, trans., *The Acts of the Council of Chalcedon*, 3 vols, Liverpool: Liverpool University Press, 2005.

11. On the institutionalization of the Syrian Orthodox church in the wake of Chalcedon, see: Menze, Volker, *Justinian and the Making of the Syrian Orthodox Church*, Oxford: Oxford University Press, 2008.

12. Here I rely on the insights of: Tannous, Jack, "Syria between Byzantium and Islam: Making Incommensurables Speak," Unpublished PhD dissertation, Princeton University, 2010, pp. 213–86.

13. Khalek, *Damascus after the Muslim Conquest*, p. 49.

14. For several good introductions to relations between Christians and Muslims in the medieval period, see: Levy-Rubin, Milka, *Non-Muslims in the Early Islamic Empire: From Surrender to Coexistence*, Cambridge: Cambridge University Press, 2011; Griffith, Sidney H., *The Church in the Shadow of the Mosque: Christians and Muslims in the World of Islam*, Princeton: Princeton University Press, 2008; Fattal, Antoine, *Statut légal des non-musulmans en pays d'Islam*, 2nd edn, Beirut: Dar El-Machreq, 1995; Tritton, A.S., *Caliphs and their Non-Muslim Subjects: A Critical Study of the Covenant of 'Umar*, London: Oxford University Press, 1930.

15. The basic work in English is: Bulliet, Richard, *Conversion to Islam in the Medieval Period: An Essay in Quantitative History*, Cambridge, MA: Harvard University Press, 1979. See too the important collection of essays: Gervers, Michael and Ramzi Jibran Bikhazi, eds, *Conversion and Continuity: Indigenous Christian Communities in Islamic Lands, Eighth to Eighteenth Centuries*, Toronto: Pontifical Institute of Medieval Studies, 1990. Also: Wasserstein, David J., "Conversion and the Ahl al-Dhimma," *The New Cambridge History of Islam: Volume 4, Islamic Cultures and Societies to the End of the Eighteenth Century*, Robert Irwin, ed., Cambridge: Cambridge University Press, 2010, pp. 184–208; Humphreys, R. Stephen, "Christian Communities in Early Islamic Syria: Dynamics of Adaptation," *Money, Power and Politics in Early Islamic Syria*, J. Haldon, ed, pp. 45–56.

16. Dennett, Daniel C., *Conversion and the Poll Tax in Early Islam*, Cambridge, MA: Harvard University Press, 1950.

17. The famous verse (Quran 9:29) reads: "Fight against those who do not believe in God or the Last Day, and who do not forbid what God has forbidden by His messenger, and who do not observe the religion of truth, until they consent to pay the *jizya* willingly, being made low."

18. The bibliography on apostasy in Islamic culture is vast. For orientation: Heffening, W., "Murtadd," *The Encyclopedia of Islam, Second Edn*, Hamilton Gibb *et al.*, eds, 13 vols, Leiden: Brill, 1954–2005, here: Vol. 7, pp. 635–6; Hallaq, Wael, "Apostasy," *Encyclopedia of the Quran*, Jane Dammen McAuliffe, ed., 5 vols, Leiden: Brill, 2001–2006, here: Vol. 1, pp. 119–22; Griffel, Frank, "Apostasy," *Encyclopedia of Islam Three*, Marc Gaborieau *et al.*, eds, Leiden: Brill, 2007-, here: 2007, Vol. 1, pp. 131–4; Peters, Rudolph and Gert J.J. De Vries, "Apostasy in Islam," *Die Welt des Islams* New Series 17, 1 (1976),

pp. 1–25; Kraemer, Joel L. "Apostates, Rebels, and Brigands," *Israel Oriental Studies* 10 (1980), pp. 34–73, esp. 36–48; Friedmann, Yohanan, *Tolerance and Coercion in Islam: Interfaith Relations in the Muslim Tradition.* Cambridge: Cambridge University Press, 2003, pp. 121–59; Cook, David, "Apostasy from Islam," *Jerusalem Studies in Arabic and Islam* 31 (2006), pp. 248–88; Simonsohn, Uri, "'Halting Between Two Opinions': Conversion and Apostasy in Early Islam," *Medieval Encounters* 19 (2013), pp. 344–72.

19. For a recent argument along these lines, see: Donner, *Muhammad and the Believers*, esp. pp. 56–89.

20. This is the topic of my forthcoming doctoral dissertation at Princeton University. For introductions to the subject, see: Hoyland, Robert, *Seeing Islam as Others Saw It*, Princeton: The Darwin Press, 1997, pp. 336–86; Griffith, Sidney H., "Christians, Muslims, and Neo-Martyrs: Saints' Lives and Holy Land History," *Sharing the Sacred: Religious Contacts and Conflicts in the Holy Land, First-Fifteenth Centuries CE*, Kofsky, Arieh and Guy G. Stroumsa, eds, Jerusalem: Yad Izhak Ben Zvi, 1998, pp. 163–207; Vila, David H., "Christian Martyrs in the First Abbasid Century and the Development of an Apologetic Against Islam," Unpublished PhD dissertation, St Louis University, 1999; Foss, Clive, "Byzantine Saints in Early Islamic Syria," *Analecta Bollandiana* 125 (2007), pp. 93–119; Binggeli, André, "Converting the Caliph: A Legendary Motif in Christian Hagiography and Historiography of the Early Islamic Period," *Writing 'True Stories': Historians and Hagiographers in the Late Antique and Medieval Near East*, Arietta Papaconstantinou with Muriel Debié and Hugh Kennedy, eds, Turnhout: Brepols, 2010, pp. 77–103.

21. Eulogius of Cordoba, "Liber apologeticus martyrum," *Patrologia Latina*, J.-P. Migne, ed., 221 vols, 1844–64, here: Vol. 115, p. 862 (in which he calls the Muslim prayer an *impietatis ruditum*).

22. For good introductions to the history of Syriac language and culture, as well as its place in the contemporary Middle East, see: Brock, Sebastian with David G.K. Taylor, eds, *The Hidden Pearl: The Syrian Orthodox Church and its Ancient Aramaic Heritage*, 4 vols, Rome: Trans World Film Italia, 2001. Also: Brock, Sebastian, *An Introduction to Syriac Studies*, 2nd edn, Piscataway: Gorgias Press, 2006. The field of Syriac studies in English in recent decades owes much to this foundational work: Murray, Robert, *Symbols of Church and Kingdom: A Study in Early Syriac Tradition*, London: Cambridge University Press,

1975. On language change in the early Islamic Middle East, see: Wasserstein, David J., "Why Did Arabic Succeed Where Greek Failed? Language Change in the Near East after Muhammad," *Scripta Classica Israelica* 22 (2003), pp. 257–72; Hoyland, Robert, "Language and Identity: The Twin Histories of Arabic and Aramaic (and: Why Did Aramaic Succeed Where Greek Failed?)," *Scripta Classica Israelica* 23 (2004), pp. 183–99.

23. See, for example: Payne, Richard, "Monks, Dinars and Date Palms: Hagiographical Production and the Expansion of Monastic Institutions in the Early Islamic Persian Gulf," *Arabian Archaeology and Epigraphy* 22 (2011), pp. 97–111; Carter, R.A., "Christianity in the Gulf during the First Centuries of Islam," *Arabian Archaeology and Epigraphy* 19 (2008), pp. 71–108.

24. Dalrymple, William, *From the Holy Mountain: A Journey in the Shadow of Byzantium*, London: HarperCollins, 1997, pp. 186–91.

25. For the important studies of the topic, see: Nöldeke, Theodor, "Hatte Muhammad christliche Lehrer?," *Zeitschrift für Deutschen Morgenländischen Gesellschaft* 12 (1858), pp. 699–708; Carra de Vaux, Baron Bernard, "La légende de Bahira," *Revue de l'orient chrétien* 2 (1897), pp. 439–54; Gero, Stephen, "The Legend of the Monk Baḥīra, the Cult of the Cross and Iconoclasm," *La Syrie de Byzance à l'Islam*, Canivet, P. and J.-P. Rey-Coquais, eds, pp. 47–57; Szilágyi, Krisztina, "Muḥammad and the Monk: The Making of the Baḥīra Legend," *Jerusalem Studies in Arabic and Islam* 34 (2008), pp. 169–214; Roggema, Barbara, *The Legend of Sergius Baḥīrā: Eastern Christian Apologetics and Apocalyptic Response to Islam*, Leiden: Brill, 2009.

26. Al-Azdi, *Tarikh futuh al-Sham* [*History of the Conquest of Syria*], 'Abd al-Mun'im 'Abdullah 'Amir, ed., Cairo: Mu'assasat Sijil al-'Arab, 1970, pp. 115–16.

27. Quoted Dawn, C. Ernest, "From Ottomanism to Arabism: The Origin of an Ideology," *The Modern Middle East: A Reader*, Hourani, Albert, Philip Khoury, and Mary C. Wilson, eds, London: I.B. Tauris, 2004, pp. 375–93, here: p. 388.

28. On the events of 1860 and their role in forging a "sectarian" culture on Mount Lebanon, see: Makdisi, Ussama, *The Culture of Sectarianism: Community, History and Violence in Nineteenth Century Mount Lebanon*, Berkeley: University of California Press, 2000.

29. On the spillover of violence from Mount Lebanon into Damascus, especially to Christian areas such as Bab Touma: Fawaz, Leila Tarazi,

An Occasion for War: Civil Conflict in Lebanon and Damascus in 1860, London: Centre for Lebanese Studies, with I.B. Tauris, 1994; and on conflicting memories of the violence: Rogan, Eugene, "Sectarianism and Social Conflict in Damascus: The 1860 Events Reconsidered," *Arabica* 51 (2004), pp. 493–511.

3. OUTSIDERS BECOME INSIDERS: SECTARIANISM IN SYRIA

1. Full quote: "I believe that the earth is very large and that we who dwell between the Pillars of Hercules and the river Phasis live in a small part of it about the sea, like ants or frogs about a pond, and that many other people live in many other regions"; see: Plato, *Phaedo*, 109a-b; Lamb, W.R.M., trans., *Plato in Twelve Volumes*, Cambridge, MA: Harvard University Press, 1966, here: Vol. 1, pp. 374–5.
2. Stein, Gertrude, *Everybody's Autobiography*, New York: Random House, 1937, p. 289.
3. For a good overview of the demography and geography of Syria's sects, as well as their role in political life over the past fifty years, see: Dam, Nikolaos van, *The Struggle for Power in Syria: Politics and Society under Asad and the Ba'th Party*, 4th edn, London: I.B. Tauris, 2011, esp. pp. 1–14.
4. The view is summed up at various points in the useful survey of modern Middle Eastern history: Gelvin, James, *The Modern Middle East: A History*, 3rd edn, New York: Oxford University Press, 2011, pp. 79–81, 96–9, 193. See also: Makdisi, *The Culture of Sectarianism*, especially the introduction, pp. 1–14.
5. To provide but two examples see the 13th/14th century polemical tract in Arabic that accuses Christians and Jews of various kinds of political disloyalty, with respect to Mongols and Crusaders. It is clear that for its author, religious identity is one of the main dividing and uniting principles of social and political life: Gottheil, Richard, "An Answer to the Dhimmis," *Journal of the American Oriental Society* 41 (1921), pp. 383–457. There was also a longstanding discussion among medieval Muslim scholars about the permissibility of non-Muslims serving in the Muslim state—most were skeptical of their loyalties; see: Yarbrough, Luke B., "Upholding God's Rule: Origins of Juristic Opposition to the State Employment of Non-Muslims," *Islamic Law and Society* 19 (2012), pp. 11–85.
6. For example, early Muslims believed that a righteous imam—or caliph—had the power to lead his caravan of followers to salvation,

while a misguided imam was destined to lead his caravan to perdition; see: Crone, Patricia, *God's Rule: Government and Islam*, New York: Columbia University Press, pp. 21–3.

7. Burns, *Monuments of Syria*, pp. 116–20; and the recent collections of essays: Brody, Lisa R. and Gail L. Hoffman, eds, *Dura-Europos: Crossroads of Antiquity*, Chestnut Hill, MA: McMullen Museum of Art—Boston College, 2011; Chi, Jennifer Y. and Sebastian Heath, eds, *Edge of Empires: Pagans, Jews, and Christians at Roman Dura Europos*, New York: Institute for the Study of the Ancient World, 2011.

8. On the art of these buildings, see: Weitzmann, Kurt and Herbert Kessler, *Frescoes of the Dura Synagogue and Christian Art*, Washington, DC: Dumbarton Oaks Research Library and Collection, 1990.

9. For introductions to 'Alawi history and thought, see: Halm, Heinz, "Nuṣayriyya," *Encyclopedia of Islam, Second Edn*, Vol. 8, pp. 145–8; Bar Asher, Meir and Aryeh Kofsky, *The Nuṣayrī-'Alawī Religion: An Enquiry into its Theology and Liturgy*, Leiden: Brill, 2002; Friedman, Yaron, *Nuṣayrī-'Alawīs: An Introduction to the Religion, History and Identity of the Leading Minority in Syria*, Leiden: Brill, 2010; Winter, Stefan, *The 'Alawis of Syria: A Secular History* (forthcoming); I thank Stefan Winter for sharing with me a chapter of his unpublished work.

10. For the complex social, political, and legal relationships between Muslims and non-Muslims in the late Ottoman empire, see: Reilly, James A., "Inter-confessional Relations in Nineteenth-Century Syria: Damascus, Homs, and Hama Compared," *Islam and Christian-Muslim Relations* 7 (1996), pp. 213–24; Al-Qattan, Najwa, "Dhimmis in the Muslim Court: Legal Autonomy and Religious Discrimination," *International Journal of Middle East Studies* 31 (1999), pp. 429–44; eadem, "Litigants and Neighbors: The Communal Topography of Ottoman Damascus," *Comparative Studies in Society and History* 44 (2002), pp. 511–33.

11. On the *Tanzimat* generally, see: Hanioğlu, Şükrü, *A Brief History of the Late Ottoman Empire*, Princeton: Princeton University Press, 2008, pp. 72–108; Findley, Carter, *Turkey, Islam, Nationalism, and Modernity: A History, 1789–2007*, New Haven: Yale University Press, 2010, pp. 76–132. For two classic, but now slightly outdated views: Lewis, Bernard, *The Emergence of Modern Turkey*, Oxford: Oxford University Press, 1961, pp. 74–128; Berkes, Niyazi, *The Development of Secularism in Turkey*, Montreal: McGill University Press, 1964, pp. 89–250.

12. For English translation of the document, see: Hurewitz, J.C., ed., *The Middle East and North Africa in World Politics: A Documentary Record*, 2nd edn, 2 vols, New Haven: Yale University Press, 1975, Vol. 1, pp. 269–71.

13. For English translation of the document, see: Hurewitz, *The Middle East and North Africa in World Politics*, Vol. 1, pp. 315–18.

14. For discussion of the impact of the *Tanzimat* on the minorities of the Ottoman Empire, especially in Arab lands: Rogan, Eugene, *The Arabs: A History*, New York: Basic Books, 2009, pp. 88–98; Masters, Bruce, *The Arabs of the Ottoman Empire, 1516–1918: A Social and Cultural History*, Cambridge: Cambridge University Press, 2013, pp. 157–91.

15. For an excellent study of this process, especially among the Christians of northern Syria, see: Masters, Bruce, *Christians and Jews in the Ottoman Arab World: The Roots of Sectarianism*, Cambridge: Cambridge University Press, 2001.

16. Makdisi, Ussama, *Artillery of Heaven: American Missionaries and the Failed Conversion of the Middle East*, Ithaca, NY: Cornell University Press, 2008; idem, *The Culture of Sectarianism*, pp. 88–94.

17. Braude, Benjamin, "Foundation Myths of the Millet System," *Christians and Jews in the Ottoman Empire: The Functioning of a Plural System*, Benjamin Braude and Bernard Lewis, eds, 2 vols, New York: Holmes and Meier, 1982, Vol. 1, pp. 69–88.

18. Masters, Bruce, "The 1850 Events in Aleppo: An Aftershock of Syria's Incorporation into the Capitalist World System," *The International Journal of Middle East Studies* 22 (1990), pp. 3–20; with further comment idem, *Christians and Jews*, pp. 130–68.

19. One can see the plurality of ideologies generated by the reform era in the competing movements that gripped the Ottoman Empire just before and during the war: Kayalı, Hasan, *Arabs and Young Turks: Ottomanism, Arabism, and Islamism in the Ottoman Empire, 1908–1918*, Berkeley: University of California Press, 1997.

20. On the reign of Abdülhamid, generally, see: Hanioğlu, *A Brief History of the Late Ottoman Empire*, pp. 109–49; Findley, *Turkey, Islam, Nationalism, and Modernity*, pp. 133–91.

21. My thinking here is greatly influenced by: Deringil, Selim, *The Well-Protected Domains: Ideology and Legitimation of Power in the Ottoman Empire, 1876–1909*, London: I.B. Tauris, 1998; also, see: Fortna, Benjamin, *Imperial Classroom: Islam, the State, and Education in the Late Ottoman Empire*, Oxford: Oxford University Press, 2002.

22. Deringil, *Well-Protected Domains*, p. 75.

23. Though now outdated, the essential study of the *Nahda* period remains: Hourani, Albert, *Arabic Thought in a Liberal Age, 1798–1939*, London: Oxford University Press, 1962; on the rise of Arab nationalist politics in the early twentieth century, see: Dawn, "From Ottomanism to Arabism"; Kayalı, *Arabs and Young Turks*; Watenpaugh, Keith David, *Being Modern in the Middle East: Revolution, Nationalism, Colonialism and the Arab Middle Class*, Princeton: Princeton University Press, 2006. On competing scholarly approaches to origins of Arab nationalism: Khalidi, Rashid, "Arab Nationalism: Historical Problems in the Literature," *American Historical Review* 96 (1991), pp. 1363–73. For an early effort to record the history of the Arab nationalist movement—as much a work of scholarship as one of advocacy by one of Arabism's most impassioned supporters: Antonius, George, *The Arab Awakening: The Story of the Arab National Movement*, Philadelphia: J.B. Lippincott Company, 1939.

24. My analysis owes to: Provence, Michael, *The Great Syrian Revolt and the Rise of Arab Nationalism*, Austin: University of Texas Press, 2005.

25. On the culture of the urban notables in Syria, who facilitated Ottoman rule and, later, the French Mandate, see the foundational article: Hourani, Albert, "Ottoman Reform and the Politics of Notables," *The Modern Middle East: A Reader*, pp. 83–109; also: Khoury, Philip, *Urban Notables and Arab Nationalism: The Politics of Damascus, 1860–1920*, Cambridge: Cambridge University Press, 1983; idem, *Syria and the French Mandate: The Politics of Arab Nationalism, 1920–1945*, Princeton: Princeton University Press, 1987. It is best to see Provence, *The Great Syrian Revolt*, partly as a reaction to the work of Khoury, who regards the urban aristocracy as playing the key role in nationalist activity in the inter-war period; Dawn attributes it to humbler groups in society, including the Druze.

26. For more on 'Aflaq and early Baathist history, see: Kamel, Abu Jaber, with forward by Philip K. Hitti, *The Arab Ba'th Socialist Party: History, Ideology, and Organization*, Syracuse: Syracuse University Press, 1966, pp. 1–32; Devlin, John F., *The Ba'th Party: A History from its Origins to 1966*, Hoover Institution Press: Stanford, CA, 1975, pp. 1–22; Heydemann, Steven, *Authoritarianism in Syria: Institutions and Social Conflict, 1946–1970*, Ithaca, NY: Cornell University Press, 1999; also: Haim, Sylvia, ed., *Arab Nationalism: An Anthology*, Berkeley: University of California Press, 1976, pp. 3–72, 242–9; for general Baathist history, in Iraq and in Syria: Batatu,

Hanna, *The Old Social Classes and the Revolutionary Movements of Iraq: A Study of Iraq's Old Landed Commercial Classes and of its Communists, Ba'thists, and Free Officers*, Princeton: Princeton University Press, 1978, pp. 722–48.

27. 'Aflaq, Michel, *Fi sabil al-Ba'th* [*In the Way of the Ba'th*], Beirut: Dar al-Tali'a, 1963, pp. 122–33; see in the same book 'Aflaq's speech, "The Eternal Arab Message," pp. 97–105.

28. *Ba'th Regional Command Collection*, 3156_0000 (0101–0111), Hoover Institution, Stanford University, March 1995; I thank Samuel Helfont for this reference.

29. On the role of the 'Alawis in Syria during the French Mandate, see: Seale, Patrick, *Asad of Syria: The Struggle for the Middle East*, London: I.B. Tauris, 1988, pp. 14–23; Moosa, Matti, *Extremist Shiites: The Ghulat Sects*, Syracuse, NY: Syracuse University Press, 1987, pp. 280–91. Generally: White, Benjamin Thomas, *The Emergence of Minorities in the Middle East: The Politics of Community in French Mandate Syria*, Edinburgh: Edinburgh University Press, 2011.

30. For further discussion of the 'Alawite region during the Mandate period, especially its changing administrative status and the political movements inside it see Rabinovich, *The View from Damascus*, pp. 81–110; the anecdote about the grandfather of Hafez al-Asad comes from Doran, Michael, "Syria's Coming Sectarian Crack-Up," *The Wall Street Journal*, 13 August 2012.

31. On the rise of the Baath Party among Syria's peasant classes, with comment on the role of the minority communities and the presidency of Hafez al-Asad, it see: Batatu, Hanna, *Syria's Peasantry, the Descendants of its Lesser Rural Notables, and their Politics*, Princeton: Princeton University Press, 1999.

32. Van Dam, *The Struggle for Power in Syria*, pp. 76–7.

33. See now, Lefèvre, Raphaël, *Ashes of Hama: The Muslim Brotherhood in Syria*, London: Hurst, 2013.

34. "Wathiqa: 'Ahd wa-mithaq Ikhwan fi Suriya" [Document: The Covenant and Pact of the Brotherhood in Syria], *Al-Jazeera Net*, 25 March 2012; accessible online: http://www.aljazeera.net/news/pages/3d4903fd-26a7–4979–8dc7-d3f05a9ffd9a

35. For discussion of the incident, see: Rogan, *The Arabs*, p. 406; the most thorough analysis of the Islamist uprising that followed the attack is: Lobmeyer, Hans Günter, *Opposition und Widerstand in Syrien*, Hamburg: Deutsches Orient-Institut, 1995.

4. GUARDIANS OF THE HOMELAND: STATE AND SOCIETY IN SYRIA

1. On the great pilgrimage site of St Sergius at Rusafa: Fowden, Elizabeth Key, *The Barbarian Plain: Saint Sergius between Rome and Iran*, Berkeley: University of California Press, 1999, pp. 60–100.

2. On the Umayyad complex at Qasr al-Hayr al-Sharqi: Grabar, Oleg, ed., *City in the Desert: Qasr al-Hayr East*, Cambridge, MA: Center for Middle Eastern Studies of Harvard University, 1978.

3. For an excellent study of the cult of personality surrounding Hafez al-Asad, see: Wedeen, Lisa, *Ambiguities of Domination: Politics, Rhetoric, and Symbols in Contemporary Syria*, Chicago: University of Chicago Press, 1999.

4. The traditional image of the imperial cult—as shaped by accounts of Christian martyrdom—was challenged by Simon Price, who argued that Greek cities embraced the cult in order to make sense of their subjugation by an outside power, less because the imperial court needed to enforce loyalty among its subjects: Price, S.R.F., *Rituals and Power: The Roman Imperial Cult in Asia Minor*, Cambridge: Cambridge University Press, 1984.

5. For the question of the dissimulation of political beliefs in favor of the regime-sanctioned beliefs, see: Wedeen, Lisa, "Acting 'As If': Symbolic Politics and Social Control in Syria," *Comparative Studies in Society and History* 40 (1998), pp. 503–523; and in the aforementioned book: eadem, *Ambiguities of Domination*, pp. 67–86.

6. Madison, Lucy, "Clinton: No military action for now," *CBS News: Face the Nation*, 27 March 2011; accessible online: http://www.cbsnews.com/8301–3460_162–20047627/clinton-no-military-action-in-syria-for-now/

7. Buck, Joan Juliet, "A Rose in the Desert," *Vogue* [US edn], March 2011; the article provoked such controversy that *Vogue* removed the article from its online servers; a website belonging to an employee of the Syrian government news agency hosted an electronic version independently for a time, but this too has disappeared. For coverage of the article and *Vogue's* attempts to quell the firestorm, see: Fisher, Max, "Vogue Defends Profile of Syrian First Lady," *The Atlantic*, 28 February 2011, accessible online: http://www.theatlantic.com/international/archive/2011/02/vogue-defends-profile-of-syrian-first-lady/71764/; Weiss, Bari and David Feith, "The Dictator's Wife Wears Louboutins," *The Wall Street Journal*, 7 March 2011, accessible online: http://online.wsj.com/article/SB10001424052748704506004576174 6

23822364258.html; a subsequent explanation by the author of the piece, who claimed to have been duped into writing it: Buck, Joan Juliet, "Syria's Fake First Family," *Newsweek*, 30 July 2012, accessible online: http://www.thedailybeast.com/newsweek/2012/07/29/joan-juliet-buck-my-vogue-interview-with-syria-s-first-lady.html; on efforts to remove the piece from the Internet: Fisher, Max, "The Only Remaining Online copy of Vogue's Asma al-Assad Profile," *The Atlantic*, 3 January 2012, accessible online: http://www.theatlantic.com/international/archive/2012/01/the-only-remaining-online-copy-of-vogues-asma-al-assad-profile/250753/

8. Shaaban, Bouthaina, "The Navi and the Palestinians," *CounterPunch*, 5–7 March 2010, accessible online: http://www.counterpunch.org/2010/03/05/the-navi-and-the-palestinians/. Shaaban has recently published her memoirs from the final years of Hafez al-Asad's reign as president: eadem, *Damascus Diary: An Inside Account of Hafez al-Assad's Peace Diplomacy, 1990–2000*, Boulder, CO: Lynne Rienner, 2013.

9. Kershner, Isabel, "Israeli Soldiers Shoot at Protesters on Syrian Border," *The New York Times*, 5 June 2011, accessible online: http://www.nytimes.com/2011/06/06/world/middleeast/06mideast.html?pagewanted=all

10. For a detailed description of the conflict: Oren, Michael, *Six Days of War: June 1967 and the Making of the Modern Middle East*, Oxford: Oxford University Press, 2002.

11. Burns, *Monuments of Syria*, pp. 162–75; Browning, Iain, *Palmyra*, London: Chatto and Windus, 1979; also: Seyrig, Henri, Robert Amy, and Ernest Will, *Temple de Bêl à Palmyre*, 2 vols, Paris: Librairie Orientaliste Paul Geuthner, 1975.

12. Young, Gary K., *Rome's Eastern Trade: International Commerce and Imperial Policy, 31 BC–AD 305*, London: Routledge, 2001, pp. 136–86.

13. For the general context: Bowersock, Glen W., *Roman Arabia*, Cambridge, MA: Harvard University Press, 1983, pp. 123–37. A recent biography: Southern, Pat, *Empress Zenobia: Palmyra's Rebel Queen*, London: Hambledon Continuum, 2008; Stoneman, Richard, *Palmyra and its Empire: Zenobia's Revolt against Rome*, Ann Arbor, MI: University of Michigan Press, 1992. On the afterlife of Zenobia as a literary and cultural figure, see: Winsbury, Rex, *Zenobia of Palmyra: History, Myth, and the Neoclassical Imagination*, London: Duckworth, 2010.

14. Tlass, Moustafa, *Zenobia, the Queen of Palmyra*, Damascus: Tlass House, 2000 (published originally as: *Zanubiya malikat Tadmur* [*Zenobia, the Queen of Tadmur*], 1985).

15. Rogan, *The Arabs*, pp. 405–6.

16. Kramer, Martin, "Syria's Alawis and Shi'ism," *Shi'ism, Resistance, and Revolution*, Martin Kramer, ed., Boulder, CO: Westview Press, 1987, pp. 237–54.

17. This and much of the following analysis owe to the insights of the following work: Pierret, Thomas, *Religion and State in Syria: The Sunni Ulama from Coup to Revolution*, Cambridge: Cambridge University Press, 2013; for Sa'id Ramadan al-Bouti, pp. 106–11.

18. On the changing status of Sunni scholars in Syria over the twentieth century, which provides the essential backdrop for these events, see: Commins, David Dean, *Islamic Reform: Politics and Social Change in Late Ottoman Syria*, New York: Oxford University Press, 1990.

19. Muir, Jim, "Syria 'death video' of Sheikh Bouti poses questions," *BBC News, Middle East*, 9 April 2013, accessible online: http://www.bbc. co.uk/news/world-middle-east-22086230

20. See the new biography of Qutb and his influence on the Muslim Brotherhood, among other groups: Calvert, John, *Sayyid Qutb and the Origins of Radical Islamism*, New York: Columbia University Press 2010; for Qutb's American sojourn, see pp. 139–56. For translation from Qutb's work, "The America I have seen", see the following anthology: Abdel Malek, Kamal and Mouna El Kahla, eds, *America in an Arab Mirror: Images of America in Arabic Travel Literature, 1668 to 9/11 and Beyond*, 2nd edn, New York: Palgrave Macmillan, 2011, pp. 20–22.

5. A VIEW FROM THE EDGE: WAR IN SYRIA

1. Solomon, Jay and Bill Spindle, "Syria Strongman: Time for 'Reform'," *The Wall Street Journal*, 31 January 2011, accessible online: http://online.wsj.com/article/SB10001424052748704832704576114340735033236.html

2. Kassir, Samir, *Beirut*, M.B. DeBevoise, trans., Berkeley: University of California Press, 2010, pp. 80–159; also: Hanssen, Jens, *Fin de siècle Beirut: The Making of an Ottoman Provincial Capital*, Oxford: Clarendon Press, 2005.

3. On the history of the Maronites generally, see: Moosa, Matti, *The Maronites in History*, Syracuse: Syracuse University Press, 1986.

4. My analysis owes much to the now classic work: Salibi, Kamal, *A House of Many Mansions: The History of Lebanon Reconsidered*, London: I.B. Tauris, 2009 (published originally 1988); and more recently: Firro, Kays, *Inventing Lebanon: Nationalism and the State under the Mandate*, London: I.B. Tauris, 2003. For a forceful articulation of the view of Syrian particularism—being neither Arab nor Muslim in character—penned by a Belgian Jesuit resident in Beirut in the early twentieth century see: Lammens, Henri, *La Syrie: précis historique*. 2 vols. Beirut: Imprimerie Catholique, 1921.

5. On the historical marginalization of Lebanon's Shi'i community, see: Ajami, Fouad, *The Vanished Imam: Musa al-Sadr and the Shia of Lebanon*, Ithaca, NY: Cornell University Press, 1986, pp. 52–84.

6. For general comment on the Palestinian refugees, many of whom went to Lebanon, see: Morris, Benny, *The Birth of the Palestinian Refugee Problem, 1947–1949*, Cambridge: Cambridge University Press, 1987.

7. For gripping accounts of the Lebanese Civil War by two esteemed journalists, see: Fisk, Robert, *Pity the Nation: Lebanon at War*, 3rd edn, Oxford: Oxford University Press, 2001; Friedman, Thomas, *From Beirut to Jerusalem*, New York: Farrar, Straus, Giroux, 1989.

8. On 'Aflaq, Saadeh, and the Greek Orthodox milieu from which they came, see: Sab', Mishal, *Sa'ada wa-'Aflaq fi al-fikr al-siyasi al-Urthudhuksi* [*Saadeh and 'Aflaq in Orthodox Political Thought*], Beirut: Manshurat Afaq Jami'yya, 2005; an introduction to the origins and principles of the SSNP: Zuwiyya Yamak, Labib, *The Syrian Social Nationalist Party: An Ideological Analysis*, Cambridge, MA: Center for Middle Eastern Studies of Harvard University, 1966; general discussion in Rabinovich, *The View from Damascus*, pp. 124–7.

9. Blanford, Nicholas, *Killing Mr Lebanon: The Assassination of Rafik al-Hariri and its Impact on the Middle East*, London: I.B. Tauris, 2006.

10. For example, this article from the spring of 2012, which hailed Beirut as a haven of fun in a region teeming with tumult: Barnard, Anne, "Resurgent Beirut Offers Haven Amid Turmoil of Arab Spring," *The New York Times*, 13 April 2012, accessible online: http://www.nytimes.com/2012/04/14/world/middleeast/resurgent-beirut-offers-a-haven-in-the-arab-spring.html?pagewanted=all.

11. MacFarquhar, Neil and Hwaida Saad, "Kidnapping in Syria Fuels Unrest in Lebanon," *The New York Times*, 22 May 2012, accessible online: http://www.nytimes.com/2012/05/23/world/middleeast/abduction-of-lebanese-shiites-in-syria-stokes-new-tensions.htm.

12. For a famous critique of the challenges of Arab nationalism, long before the Arab Spring, see: Ajami, Fouad, *The Arab Predicament: Arab Political Thought and Practice Since 1967*, 2nd edn, Cambridge: Cambridge University Press, 1992.

13. For a study of wartime political posters belonging to the Phalange and other factions, see: Maasri, Zeina, *Off the Wall: Political Posters of the Lebanese Civil War*, London: I.B. Tauris, 2009.

14. For an eyewitness account of the aftermath of the massacre, see: Fisk, *Pity the Nation*, pp. 359–400; on the alliance between the Maronites and the Israelis during the war: Schulze, Kirsten E., *Israel's Covert Diplomacy in Lebanon*, New York: St Martin's Press, 1998, pp. 81–145.

15. MacFarquhar, Neil, "Car Bomb Kills Figure in 1982 Lebanese Massacre," *The New York Times*, 25 January 2002, accessible online: http://www.nytimes.com/2002/01/25/world/car-bomb-kills-figure-in-1982-lebanese-massacre.html; his supporters maintain a website in his memory: http://eliehobeika.com/index.html.

16. My summary draws on the following research: Volk, Lucia, *Memorials and Martyrs in Modern Lebanon*, Bloomington, IN: Indiana University Press, 2010.

INDEX